SITUATING "RACE" AND RACISMS
IN TIME, SPACE, AND THEORY

Situating "Race" and Racisms in Time, Space, and Theory

Critical Essays for Activists and Scholars

Edited by

JO-ANNE LEE AND JOHN LUTZ

McGill-Queen's University Press
Montreal & Kingston · London · Ithaca

© McGill-Queen's University Press 2005
ISBN 0-7735-2886-5 (cloth)
ISBN 0-7735-2887-3 (paper)

Legal deposit second quarter 2005
Bibliothèque nationale du Québec

Printed in Canada on acid-free paper that is 100% ancient forest free (100% post-consumer recycled), processed chlorine free.

This book has been published with the help of grants from the Canadian Federation for the Humanities and Social Sciences, through the Aid to Scholarly Publications Programme, using funds provided by the Social Sciences and Humanities Research Council of Canada, the Canadian Race Relations Foundation, and the University of Victoria.

McGill-Queen's University Press acknowledges the support of the Canada Council for the Arts for our publishing program. We also acknowledge the financial support of the Government of Canada through the Book Publishing Industry Development Program (BPIDP) for our publishing activities.

Library and Archives Canada Cataloguing in Publication

Situating "race" and racisms in time, space, and theory: critical essays for activists and scholars / edited by Jo-Anne Lee and John Lutz.

Includes index.
ISBN 0-7735-2886-5 (bound). – ISBN 0-7735-2887-3 (pbk.)

1. Race. 2. Racism. I. Lee, Jo-Anne, 1948– II. Lutz, John S. (John Sutton), 1959–

HT1521.S534 2005   305.8   C2004-906646-3

This book was typeset by Dynagram Inc. in 10/12 Sabon.

Contents

Acknowledgments   vii

Preface   ix

Introduction: Toward a Critical Literacy of Racisms, Anti-Racisms, and Racialization   3
JO-ANNE LEE AND JOHN LUTZ

Deconstructing Race, Deconstructing Racism
(with Postscript 2004)   30
A CONVERSATION BETWEEN JEANNETTE ARMSTRONG AND ROXANA NG

On Being and not Being Brown/Black-British: Racism, Class, Sexuality, and Ethnicity in Post-Imperial Britain (with Postscript 2004: The Politics of Longing and (Un)Belonging, Fear, and Loathing)   46
ALI RATTANSI

Mixed Metaphors: Positioning "Mixed Race" Identity   77
MINELLE MAHTANI

Turning In, Turning Out: The Shifting Formations of "Japanese Canadian" from Uprooting to Redress   94
ROY MIKI

Racist Visions for the Twenty-First Century: On the Banal Force of the French Radical Right   114
ANN LAURA STOLER

Unravelling South Africa's Racial Order: The Historiography of Racism, Segregation, and Apartheid   138
PAUL MAYLAM

A Critical Discourse Analysis of the *Globe and Mail* Editorials on Employment Equity   161
FRANCES HENRY AND CAROL TATOR

Orientalizing "War Talk": Representations of the Gendered Muslim Body Post-9/11 in *The Montreal Gazette*   178
YASMIN JIWANI

Contributors   205

Index   209

Acknowledgments

The book has its origins in the History of Racialization Group of the University of Victoria, a group of graduate students vibrant in the late 1990s. These included Pasi Ahonen and Mrinalini Greedharry, who provided the anchor and organization for the group, and Eva Campbell, Karen Duder, Jennifer Fraser, Joel Freedman, Masumi Izumi, Susan Johnson, John Lutz, Jason Miller, Georgia Sitara, and Christie Shaw.

The reading group started as a place to bring scholars, activists, and artists – as well as people who were all three – into dialogue and were joined in this by Elias Cheboud, Winnie Lee, Tomoko Okada, and Jean McRae of the Inter-Cultural Association; Harinder Dhillon of the Capital Region Race Relations Association; Fred Eckert-Maret, Rahngild Watson Reinartz, and Dave Southern of the Vancouver Immigrant and Refugee Centre Society; Janice Simcoe of the Victoria First Nations Interagency Team; Greg Blue, Dennis Flewelling, and Elizabeth Vibert (History), Annalee Lepp and Jo-Anne Lee (Women's Studies), John McLaren (Law), Linda Sproule-Jones (Equity Office), David Turner (Social Work), and Rennie Warburton (Sociology) of the University of Victoria. The result was the "Making History, Constructing Race" conference held in Victoria in 1998 and the start of a conversation that resulted in this book.

The project was assisted along the way by several student research and conference assistants, including Blair MacDonald, John Threlfall, Haydn Lansdell, Mrinalini Greedharry, and finally, the meticulous editorial assistance of Melinda Maunsell, who also prepared the index. Thanks also to Imogen Brian who edited the manuscript for McGill-Queen's.

Conferences and books require funding, and for this we wish to thank the generous help of the Canadian Race Relations Foundation, the Social Sciences and Humanities Research Council of Canada, and the University of Victoria.

Preface

The spark for this book came from a group of graduate students led by Pasi Ahonen and Mrinalini Greedharry, from the departments of History and English respectively, who formed the "History of Racialization" reading group (HORG) at the University of Victoria, in Victoria, Canada. The group drew in scholars and students from History in Art, Women's Studies, Political Science, and Sociology, as well as from their own departments.

HORG's objectives were to learn more about the history of race and racialization and to connect their learning to practice in order to do something about racism. The group made connections with local anti-racism organizations and activists, and together they dreamed up a conference to bring scholars, activists, film makers, and other artists into conversation with each other.

Three hundred registrants from Australia, Brazil, Canada, Great Britain, Israel, Japan, Mexico, South Africa, and the United States assembled in Victoria in October 1998 for the conference, "Making History: Constructing 'Race'." They learned about racism/anti-racism from the perspectives of activists, artists, scholars, and victims from different countries, ethnicities, and races. Community-oriented anti-racism workshops were juxtaposed with academic papers and artistic representations of race in our society.

It was the organizers' dream that something of that learning be captured and passed on to others. This collection is a partial fulfillment of that dream. It is part of an ongoing conversation that develops some of the seminal thoughts presented at that remarkable event. It starts with the discussion that kicked off the conference and includes five of the key presentations. The events preceding 1998 – the collapse of Apartheid in South Africa, the first Gulf War, and the end of the Cold War, to name only three – created a fertile backdrop to the conference discussions. Since then, dramatic events have shaken the world again. Most dramatic were the 11 September 2001 attacks on the World Trade Centre in New York and their fallout: the Afghan War, the Iraq War, and anti-Islamic agitation around the Western world.

The authors have all updated their thoughts in light of these changes in the world and the current debates. Among these foundational pieces are a series of newly commissioned papers that round out a collection that is current, provocative, and practical. We present these essays in the spirit of listening, learning, and working towards the eradication of racism.

Jo-Anne Lee
John Lutz

SITUATING "RACE" AND RACISMS
IN TIME, SPACE, AND THEORY

JO-ANNE LEE AND JOHN LUTZ

Introduction: Toward a Critical Literacy of Racisms, Anti-Racisms, and Racialization

THINKING CRITICALLY ABOUT "RACE," RACISMS, AND RACIALIZATION

Racism is not what it used to be. Ideas of "race," racisms, and anti-racisms are in constant motion, and our understanding evolves as they take new forms. This volume is aimed at a wide audience of those people who care about understanding, tracking, and opposing all racisms in their multiple forms. It offers concepts, language, analysis, and practical tools to activists and researchers. Each of the eight chapters in this book is a step toward new critical readings of "race," racisms, anti-racisms, and racialization. The contributions come from Canadian, American, British, and South African scholars who analyze racisms across three continents. Although each uses concrete historical or contemporary examples drawn from specific national experiences, the focus is on using new analytical tools and posing new questions about racisms. Each author explores possibilities for new critical literacies to understand the persistence of and transformations in established and emergent forms of racisms.

The book engages what Ann Laura Stoler, in her essay in this volume, calls the "politics of comparison," in which similarities and differences among racisms in different times and places are addressed. Stoler's observations, for example, about the relationship between racist practices and not-so-fringe political groups in France offer insights into the rise of similar far right groups in Britain, North America, Australia, and a host of other countries. Although racism in South Africa is clearly different from that in Canada or the United States, might the tools that Paul Maylam's essay gives us for reading the histories of race be applicable to other national histories? Are these insights, and those from the other chapters, transferable to all racisms across time and space? The contributors to this volume raise these and other uncomfortable questions about theories and practices of racisms and anti-racisms.

One of the central challenges in the politics of comparisons is that our terminology often seems to have come from nineteenth-century world views of inheritable racial traits. Words such as *Indian blood*, *mixed-blood*, *half-breed*, and *miscegenation* are historic artifacts steeped in biological determinism. This is also true of shorthand labels such as *Red*, *White*, and *Black* that presume and reify racial identities based on imagined skin colour. Canada's commonplace official terms "visible minorities" and "women of colour" may sound offensive to those who struggle against racisms' affronts elsewhere. Even to challenge racial ideas invokes the label "anti-racist" and replicates outdated notions, raising the need for a new critical literacy of anti-racisms that is not just reactionary to racism. Instead of seeing racism as "the thing" to oppose, we need a clearly articulated vision of a post-racist world and strategies to move forward. For this to happen, scholars and activists also need a "literacy of listening." Much of what needs to be done involves talking and listening across differences; if we learn how, we can listen to written stories too, hearing old stories in new ways.

By calling for a critical literacy of "race," racisms, anti-racisms, and racialization, we are not simply asking for new words, meanings, and concepts, although this is part of the task. We point toward the need for critical "readings" of how power operates and how it transforms, and reforms, social relations, through racial categories and consciousness. We call attention to the particularities of racializations as they mutate and take hold on new ground. To counter the insidious, commonsensical nature of racial consciousness, new critical literacies must involve processes of "cognitive decolonization," so that it is possible to really see, hear, and understand where that consciousness comes from. Several writers in this collection argue the need for scholars and activists of anti-racisms to be self-reflective in their use of analytical and practical tools. Given the chameleon-like nature of racisms, which easily adapt to shifting demands of power, it would be unwise to believe that racisms can be identified once and for all. No single conceptual tool or framework will work to uncover the operations of racial discourses and practices in all times and places.

Accepted terms and concepts for talking about "race," racisms, and anti-racisms are problematic, because meanings attached to words form a system of representation about people that comprise racial ideologies. Power operates by fixing these ideologies as common sense. Underlying all the chapters is a notion that racist ideologies are deployed by those with wealth and power to achieve cultural hegemony;

a condition where the self-serving world views of an elite few become so widely disseminated, so often taught and repeated, that they become "common sense" and internalized – even by those who are oppressed by these very ideas. "Race" remains such a common-sense idea that this way of thinking is hard to break out of (Hall 1997).

Fortunately, as Stuart Hall (1997) argues, following Gramsci, cultural hegemony is never complete and is always being contested. A few intellectuals in each generation are able to "free thought from what it silently thinks, and so enable it to think differently" (Foucault 1977, 9). Not all cultural practices are incorporated into the hegemonic system, and words and terms have many meanings that have been subordinated to power but that still circulate outside the gaze of disciplinary power.

Historians point out that we do not start each new era with a clean slate; instead, we stand on the bedrock of earlier forms of racial consciousness and practices of racial exclusion and inclusion. Foucault suggests that each new way of thinking about a social phenomenon has its own archaeology and genealogy. Postmodernist social theory has challenged the ideas of a single "truth" discoverable through objective sciences and of universal explanatory "laws" of social behaviour. Seen through postmodernist lenses, scientific knowledge is not neutral, only another truth claim linked to relations of power (Latour 1987). Because knowledge is linked to power and, in turn, linked to the production of subjectivities and consciousness, the way we talk and think about subjects helps to produce and maintain social inequality.

There are indications at the beginning of the twenty-first century of a growing awareness of the profoundly sedimented nature of "race" thinking on "race" consciousness (Goldberg 1993). Mounting evidence demonstrates that scientific and popular discourses on "race" and racisms arose simultaneously with modernity in the European "Enlightenment" era (although its roots go back much further). In the late seventeenth and eighteenth centuries, the invention of race classification systems, based on scientific investigation of so-called natural, inherited, biological differences among different groups of humans, strengthened racist ideologies. These "scientific" approaches, such as craniometry, ethnology, and evolutionary human anthropology, informed social engineering policies such as the eugenics movement, and were used to justify racisms and racist practices and to rationalize claims of natural superiority. Goldberg and others argue that the rise of modernity corresponds to the rise of racism and that the two are tightly interwoven.

Martin Bernal and Edward Said, to differing degrees, have moved academic thought to recognize and acknowledge the legacy and implications of racialized colonial discourse in contemporary social theory.

Their work profoundly unsettles received knowledge about the origins of Western civilization and thought (Young 1995, 151–69). In approaches familiar to feminist scholarship, both scholars contest the notion of an objective, neutral social science standing outside the dominant social values of the society in which the researcher is situated. Martin Bernal's (1987) study, *Black Athena,* documents the racial biases underlying the attempts of European archaeologists and classicists of the nineteenth and twentieth century to reinterpret the roots of Greek and Roman civilization through what he calls the "Aryan model." Bernal links the development of "classical studies" of Greece and Rome in the nineteenth century to the deployment of a new form of scholarship that tried to modify the established account of the beginnings of Greek civilization. Traditional accounts acknowledge the importance of Egyptian culture in the formation of classical Greek culture, but the Aryan model proposed that Greek and Roman civilizations developed with minimal influence from African and Semitic cultures.

Edward Said's 1979 study of Western scholarship on "the Orient" documents the rise of a discipline and discourse called "Orientalism," a study of the imagined "Orient" and "Orientals." Said [pronounced Sie-eed] demonstrates that Orientalism provided the language and conceptual frameworks for the colonizers to understand and govern the "Orient." Yet the scholarly knowledge generated by "Orientalists" had little to do with the actual lived reality of those it pretended to represent and instead reflected the fantasies and desires of the colonizers. Said's work has since spawned a large body of subsequent research on the ideological practices of colonialism, particularly in cultural studies of racism where his approach has helped to uncover the discursive and symbolic practices involved in constituting non-Europeans as "Others." All the authors in this volume owe a debt to Said; Jiwani's essay in this volume explicitly deploys his insights on "othering" – creating others – in her analyses of media reports in the weeks following the attack of 11 September 2001.

Sociologist Robert Miles (1989) provides a way of thinking about the social production of race consciousness through the term *racialization*, which he defines as "a representational process whereby social significance is attached to certain biological (usually phenotypical) human features, on the basis of which those people possessing those characteristics are designated as a distinct collectivity" (74). Miles further argues that the characteristics signified as "racial" vary historically and are not restricted to physical features. By naming the process, Miles allows scholars to put their focus on the historic and contemporary creation of racial categories instead of just taking race as a given and writing about "race relations."

Understanding "race," racisms, and racialization as social processes and not innate biological givens leads to analyses that attend to historically specific and variant conditions and continuous and discontinuous forms of racisms from one historical period and place to another. Most feminist anti-racist scholars understand racisms as necessarily intersecting with other systems of structured inequality: gender, nationality, language, class, sexuality, and ability, among others (Anthias and Lloyd 2002; Dua and Robertson 1999; hooks 1984; Mohanty, Russo, et al. 1991). They further argue that we cannot fully understand racisms' exclusions and subordinations without comprehending the mechanics of sexuality that underpin its discourses and practices. The sexual desires, fantasies, and fears of white, heterosexual males and females constitute masculine and feminine Others as objects to be feared, desired, exploited, and dominated. Female and male Others were and still are represented as either hypersexual, with insatiable sexual appetites; over-endowed with sexual prowess or organs; and/or lacking in civility due to inherently immoral sexual behaviours that are devoid of all modesty (Gilman 1985; Jiwani 1992; Loomba 1998; Stoler 1995; Young 1995). White culture's contradictory and mutual fascination with and terror of sexualized Others – perceived as threatening to the imagined purity of the white race – has fuelled some of the most extreme acts of genocide and violence against Others. When linked to productive powers of representation, the most damaging aspect of these sexually driven, often unconscious characterizations is that white representations of Otherness are consumed not only by whites, but also by those racialized Others who internalize racialized Otherness as normal and natural. This double consciousness of self and Other is powerfully addressed by Franz Fanon in his seminal book, *Black Skin, White Masks*.

Most anti-racist activists still tend to see racisms as though they were separate from other systems of inequality. According to Bonnett (2000), anti-racists still largely view racism as negative because it is "socially disruptive, foreign, sustains the ruling class, hinders the progress of 'our' community, is an intellectual error, distorts and erases peoples' identities, and is anti-egalitarian and socially unjust" (4–7). To this should be added the insights of anti-racist feminist scholars and activists who point out the need to acknowledge the centrality of gender and sexuality to the perpetuation and maintenance of a white supremacist racial order (Bhavnani 2001; hooks 1994). Feminists view racism as bad, not only for the reasons listed above, but also, and perhaps most importantly, because it is a linchpin that sustains a world order built on interlocking systems of gender, heterosexism, white supremacism, ableism, fundamentalisms of all sorts, classism, colonialism, and neo-colonialism (Loomba 1998; hooks 1994).

Modernist Views of "Race"

Critical race scholars have linked the idea that race is an autonomous or semi-autonomous structure to modernist science and social science. Bernal (1987) and Said (1979), among others, depart dramatically from the entire corpus of modernist research into "race" and racisms that searched for a general theory of race and racism capable of transcending historical variations and localized particularistic experiences. Today problems with modernist thinking about "race" and racism seem all too evident. Older debates over whether or not races existed, how to measure and classify races, the existence (or not) of innate racial differences among humans, and whether racisms were a matter of irrational behaviour or instrumental ideologies of capitalism never really questioned the reality of separate "races." Modernist approaches relied on the same taken-for-granted racial categories to interpret data. Moreover, in attempts to explain the persistence of racism, some approaches tended to be reductionistic and to see "race" as a derivative of something else (Goldberg 1990).

Modernist views of "race" are strongly linked to the rise of liberal philosophies, but this does not mean that liberalism or Marxism supplanted and displaced older conservative views of "races." These older views of race are still very much alive today and, as Taguieff (1990) points out in France, (and in other Western countries), get reworked and strengthened to the point of displacing liberal views. Conservative views of "race" hearken back to the time when society was divided into estates, castes, and classes, and to beliefs that this was not only natural but also desirable. Conservatism, associated historically most closely with the European nobility and clergy (but shared in other traditional cultures), held that the differences in society were ordained by God and that they should be maintained and protected. In this philosophy, every person had a place in a "great chain of being" that was not to be disturbed. From a conservative point of view, maintaining separation between "races" is normal and a desirable way of maintaining "natural" boundaries.

Liberalism is closely associated with the rise of the middle class and the assault on inherited privilege. While conservatism was linked with feudalism and was "pre-modern," the liberal emphasis on the self-sufficiency of the individual linked it to capitalism, democracy, and modernism. Liberal individualism, a dominant theme in modern, enlightenment philosophy, presumes that individuals are equal in their ability to make rational choices and equal in rights and responsibilities of citizenship. Liberalism sees racism as an individual pathology – an outcome of an individual's irrational prejudices – and not a widespread societal problem. Within this framing, anti-racism takes an individualistic approach favouring moral education, promoting greater cultural knowledge of Others, and undertaking psychological profiling and testing to identify those individuals susceptible to racist intolerance for anti-racist educational and informational programs.

Liberal individualism also underpins a legalistic understanding of racism as a transgression of the rights to which each person is entitled in a liberal democracy. Those whose rights are abused, and whom the state recognizes as a rights-bearing citizen, may ask for legal remedies of punishment, protection, and compensation. However, because this view fails to challenge the assumed naturalness of "races" and fails to acknowledge internalized assumptions and biases that blind the law and the justice system to their own distortions, the juridical approach to racism is unable to transcend its own complicity in the production and reproduction of racism.

The modernist response took another form in addition to liberalism. Materialism, or as it is also called, Historical Materialism, or Marxism, moved the emphasis from individuals to classes and from people to the relationship between people and the mode of production. The materialist approach focused on the relations of production of wealth, that is the process by which goods and services are produced and how the profit or surplus of that production was distributed. In explaining the unequal distribution of wealth, materialists point to the relations between capital and labour classes that benefit and enrich the wealthy. Classical Marxist explanations have been criticized for claiming that racism is a by-product of capitalism. In this view, racism is a false consciousness or a false ideology produced by capitalists and the capitalist state to divide the working class, to force the different components to compete with each other, thereby keeping wages low.

As a false consciousness, Marxists believe that racism will be addressed after overcoming class exploitation, because racism, as ideology, operates to prevent the workers from forming a common consciousness about the roots of their oppression under capitalism. In other words, to eliminate racism, it is first necessary to overthrow capitalism. Although this theory is useful in highlighting the social basis of racist ideology and refuting the belief that race and racism are natural, Marxist explanations privilege class relations as the primary determining factor of racially based inequality to the exclusion of others. The materialist position ignores relationships between racism and other ideologies, such as nationalism, ethnicity, and gender. More generally, the materialist approaches fail to account for racial ideologies that run counter to capitalist interests, such as the elimination of slavery or human rights legislation.

In its two main forms, liberalism and materialism, modernism represented a movement away from a spiritual view that saw humans in terms of their relationship with the natural and immaterial world. Modernist thinkers embraced secularism, rationality, empiricism, objectivity, and efficiency, while emphasizing the notions of progress and linear history.

Postmodernist Views

The chaos of the First and Second World Wars undermined, for many artists and intellectuals, the modernist belief that civilization would follow a natural progression through rationality and improved technology to achieve the perfect society. The post-war years produced a philosophic and aesthetic stance that became known as postmodernism. As a social and philosophical perspective, postmodernism does not see the world unfolding according to a divinely ordained timeline in which each society is continually approaching a perfect state, with European societies assumed to be the most advanced, and all others ranked according to their place on that scale. When postmodernist perspectives, and there are many variations, are applied to racisms, they raise many new questions about how and why race consciousness develops, the role that science plays in creating the fact of race, and the way modernist histories deny the continuing interaction between the past and the present. Because linearity is disrupted by postmodernism, what happened in the past is not seen as behind us, rather it is always with us as a reservoir that is being tapped constantly to support racist ideas. Although racism is being acted out continuously in our society and finds new modes of expression, it is a profoundly historical phenomenon. To understand and combat racism, we must understand its complex and multiple historical beginnings.

Postmodern approaches have brought a new language and analytic tools to understand and oppose racisms, but there are, still, distinct limits to postmodern approaches (Rattansi 1994; 1995). Changing concepts of "race," different manifestations of racisms, and intricate complexities of racializations require activists and scholars to develop a broad range of tools to analyze racial formations as they exist and change across space, time, and theory. Critical self-reflection becomes crucial in assessing where we have come from and where we are heading.

Analytically, postmodernism has tended to focus on language, discourse, and representation and has been less attentive to material experience and practical implications. In this collection, Paul Maylam speaks of a tendency in postmodern South African historiography to fail to draw links to material conditions – capitalism and the economy.

Roxana Ng also reminds readers that the lives of immigrant women garment workers are shaped by their shifting relations to the mode of production and that the material basis of their lived experiences cannot be explained without investigating the actual conditions that organize their work.

Postmodern-influenced frameworks have also focused needed attention on the subjectivity of the observer/researcher. As researchers, we cannot separate ourselves from the society we seek to understand; we too participate in shaping and representing the society in which we live. Moreover, as stated earlier, fantasy, imagination, and desire play a critical role in shaping our perceptions and representations of the material world.

Maylam also points out that the historiography of racial differences in South Africa has much to do with the politics and ideologies prevalent at the time each historian was writing. In other words, South African historians writing about apartheid were part of the social formation, and their writings often reflected an unconscious absorption into the discourses of the dominant racial order. Against objective knowledge taken as fact, postmodernism recognizes subjective experiences and multiple bases for knowing. Facts formerly asserted as truth are now seen as merely interpretations fixed and institutionalized through power, discourse, and cultural practices. They draw attention to the social processes that construct meaning, including modes of representation. The questioning of the notion of progress has brought new forms of racisms into the analytic field in a way that modernist approaches could not have done. By asking how race has taken on different roles and different meanings in different places and periods, postmodernist social theory allows us to think critically about race and how it changes over time and across space (Goldberg 1993; Rattansi 1994).

This volume moves in a direction mapped by Rattansi (1994; 1995) through nuanced postmodern framings for understanding racisms and racializations as processes that are actively constructed, have multiple historical roots, and constantly undergo change in response to antiracist opposition and changing contexts. Such a framing takes the strengths of postmodernist approaches, namely their focus on ideology, and merges them with elements of the materialist approach, which emphasizes the material power relations embedded in modern capitalism. Both types of approach focus on structure: for materialists, it is the social institutions of capitalism that limit human scope for action and freedom; for postmodernists, the focus is on discursive structures. Each focuses on a different kind of agency. The postmodernist approach emphasizes the multiple and overlapping identities (subject position) of all actors. The modernist materialist approach emphasizes individual political and group (class) action and resistance.

Finally, we are inheritors of a legacy of racialized thought, and as scholars and activists we must therefore adopt ethical self-consciousness by situating ourselves within and not outside our discursive legacy. As Rattansi (1994) suggests (and we agree), sensitive postmodern framing and materialist analysis offer tentative ground from which to diagnose the changing pulse of racisms at the beginning of the twenty-first century but no simple answers.

SITES/PROCESSES FOR PRODUCING AND REPRODUCING RACIALIZING DISCOURSES AND REPRESENTATIONS

Postmodernist approaches have strongly influenced contemporary understandings of how racialization operates in and through a range of subjectivities and identities. While we discuss the racial state, nation formation, multiculturalism, whiteness, cultural racisms, and the media as analytically distinct, in reality these sites and processes are tightly interwoven and mutually reinforcing.

Racialized Subjectivities and Identities

Post-structural and post-colonial psychoanalytic approaches explicated by Stuart Hall (1996), for example, view individuals not as unitary, coherent, and already constituted subjects, but as holding multiple, open, and porous subjectivities that are always under formation. Yet these are not free-floating identities. In engaging in a sophisticated analysis of identities and representation, analysts have identified the central role of the nation state (which we discuss later in this Introduction) in producing and reproducing racialized subjective identities. They have also identified hidden strategies of resistance to the subjectifying powers of the state that undermine too-facile, premature predictions of the effects of state policies. Where earlier race theories assumed fixed oppositional binaries of black/white, native/non-native, for example, postmodern approaches in their nuanced incarnations remind us of the open, contingent, and contextual bases of discourses about "race," racisms, anti-racisms, and racialization. The black/white, white/non-white politics of racism and anti-racism tended to exclude multi-racial, multi-ethnic interactions from analysis and left no room for recognizing "mixed-raced" groups' self-understandings or the modes of resistance taken up by those seen as "in-between." "Mixed-raced" and hyphenated citizen-subjects have long been articulating and constructing "new ethnicities" (Cohen 1997; Hall 2000; Gilroy 1993; Parker and Song 2001).

To approach the debate over essentialism and anti-essentialism from the place of the racialized subject as a knowing subject who occupies the inside of an imposed category is quite different from approaching it as one who stands, consciously or unconsciously, as the imposer or border guard of categorical differences (Werbner 1997). The viewpoint of those who stand in both places, such as Minelle Mahtani's mixed-race women who enact their self-awareness and intentionality through self-naming, is different again. Their self-naming of their politicized identities is not a natural outcome of an organic, unreflective articulation, but comes from an awareness of where they fit into the dominant racial order. They use names such as "tricksters," and "spies" to reflect their mobile self-identities across the racial divide. Yet as Mahtani cautions, hybridity in itself does not guarantee political consciousness of racism, despite its conceptual popularity as an alternative to essentialized, binary categories of identities. Rattansi and Miki in their essays also address the question of how racialized identities are formed and reformed through time and space.

Postmodernist frameworks regard racial identity as arising out of historical circumstances, not as something primordial or innate. However, in political struggles, some marginalized groups continue to use variants of modernist, biological race thinking, which formerly had been used to force them to the margins, as a mobilizing strategy. For example, some aboriginal leaders argue that there is something essentially different about their world views and lived experiences as "a people," which stems from their innate spirituality and traditional cultures, as a way to build pride and mobilize resistance (Alfred 1999; Sioui 1992). Moreover, many marginalized groups take no comfort in the notion that the racisms they experience are not based on essential difference. To essentialize or not? For some racialized minority groups whose entire past has been distorted and corrupted through colonialism, restoring an imagined wholeness as an anti-colonial reclamation project remains crucial. Holding tight to a sense of ethnic identity for minoritized communities can be positive in building resistance, as long as we see ethnicity as culturally formed and identity as an ongoing project of formation (Hall 1992; Rattansi this volume). Paul Gilroy (1993) in *The Black Atlantic* warns however that appeals to primordial essences, especially those based on territorial claims of "the land" or "the continent," are dangerous because of their presuppositions. The promotion and adoption of selective particularities risks returning to discourses and practices of enforced categorical difference. Postmodernist analytical frameworks draw attention to the dangers of strategic essentialism as an anti-racism strategy. Although empowering in their naming a common lived experience and history of oppression, essentialisms also contain within them the seeds of their own failings. For these reasons, concepts that refuse borders and confinement, such as diaspora, third space, hybridity, multiplicity, metissage, transnationalism, and other spatial metaphors of movement, have been reclaimed, resignified, and reinterrogated in recent critical anti-racist thought (Werbner and Modood 1997).

Racial States, Nation Formation, Multiculturalism, and Hyphenated and Mixed-Race Identities

In considering the continuing salience of "race," scholars have foregrounded the centrality of ideologies of nationalism and national cultural identity produced by the state (Gilroy 1987; Omi and Winant 1986).

Studies of the racial formation of nations and states in Britain, the United States, and Canada (Anthias and Yuval-Davis 1991; Bannerji 2000; Gilroy 1987; Goldberg 2002; Omi and Winant 1986; Razack 1998; 2002) demonstrate that racisms have been central to the formation of the state and the nation. In all states, racist ideologies are deployed in forming the nation and nationalism and in constructing national identities. Great effort is devoted to managing cultural identity through discursive strategies, because the loyalty of the national subject/citizen cannot be left to chance. The racial state must ensure its own continuity, after all. Thus racial discourses may be presented as positive and productive and may not always appear blatantly negative and oppressive. In other words, racism is knitted into the fabric of state discourses, practices, and ideologies and is thoroughly institutionalized and systemized (Winant 1994). As Western nations feel the intensification of migration from the non-West under the pressure of capitalist globalization, the state's role in managing the conditions of its own hegemonic renewal becomes more subtle and indirect. Today racial exclusions no longer require overt discriminatory acts.

Take multiculturalism as social policy and social reality, for example. Rattansi observes that multiculturalism meanders in an indirect fashion, allowing brown/black Britishers to stake a claim to the "motherland," to set down roots, and to belong and not belong to the nation, but that this circuitous and often dangerous adventure offers no destination of full inclusion. The emergence of mixed and multiple hybrid and hyphenated bodies as subjects and citizens, and postmodern discourses of hybridity and diaspora, are additional challenges to old racial binaries of black and white. However, as Rattansi points out in his essay, the point is not, as in some cruder forms of postmodernist theorizing, that all identities are in play, decentred, and unstable, but that the "particularities and peculiarities of any unique indemnificatory configuration need to be carefully plotted and narrated precisely because of the complex historical and contextual features which condition the formation and re-formation of all identities" (Rattansi this volume, 54). Rattansi argues for empirical studies of the relative stability and instability of identities and their specific particularities, fragilities, and vulnerabilities.

Rattansi observes that hyphenation of citizenship, toward whiteness or toward "blackness" (in the British context) or "multiculturalness" (in the Canadian context), does not necessarily mean an easy mixture or the creation of a new cultural identity. These hyphenated combinations are displayed in syncretic cultural forms, as well as embodied in the physical features of young men and women. Racial significations and meanings still impose their meanings on hybrid selves. As a response, Hall's (1992) "new ethnicities" best captures the emergence of a new social category that challenges the national policing of older borders between black and white. Rattansi also addresses gender and sexualities, class and religion as they are affected by and productive of new identities of black Britishness, as well as the promiscuous cultural influences on blackness, coming from South Asia, Africa, America, and the Caribbean, that are themselves impure, hybrid combinations. Whether the potential creation of new cultural practices by hyphenated youth with black-brown-Asian backgrounds in Britain and by "multicultural" or multi-hyphenated youth in Canada and the United States will offer resources to anti-racisms remains a difficult and open question. However, it may profoundly impact the meaning of citizenship in Britain and the British settler colonies (Canada, United States, Australia, and New Zealand) because none of these show strong signs of de-raciation or de-ethnicization away from normative and hegemonic whiteness as cultural identity of citizenship.

A racial politics that remains locked into a white/black oppositional binary as a way of mobilizing the anti-racist movement will be unable to address new forms of racializations and emerging horizontal racisms across and between differently racialized ethnic groups.

Cultural Racisms

Defending the racial nation-state against a perceived invasion of Others has given rise to new forms of racisms, one of which is captured in the concept "cultural racism" (Taguieff 1990). This "new" form of racism no longer depends on "scientific" or "biological" differences to justify discriminatory practices. Rather, cultural racisms signify Otherness in new ways. They point to "essential" cultural behaviours that are different from "ours." "They are not like us" becomes the basis for exclusionary and discriminatory practices. Without explicit reference to biology or even to hierarchy, these are usually at issue when someone says, "I do not object to *them* wearing (a turban, a scarf, burka) in their *own* country, but they cannot do it here." Some people, the argument goes, are unassimilatable to "our" way of life because of their inherent cultural differences. But these attitudes are not entirely new. Contemporary forms of cultural racisms draw upon long-standing conservative beliefs that it is necessary to segregate those who are "different," although cultural symbols and ways of living rather than physical characteristics are now being used to signify difference. Older discourses of national cultural identity are being reworked but retain their appeal to traditional views of the nation as the symbol of civilization, progressivism, ethnic superiority, peoplehood, and so on, all as a God-given endowment to some but not others. "Rightful" citizens are called upon to defend this legacy by excluding those who are accused of not belonging to the nation.

In examining the rise and decline of the Front Nationale in France during 1998 and 1999, Stoler raises questions about whether there is anything really "new" about these so-called cultural racisms, or whether cultural racisms are more a consequence of how analysts choose to represent and interpret these instances. She points out that racisms worked out by colonial administrators in the Dutch colonies in the nineteenth century were not derived from strict scientific classifications, but from flexible cultural criteria whose "malleability was a key to the sliding scale along which economic privilege was protected and social entitlements were assigned" (Stoler this volume, 134). In short, Stoler argues that the openness that we perceive in contemporary racisms and "race" may be a product of the fluidity inherent in the concepts themselves and not "a hallmark of our postmodern critique – much less our post-colonial moment" (134). Yet Stoler cautions against a too-simplistic, derivative analysis that simply reinterprets what is known about racism's eighteenth and nineteenth century forms. Racism is known to rupture with the past and at the same time, selectively and strategically recuperate earlier forms of racisms; thus we cannot think that an explanation of earlier forms can be simply projected into the present or that racisms will remain constant over time.

Older sites of regulation can be resignified. Stoler's analysis of the rise of the new right in France and Jiwani's analysis of media coverage highlight the hegemonic nation's use of discourses of the "family," a traditional site for controlling women. Women (particularly those who are seen to "naturally" belong to the nation) are being called on to police public and private, moral and immoral, secular and religious boundaries of the nation. Stoler and Jiwani observe that contemporary gendered discourses of racism resurrect older colonial racisms that drew on cultural discourses of family and parenting to create and sustain racial divisions.

This recuperating tactic is made more clear by analyzing debates over multiculturalism. In these debates, conservatives have taken over terrain once occupied and now vacated by the left. Conservatives reject multiculturalism on the basis that it erodes the national culture, promotes destabilization and disunity, and leads to social confusion and conflict. The Left also rejects multiculturalism, but for different reasons. They see it as a ploy by the state to delude ethnic groups into believing that they have cultural rights without offering meaningful changes in the political, economic, or social rights of citizenship. Multiculturalism is perceived as a false ideology that disguises racism and exploitation by celebrating ethnicity. From a leftist perspective multiculturalism in Canada is the state's liberal response to racial, ethnic, and cultural diversity, in that it attempts to respond to ethnic particularities as a step toward achieving integration into a universal, inclusive national culture. Through multiculturalism as national policy, the state hopes that individuals will feel more secure in their ethnic identities so that they will be more willing to assimilate fully into the national culture. Official multiculturalism assumes the national culture as the existing, normative, national culture of hegemonic whiteness. Liberal multiculturalism does not address racism systematically, because racism is viewed as an individual pathology and not seen as part of the social order.

Furthermore, the older consensus between the Left and liberals over civil and cultural rights has broken up and has not been replaced by consensus over social justice and equality. Shared responsibility for correcting past injustices to indigenous peoples, blacks, Asians, sexual minorities, those with disabilities, and women simply has been sidelined to the courts. The once promising consensus on universal human rights has been heavily eroded in the neo-conservative era. Instead, individuals who would have benefited most from the ideals of universal human rights – immigrants and refugees – have been cynically constituted as undeserving racialized Others: enemy aliens or the enemy within. National borders have not been loosened, as was hoped under the earlier vision of a global village; instead, they have been refortified. Unless immigrants can demonstrate their use to the nation through their labour power or capital resources, they are not welcomed in any Western nation.

Whiteness

The essays in this collection challenge us to think about who is white and what whiteness means. Anti-racisms have tended not to interrogate whiteness, holding whiteness as the convenient norm (Bonnett 2000). But by naming "whiteness" as a racialized identity and cultural formation constructed alongside others, we have a new tool for understanding racisms. However, as in all forms of othering, stereotypes and generalizations hide and obscure multiple variants of being and becoming "white." All the authors in this collection are in dialogue with unacknowledged, taken-for-granted assumptions of whiteness as the hegemonic norm. They join an explosion of writings on whiteness written from an anti-racist perspective in the past ten years that have sought to investigate the social and historical construction of whiteness and that have tried to bring a complex, nuanced understanding of the many layers of whiteness (Dyer 1997; Frankenberg 1993, 1997; Roediger 1991; Rothenberg 2002; Ware 1992).

Whiteness as a cultural formation has been normalized to the point that it is taken for granted as the absent centre against which everything is silently compared. But whiteness has differing effects and consequences for phenotypical and cultural whites, making it necessary to complexify the anti-racist project of decentring and exploding myths of whiteness. By *cultural whites* we mean those who grow up under whiteness as a hegemonic cultural formation and learn to perform, act, and think white, but because they are racialized as Other, gain none of the benefits.

Mahtani, Miki, and Rattansi help to unpack the differing implications of whiteness for individuals of "mixed race" or multiple ethnicities. White national ethnicity compels those of non-phenotypical "whiteness" to adopt hyphenation as a response to their ambivalent citizenship identity in white settler and colonizing nations. National identity formation is a flexible process that works to stabilize the nation by destabilizing those on the frontiers of the hyphen-blackness, -brownness, -redness and all the mixtures inside and between (Rattansi). Mahtani's studies with mixed-race women, who inhabit collapsed borders but who must still live within a hierarchically striated continuum of white/non-white, indicate that whiteness has its limits as an elastic and inclusive category – but that these limits are being watched, tested, and pushed by mixed-race women who see themselves as active agents of racial subversion. As Mahtani's studies show, the lives of hyphenated subject-citizens must be taken up in the larger project of developing broader critical literacies for reading changing racisms and racialization.

Introduction

How can whites and mixed whites be brought into the anti-racism movement? This question has centred on whether getting whites to admit their unacknowledged privileges of whiteness remains within a "confessional" mode (Rothenberg 2002) whereby they confess and apologize for their unearned privileges, which does little to dismantle the structures of white supremacy. Should we be investigating how individuals become white and the privileges of whiteness? This question is now being posed in anti-racist circles. Some argue that if we fail to investigate how whiteness is formed, whiteness remains normalized as the hegemonic, naturalized, unmarked, and absent centre. Whites will then continue to be able to claim ignorance about their identity. Others argue that whiteness studies simply return the gaze to whiteness.

While agreeing that whiteness is not fixed and given, scholars differ as to how to explain the production and persistence of whiteness as a changing cultural and historical formation. Roediger (1991) and Ware (1992) have shown whiteness to have been created in the United States as a project of American capitalism and labour organizations. However, whiteness as a hegemonic cultural formation has also served the interests of nation formation and empire building from the colonial period onward (McLintock 1995). Maylam shows that history, when written by whites, often reflects the cultural conditions in which the historians live, and so contributes to the "normalcy" of whiteness. Jiwani and Henry and Tator, analysts of racism and the media, demonstrate the cultural (white) embeddedness of newspaper accounts of contemporary events.

Given the fully entrenched and concretized nature of whiteness in history and culture, will anti-racists' efforts to morally educate whites about the privileges and unearned benefits that accrue from their passive acquiescence to racisms be effective in the long run? Will greater awareness of the experience of suffering do anything except make whites feel guilty? What changes will recognition and confessions of white guilt do for those who remain marginalized and exploited? Will initiatives such as racism awareness training, or cultural diversity training – two models of practice that are intentionally aimed at the majority population and liberal organizations – do anything to transform institutional structures? Does destabilizing whiteness do anything to undermine its normative powers? For example, when white, suburban and urban youth symbolically appropriate black urban youth culture, or orientalize their bodies in piercings, tattoos, bindis, and eyeliner in ways that are meant to transgress white normativity, it does nothing to dismantle white normativity or privilege, or change the rates of violence, incarceration, unemployment, or sexual exploitation that disproportionately affect minority youth. All it does is allow these white youth to appear "cool" in the eyes of their peers, returning privilege and power to white normativity.

The Media and Representations

Essays by Henry and Tator and Jiwani demonstrate the collusion of racial state apparatuses and agents in perpetuating the myths of the hegemonic nation. However, it is important to acknowledge that the state is not a coherent monolith that acts consistently and exclusively in the interests of dominant power. Anti-racisms, for example, have historically developed through a dialectical process of incorporation and resistance in, through, and with the state, and the media is also a place for oppositional voices (Goldberg 2002; Omi and Winant 1986). Yet the asymmetry of control and access privileges certain voices and views over others. On the one hand, the liberal state's need to sustain its consent to rule from all citizens requires it to curb any inherent tendency toward violence and abuse. This is countered by the hegemonic bloc's deliberate and wilful use of racialized state power to produce and reproduce conditions advantageous to them. Multiple justifications are produced to rationalize their actions. The hegemonic political, social, cultural, and economic bloc, which controls the levers of state power, represents itself as being more liberal, more just, more civilized, more knowledgeable, more worthy, and more human than any other social group. This bloc uses the mass media to organize the racial, sexual, gender, religious, economic, and cultural order in ways that perpetuate their hold on power.

In their analysis of *Globe and Mail* editorials on employment equity legislation, Henry and Tator find that newspaper editorials are framed within the liberal notion of equality or equal opportunity, which is premised on a level playing field with everyone starting off at the same point. They demonstrate that liberalism in the news media reflects the views of the dominant elite and sustains the unequal racial order. Henry and Tator argue that the news media communicate only with the particular constituencies that form its readership; in the case of the *Globe and Mail*, these are the political, cultural, and economic elite in Canada. In their view, the *Globe and Mail* editorials are meant to reassure and confirm its white, male, and able-bodied readers as normal and entitled to their privileges.

Henry and Tator conclude that the "representations that permeate much of the press are not haphazard and isolated, but rather are part of a deep and complex ideological process" (174–5). The news media represents one of the central mechanisms for perpetuating racial consciousness by manufacturing shared ideologies across the state and the public.

Racisms and racialization remain very effective for mobilizing power in the interests of some (the few) over others (the many). For example, manufactured rhetoric about anti-terrorism and national security to justify military action and increased surveillance toward "the enemy" by the state/media partnership has resulted in increased racialized sexism against Muslim and Muslim-looking males and Muslim and Muslim-looking females. Citizenship and residency does not protect one against state-sanctioned racism, as Miki points out.

In France and Quebec, where laws were passed in 2004 to prohibit Muslim women and girls from wearing "head coverings" in public spaces, Muslim women were represented in the media as in need of saving from Muslim men who were portrayed as oppressing them and denying them freedoms and rights.[1]

Once again, we observe the intersection of race, sexuality, and nation interacting to racialize men and women in different ways. In moving to protect the secular nation against religious fundamentalism on the part of threats seen to be coming from Muslim males, the state required a justficatory discourse. Into this space, the media constructed representations of white, Christian males and females as saviours of deserving, educated, Muslim females against backward, oppressive, and brutal Muslim males. Once again, gender, race, religion, and class assumptions were brought together to construct Muslim males as the Other, occupying the "black" space in a black/white binary of racial politics.

Especially since the attack of 11 September 2001, when the United States' political, cultural, and military elite mobilized to racialize and demonize the entire Muslim and Arab world as "terrorists," light-skinned Muslims in North America, who previously could enter relatively easily into whiteness as long as they did not draw attention to their "difference," found themselves "marked" as Other. Since 9/11, racial boundaries have become much less permeable for Muslim and "Muslim-looking" people. New signifiers of difference were constructed around clothing, jewellery, brown-skinned bodies, cultural and religious practices, and language. This new racializing discourse is not just about skin colour, a fact that has prompted many authors in the collection to identify the rise or reawakening of cultural racisms in contemporary discourse.

IMPLICATIONS FOR ANTI-RACIST PRACTICE

The conference "*Making History, Constructing Race,*" from which most of the essays in this collection stem (with the exception of essays by Henry and Tator, Jiwani, and Mahtani), brought together scholars who struggle against racisms in university classrooms, and community organizations and workers from "the frontlines" of anti-racist struggle. It was not entirely a mutual meeting of minds. Not everyone was open to hearing divergent views. Some participants wished to hold existing boundaries in place, and many expressed deep suspicion about whether academics or practitioners "really knew" anything about racisms. Challenges and tensions erupted throughout the conference, and not surprisingly, many conflicts were over authenticity – who could speak on what issues and why – and turf – who was or was not getting resources and why. These troubling relationships and substantive disputes over representation and redistribution are in many ways refracting mirrors of debates occurring at the conceptual level about the status of "race," racisms, and racialization and the "proper" analysis to bring to the task.

The conference brought together 300 people from around the world to share concerns about racisms. It engaged the local community in thinking about racisms and anti-racisms and projected local concerns into a broader world context. The conference was a practical and symbolic example of the difficulties in working together across differences. Discussions revealed fissures, but also possibilities for alternative ways of thinking about racial difference from Aboriginal and non-Western perspectives.

As we learned in organizing the conference, listening is not always easy and is sometimes risky: tensions and conflicts are inherent in crossing disciplinary and sectoral boundaries. As anti-racists, we fight imposed ideas of difference, but as scholars and activists from diverse backgrounds, we often trip over the differences that we impose between ourselves.

The hegemony of racial thinking in our own culture means that fresh ideas and critical avenues of thinking often come to us from other cultures, if we can listen across the differences. The opening reading in this book provides an excellent example of a dialogue across differences and contributes to a new literacy of race. In the dialogue, First Nations writer Jeannette Armstrong introduces the Okanagan concept of *Enowkin* – to focus on difference as a positive thing. *Enowkin* means soliciting difference and recognizing its value. The Okanagan think that diversity brings resilience, endurance, and strength. Armstrong contrasts this to racism, an introduced system that sees difference as negative and that uses markers of difference to accord privilege to some and subjugate others. Her partner in this dialogue, Roxana Ng, uses Daoist teachings from her Chinese heritage as a platform outside Western thinking to critique racist and materialist "common sense."

Difference is a key concept, and *Enowkin* offers a new (to us) and thoughtful way to deal with it. Anti-racism is often seen to imply treating everybody the same – but we are not the same. Only through asserting our incommensurability have we broadened the horizons of studies and actions in "race," racism, racialization, and anti-racism (Bulmer and Solomos 1999). If a new literacy requires language that is more than just about being anti-racist, *Enowkin* offers just such a possibility. When difference is considered something to be embraced, not surmounted or transcended, and when human diversity is seen to be as desirable as biodiversity, we will be able to build the coalitions to create a world beyond racism.

In aiming to organize for a non-racist future, these essays offer practical tools for understanding how "race" is constantly being reformulated and redeployed to meet the changing needs of different states, corporate capitalism, nativist labour, and even disadvantaged racialized groups themselves.

Henry and Tator and Jiwani offer a language and a grid for reading between the lines of media reporting. Drawing attention to the corporate ownership of the major newspapers and the link between the ruling elite and governing parties, their chapters show how "common sense" is shaped by media reports to suit particular agendas. As mentioned earlier, the North American media is particularly concentrated in a few hands and offers only a narrow range of conservative to liberal views, but in his postscript, Rattansi shows that the British media is not so different. The two studies show how subtle and not-so-subtle use of language, story selection, and focus helps to build a consensus that there is no racism in our countries and, therefore, no affirmative action or structural change is needed. Rather, the reading (and viewing) public is constantly assured that liberal capitalist society is the pinnacle of progress and that all other cultures and races are deficient by comparison. Problems in other countries and regions are "the result of their backwardness," not, our media assure us, of any structural problems with capitalism or our own racism.

Against an overemphasis on representational politics of racism and racialization and the power of the media, however, Roxana Ng examines the lives of garment workers and shows how a racialized global capitalist order shapes the context for peoples' relationship to the mode of production and unifies garment workers in their common context of labour as racialized women. Their work is organized in similar ways, no matter if they work in downtown Toronto or Sri Lanka. Ng points out that wage labour is not a neutral category into which individuals are incorporated in undifferentiated ways. Through fundamentally raced, classed, and gendered processes, wage labour is transformed into piecework. Global capitalism has drawn upon and reworked already existing racial, sexual, gender, and class order to reposition racialized women garment workers in relation to mode of production in new ways. Factory work had the potential at least for collective organizing, but when homeworkers are separated and working out of their homes, they are isolated and without access to an organized voice, making them vulnerable to further exploitation.

Ng points out that the "needs" of the marginalized have been expelled from the state as part of the transformations occurring in global capitalism. The neo-liberal state no longer takes responsibility for those harmed by the market. Today the neo-liberal state rejects responsibility for those who suffer and fall through the social safety net. Marginalized individuals have become the responsibility of "private" organizations in civil society – the churches, the charities, family, service groups, and self-help organizations – and in the process, citizenship rights, benefits, and responsibilities are being reorganized so that those most marginalized assume a disproportionate share of the burden of neo-liberal policies. The retreat of the state from civil society in Western democracies has weakened the gains of anti-racism and feminist social movements.

If these chapters teach us how to deconstruct newspaper reports, Maylam's chapter offers tools for critically reading academic history. Although Maylam's specific example is historical writing in South Africa, the phases of race-analysis that he charts can be discerned in most Western historiography. The benefit of the South African example is that the positions were so polarized by apartheid that the role of ideology and authorial positioning is very clear. Maylam partly answers Stoler's question: Are racisms changing or just our analyses of them? Certainly our analyses have shifted dramatically. Like newspapers, they need to be read with a "critical literacy," and these essays provide several tools.

Stoler, Rattansi, and Miki also provide practical suggestions for moving forward. Stoler proposes that the role of academics is to track racisms' archived and buried traces. It is the buried traces, the sedimented accretions that form the usually unchallenged assumptions of our institutions, that activists need to challenge. Specifically, she points to the demonization of racist parties in France and argues that we make a strategic mistake if we organize only against fringe political groups. These are only the visible extremes, important for opening a discursive space for racisms, but a minor part of an entrenched racist culture and infrastructure. More important, Stoler says, is to understand "why racism is so easy to think" for the masses who do not identify with the extremists.

Rattansi explores the implications of the 9/11 phenomenon on race in Britain. He sees a turning away from diversity as a public good and multiculturalism as public policy and toward an insistence on homogeneity in culture and race. He draws out some of the renewed strategies of extremist racist parties, the (formerly) liberal state, and the British media to make aliens of non-white, and especially Islamic British. His work suggests that acceptance of diversity in Britain today is a fragile veneer over deeper racist structures and one that is easily broken through by "crisis."

The fragility of the non-racist veneer in wartime Canada is the focus of Roy Miki's exploration of hyphenated identities centred on Japanese-Canadians. Miki shows the dialogical (Bakhtin 1996) nature of identity, constantly in a state of negotiation between, in this case, the Canadian (personified by the state) and the Japanese-Canadian (personified by a committee of representatives seeking redress for historical wrongs). His chapter has particular implications for identities based on a historical wrong. So long as the wrong remains unacknowledged or unrepented by the state/mainstream, it can impart a centrifugal pull, drawing the subject group together. When the state apologizes and "re-dresses" the alien in the clothes of the citizen, the glue that held the hyphen in place dissolves and identities are forced to reform. Mahtani, like Miki and Rattansi, points to the fluidity of identity and the error of taking one-dimensional, simplistic approaches to subjectification (creating one's own identity) or objectification (creating an identity for another).

CONCLUSION

In spite of the fact that "race" has historically been defined by visible difference, it is very hard to see, track, and talk about. Racisms and racializing processes undergo constant change, and scholarship and activism need to be critical, responsive, and evolving. Today we are witnessing new morphologies of race and new sites of inclusion and exclusion, accelerated by the West's response to perceived terrorist threats from the "East." Stoler asks: "What are we willing to ask about what racisms look like on the cusp of this twenty-first century? ... Are [we] equipped with the epistemic tools to understand their regimes of [moral] truth?" Are they what those who track racisms' archived and buried traces, expect them to be?" (114–115).

The contributors to this book all belong to "those" who track racism's traces, and each makes a contribution to the epistemic and practical tools for reading race today. Several of the contributors track the evolution of concepts of race and racism (Maylam, Ng's postscript), and all develop different visions that have become thinkable within the framework of postmodernism and its subsequent development. Different sites of racialization are highlighted: for Miki, Rattansi, and Mahtani, identities are in the foreground. For Stoler, Rattansi, Miki, and Maylam, nation is the key site of struggle, while for Ng and Armstrong, global capitalism is the focus. For Jiwani and Henry and Tator, the mass media is the site and critical decoding skills are the tools. Ng and Armstrong invite us to break from the hegemonic ways of thinking about race – and even the dominant critical ideologies around race – to see race from other cultural perspectives.

Clearly these are early steps. As Rattansi points out, empirical studies of actual racisms are needed. We need to be more attentive to the intersections of racisms, sexisms, classisms, ableisms, heterosexisms, citizenship classificationism, and categoricalisms of all kinds. There is also a need to study resistance to racism and racialization, the dialogic nature of the process in all its forms, both institutional and personal. The constant reinvention of nations and their relationship to global capitalism and liberal ideologies need tracing and challenging.

New critical literacies of *anti-racisms* are urgently needed. The contributions in this book point to the need for more open-ended, flexible, and intersectional views of racisms and anti-racisms; a new literacy needs to keep pace with the shifting politics of racisms as they intersect with other changing structures of inequality.

Analysts and activists can only ever offer a partial reading of contemporary events; the future remains hazy. Yet activists and scholars *cannot afford not to* look ahead. To do this, we need a new arsenal of tools, a new literacy of "race" and racism. We need to be able to look around and name the forms that racism is taking, to deconstruct them, and to work not just against racism but toward *Enowkin*.

NOTE

1 In March 2004 legislation in France banned the wearing of prominent religious symbols in schools, including Jewish and Christian iconography, but the law was initiated by concern over the rise of Islamic fundamentalism.

REFERENCES

Alfred, T. 1999. *Peace, Power, Righteousness: An Indigenous Manifesto*. Don Mills ON: Oxford.

Anthias, F., and Lloyd, C., eds. 2002. *Rethinking Anti-Racisms: From Theory to Practice*. London: Routledge.

Anthias, F., and Yuval-Davis, N. 1991. "Connecting Race and Gender." In *Racialized Boundaries: Race, Nation, Gender, Colour, and Class and the Anti-Racist Struggle*, eds. F. Anthias and N. Yuval-Davis, 96-131. London and New York: Routledge.

Bakhtin, M. 1996. *The Dialogic Imagination: Four Essays by M.M. Bakhtin*, ed. M. Holquist, trans. C. Emmerson and M. Holquist. Austin: University of Texas.

Bannerji, H. 2000. *The Dark Side of the Nation: Essays on Multiculturalism, Nationalism and Gender*. Toronto: Canadian Scholars' Press Inc.

Bernal, M. 1987. *Black Athena: The Afro-Asiatic Roots of Classical Civilization*. London: Free Association Books.
Bhavnani, K-K., ed. 2001. *Feminism and "Race."* Oxford: Oxford University Press.
Bonnett, A. 2000. *Anti-Racism*. London and New York: Routledge.
Bulmer, J., and Solomos, J., eds. 1999. *Ethnic and Racial Studies Today*. New York: Routledge.
Cohen, P. 1997. *Rethinking the Youth Question: Education, Labour and Cultural Studies*. London: Macmillan Press.
Dua, E., and Robertson, A., eds. 1999. *Scratching the Surface*. Toronto, ON: Women's Press.
Dyer, R. 1997. *White*. London and New York: Routledge.
Fanon, F. 1986. *Black Skin, White Masks*, trans. C.L. Markmann. London: Pluto Press.
Foucault, M. 1977. *The Use of Pleasure. History of Sexuality* vol. 2. New York: Vintage.
– 1980. *Power/Knowledge: Selected Interviews and Other Writings 1972–1977*, ed. C. Gordon, trans. C. Gordon, L. Marshall, J. Mepham, and K. Soper. New York: Pantheon Books.
Frankenberg, R. 1993. *White Women, Race Matters*. Minneapolis: University of Minnesota Press.
– ed. 1997. *Displacing Whiteness: Essays in Social and Cultural Criticism*. Durham, NC: Duke University Press.
Gilman, S.L. 1985. "Black Bodies, White Bodies: Towards an Iconography of Female Sexuality in Late Nineteenth-Century Art, Medicine, and Literature." *Critical Inquiry* 12, Autumn: 204–42.
Gilroy, P. 1987. *There Ain't No Black in the Union Jack: The Cultural Politics of Race and Nation*. London: Unwin Hyman.
– 1993. *The Black Atlantic: Modernity and Double Consciousness*. London: Verso.
Goldberg, D.T., ed. 1990. *Anatomy of Racism*. Minneapolis: University of Minnesota Press.
– 1993. *Racist Culture: Philosophy and the Politics of Meaning*. Oxford: Blackwell Publishers.
– 2002. *The Racial State*. Oxford: Blackwell Publishers.
Hall, S. 1992. "New Ethnicities." In *"Race," Culture, Difference*, eds. J. Donald and A. Rattansi, 252–59. London: Sage.
– 1996. "Introduction: Who Needs 'Identity'?" In *Questions of Cultural Identity*, eds. S. Hall and P. Du Gay, 1–17. London: Sage.
– 1997. "The Centrality of Culture: Notes on the Cultural Revolutions of Our Time." In *Media and Cultural Regulation*, ed. K. Thompson, 207–38. London: Sage.
– 2000. "Old and New Ethnicities." In *Theories of Race and Racism: A Reader*, eds. L. Back and J. Solomos, 144–53. London and New York: Routledge.

hooks, b. 1984. *Feminist Theory: From Margin to Center.* Boston: South End Press.
– 1994. *Outlaw Culture Resisting Representations.* New York: Routledge.
Jiwani, Y. 1992. "The Exotic, the Erotic and the Dangerous: South Asian Women in Popular Film." *Canadian Woman Studies* 13, no. 1: 42–6.
Latour, B. 1987. *Science in Action.* Cambridge: Harvard.
Loomba, A. 1998. *Colonialism/Postcolonialism.* London and New York: Routledge.
McLintock, A. 1995. *Imperial Leather: Race, Gender and Sexuality in the Colonial Context.* New York: Routledge.
Miles, R. 1989. *Racism.* London: Routledge.
Mohanty, C.T., Russo, A., and Torres, L., eds. 1991. *Third World Women and the Politics of Feminism.* Bloomington and Indianapolis: Indiana University Press.
Omi, M., and Winant, H. 1986. *Racial Formation in the United States: From the 1960s to the 1980s.* New York: Routledge and Kegan Paul.
Parker, D., and Song, M., eds. 2001. *Rethinking "Mixed Race."* London: Pluto Press.
Rattansi, A. 1994. "'Western' Racisms, Ethnicities and Identities in a 'Postmodern' Frame." In *Racism, Modernity and Identity: On the Western Front*, eds. A. Rattansi and S. Westwood. Cambridge: Polity Press.
– 1995. "'Just Framing' Racism and Ethnicity in a 'Postmodern' Framework." In *Social Postmodernism beyond Identity Politics*, eds. L. Nicholson and S. Seidman. New York: Cambridge University Press.
Razack, S.H. 1998. *Looking White People in the Eye: Gender, Race, and Culture in Courtrooms and Classrooms.* Toronto: University of Toronto Press.
– ed. 2002. *Race Space and the Law: Unmapping a White Settler Society.* Toronto: Between the Lines Press.
Roediger, D. 1991. *The Wages of Whiteness: Race and the Making of the American Working Class.* London and New York: Verso.
Rothenberg, P.S., ed. 2002. *White Privilege Essential Readings on the Other Side of Racism.* New York: Worth Publishers.
Said, E. W. 1979. *Orientalism.* New York: Vintage Books.
Sioui, G. 1992. *For an Amerindian Autohistory.* Montreal and Kingston: McGill Queen's.
Stoler, A.L. 1995. *Race and the Education of Desire: Foucault's History of Sexuality and the Colonial Order of Things.* Durham: Duke.
Taguieff, P.A. 1990. "The New Cultural Racism in France." *Telos* Spring, no. 83: 109–23.
Ware, V. 1992. *Beyond the Pale: White Women, Racism and History.* London and New York: Verso.
Werbner, P. 1997. "Essentialising Essentialism, Essentialising Silence: Ambivalence and Multiplicity in the Constructions of Racism and Ethnicity." In

Debating Cultural Hybridity, eds. P. Werbner and T. Modood, 226–56. London and New Jersey: Zed Books.

Werbner, P., and Modood, T., eds. 1997. *Debating Cultural Hybridity: Multicultural Identities and the Politics of Anti-Racism*. London and New Jersey: Zed Books.

Winant, H. 1994. "Where Culture Meets Structure." In *Racial Conditions: Politics, Theory, Comparisons*, H. Winant. Minneapolis and London: University of Minnesota Press.

Young, R.J.C. 1995. *Colonial Desire: Hybridity in Theory, Culture and Race*. London: Routledge.

A CONVERSATION BETWEEN JEANNETTE ARMSTRONG
AND ROXANA NG

Deconstructing Race, Deconstructing Racism

(with Postscript 2004)

JEANNETTE ARMSTRONG, "DECONSTRUCTING RACE"

I want to talk about the idea of race. I wanted to begin with the idea of race from my perspective as an Okanagan First Nation woman.

I know that throughout my life, I've experienced what is called racism, firsthand. I know that it's something that, in terms of theoretical construct, presents itself as a challenge to us.

I was thinking about what race and racism really are. How do they occur? How should we look at them? How should we work against them? How should we deconstruct them and put in their place something different?

Several years ago, I started thinking about the following questions: When did the idea of race first occur? How did it occur? Where are the roots of racism? I'm not a historian; however, the questions from my First Nation view may provide insight. From my Okanagan perspective, there seems to be a fundamental difference in terms of how the world is perceived and how human interaction is perceived. The question of fundamental difference in how societies, in a behavioural sense, organize themselves for survival reasons comes to mind. I go back to that question when I think about the indigenous Okanagan society that I come from. I have also looked at and examined other land-based indigenous cultures with that fundamental question in mind. One of the things I began to see and understand about indigenous cultures is that the main principle of human interaction, in a land-based culture of self-sufficiency in the natural world, is that it must be based on cooperation. Interaction has to be based on principles by which people not only respect each other in their difference but depend on those differences and understand that those differences are critical to their survival. Difference in this way is perceived from a totally different perspective. When you look at how cooperative units and collectives, which had to survive over thousands of generations, developed their societal systems and cultures, then philosophies, theories, and cosmologies related to how difference must be celebrated and embraced begin to emerge. You begin to see how difference is perceived, not as race, but as something that is valuable, something that is strengthening, and something that is absolutely necessary.

As an example, I was thinking about the meaning of the word *Enowkin*, from my perspective as an Okanagan, and I thought I would share that with you so that we can look at it as something of a framework that we might use. The word *Enowkin*, which was given to us to use as the name for our centre, is a word that is symbolic and metaphoric. Originally, the Okanagan, like the English language, like any other language, had levels of speakers or levels of language. And just as there is an academic level of language which is used in the academic institutions of learning, and you have street English, and you have baby English, it's the same in my language. In the Okanagan the word *Enowkin* comes from what might be called the academic level of language. It refers to a process that is to be engaged in to look at difference, but also to engage difference, to solicit difference, to incorporate difference, and to strengthen difference. It is a process that our leaders used. The literal translation of it is something like (the word is broken up into three or four syllables) a drop that permeates through the top of the head and suffuses the rest of the body. Something like osmosis I guess. That's the literal imagery that occurs when you say that word. But what *Enowkin* refers to is a process of building consensus. But it's not consensus as understood by the dictionary definition, or the way that it's used today, which seems to mean everybody coming to an agreement, the idea being that if everybody sort of agrees with each other then they've reached consensus. Well, when we talk about that principle of *Enowkin*, we're saying that everybody doesn't have to come to an agreement, but everybody recognizes the common ground upon which our differences rest. So when our traditional chiefs used to call for *Enowkin* they were asking people, when there was a decision to be made or a choice to be made, to gather together with the realization that each person has a different interest.

Each person, from the elders to the young people in the community; from the women, the mothers in the community, to the men, the fathers in the community; and the workers, the artists, and the musicians, has a view. In other words, everyone has a vested interest in how this decision is going to be made. So one of the first things to do is to agree that there are going to be differences in everybody's points of view. If we're going to come to a community solution, if we're going to come to solidarity, then we must understand our differences or where each person is coming from. We must actively solicit difference of opinion. Rather than try to win the argument, rather than try to tell someone, "Well you're wrong and I'm right and you've got to see it my way and I'm going to do everything I can possibly, politically, and every which other way to coerce your thinking so that it matches mine." From my view that is a dysfunctional way of doing things. There are some ground rules that are used when the *Enowkin* process is engaged. The first ground rule is that we're here to hear differing opinions, and that I must solicit the most different view to mine because only then can I recognize what's in between us as an obstacle. Only then can I recognize how I must shift in order to recognize where that difference comes from, and find a way to communicate with you the difference of my opinion. And this dynamic creates a voice in the community in terms of difference.

I think I wanted to talk about difference a little bit because when I'm looking at difference I see it as a microcosm and as a way of doing things. As an Okanagan person, I can see, fundamentally and philosophically, where the problem seems to be when we're speaking about "race." We really are speaking about the construction of race or the construction of the idea of "race" and trying to find a way to deconstruct it. When we do not operate from the philosophical idea that difference is not only natural but of critical importance, where are we operating from? When we're operating from a societal point of view that doesn't solicit difference, that doesn't embrace difference, that doesn't honour difference, where are we operating from? In other words, where are we operating from if we do not start with the view that your difference informs and enriches me, gifts and honours me? In return, it is my responsibility to try to figure out a way to incorporate that difference so that we can build on it. By the same token you have the same responsibility toward me if we're in this together, if we're in the community together.

So when I look at history and "race" and the idea of how "race" may have started, I conclude that "race" begins with the fundamental premise that someone thinks that they have more of a right to truth or to power; someone has more of a right to state what they think the world looks like and to coerce others into agreeing with that view. Somewhere along the line, some human beings began to accept that idea as a paradigm, to believe that someone over there has the right to develop the choices, to enforce the choices, to make the choices for others. So the idea, I think, of "race" fundamentally, from my perspective, is centred around the idea of supremacy – the idea of someone having more rights than others, in other words, privilege and power.

It plays itself out when you look at the history of conquest. If you look at the history of aggression, globalization wasn't just thought up a few years ago when they coined the word. Globalization is an old story, and that old story is about supremacy. That old story is about subjugation of peoples in their interactions on their lands, about making sure people who had privilege over others maintained their privilege over others. I don't think that "race" is just about colour; I think racism is about wealth and privilege. When I look at some of the issues around race, for example, I look at Europe's colonialism before it reached Canada. I think of how the Irish people and the Scottish people suffered to a great degree in the same way that we did when they were colonized. I know there was suffering, because my grandfather, who was Irish, came over during the potato famines. The Irish were left landless and destitute and were treated in much the same way as our peoples were.

When you look within the colonizers' society and at the class systems created around ideas of privilege and power, one of the things you see is that once the initial tyranny of colonization is accomplished, the idea of class is one of the easiest ways to indoctrinate a colonized population to accept, agree with, and give consent to subjugation. In a class-structured society, the privileged members of society believe that "It's better to take from them than from us, better to enslave them than us, better to make them work than us." If you look at the colonizer peoples who instituted slavery, for instance, they were doing the same things to their own impoverished classes, to their children, to their women. I read somewhere that there are children whose bones are still stuck in smokestacks in Britain where they died cleaning chimneys. These societies' own children were sent down mines; their own women worked day and night to feed their families; landless people were hanged for shooting a rabbit or a deer. These citizens were somehow "owned" by a landlord in that society. It was a simple matter to transfer those social conditions and attitudes to people of different cultures, people of another skin colour, and people of other lands. As these views became entrenched within the entire system of colonization they inevitably created the kind of systemic violence that continues in this country, in all of the Americas, and in all of the colonized countries of the world.

What is appalling to me is the complacency that condones racism and puts up with it every day under the banner of democracy, civilization, and progress. What is appalling is that nobody thinks it is racism when a native person stands up and speaks his or her language and no one understands a single word. Who decided that my language isn't valuable? Who decided that my language has no place here, on this land, when for thousands of years our people and every other First Nation in this country took care of these lands? Who decided that our cultures do not have a right to exist on the land that our ancestors took care of for thousands of years? It's the same situation in Africa, it's the same in New Zealand, it's the same in Australia, it's the same in Central and South America.

What is the United Nations when not one indigenous nation, from North, Central, or South America, sits at the table as a nation? What kind of racism are we talking about? We all believe in peacekeeping and the work of the United Nations, yet as a global institution, it feeds the acceptance of racist behaviour. When we start to look at the different guises of racism, whether under the banner of democracy or communism, socialism or fascism, they have the same effect in terms of how women, children, and the disadvantaged of any colour are treated worldwide.

I get angry when I think about the complacency, because racism is thought of as an individual issue – it is intolerable, and I fight against it. When we go to cast our votes, do we think about how we are abdicating our responsibility to a government that institutionalizes and perpetuates racism by condoning the systemic demise of peoples through massive trade agreements that unfairly exploit resources in places like Chile, Guatemala, Brazil, and Mexico? What is the Mexico–U.S.–Canada agreement if not a racist program to institutionalize the theft and piracy from peoples who have taken care of their lands for thousands of generations years from those peasant populations who have taken care of those lands in a sustainable way for centuries? These are some of the questions that I would like to bring forward to this dialogue.

ROXANA NG, "DECONSTRUCTING RACISM: WHAT DOES IT REALLY MEAN?"

Jeannette Armstrong and I have never met before today. We decided, when we met for the first time this morning, that it was fate that brought us together (of course it's really the work of the organizing committee) because you will hear in what I say resonances with what Jeannette has said.

It is a pleasure for me to be here because B.C., or more precisely Vancouver, was my first destination in Canada when my family immigrated in 1970. Circumstances don't enable me to live in B.C. now, but I have many fond memories and experiences of my time here. The early and mid-seventies were my formative years as an anti-racist feminist activist when I studied and worked in Vancouver. These early years also laid the foundation for my scholarship on immigrant women; on conceptualizing relations of race, gender and class; and on relations between community and the state that I was to develop later. It was in Vancouver that I learned to work across differences. That stood me in good stead as I moved across the country in pursuit of study and employment. So I owe a lot to B.C. I also want to take this opportunity to pay a special tribute to Barbara Roberts, who you may or may not know. Barbara was a peace activist and feminist historian who passed away in 1998 in Victoria. When I first developed my work on immigrant women, and there were few historical studies on the subject, it was to Barbara's work that I turned to fill the void. As my thesis committee member and friend, she encouraged me to wade into an area given little attention and significance at the time. Her irreverence was what inspired me to stay in the academy when most of my experiences in it, especially after I became faculty, had been very disheartening.[1] It's also an honour to be here with Jeannette. It is a historical moment when an aboriginal person and a Chinese-Canadian can be on the same panel together, given the contemporary tension between immigrant groups and aboriginal peoples. I do think we owe this to the work of the organizing committee.

The title of my talk is "Deconstructing Racism." It is interesting that although Jeannette and I didn't get together to develop our titles, they fit together very well. My talk about "Deconstructing Racism" follows logically from Jeannette's "Deconstructing Race." I will make some general comments here, just simple points, in order to stimulate conversations later on in the session as well as in the workshops. I'm going to speak from my own positioning as an immigrant woman and as a woman of colour in this country, so my vantage point is different from Jeannette's. The issue here is not agreement, it is to hear each other.

My presentation attempts to pull together pieces of work that I have done and am developing to see how they may fit together and shed light on my talk on deconstructing racism. I want to raise three general points, and then I'll move on to talk about what I mean by anti-racism.

The first point I want to make is that we need to think beyond race as a social and theoretical category. It is appropriate that the term "race" is placed in quotation marks in the title of this conference. In spite of the persistence of marking groups of people according to their supposed biological or natural characteristics, I emphasize that "race", like gender, is a purely imaginary social fabrication for the purpose of establishing a hierarchy among people. This point is similar to what Jeannette has said. However, the effect of racialization is obvious. In spite of the many common conditions shared by aboriginal peoples, African-Americans and African-Canadians, and immigrant groups in terms of their relations to the means of production, we have not been able to organize across the divide of the supposed natural differences of phenotypical characteristics. So I would say that race is the social construction, but the act and effect of this construction, racialization, have produced actual divisions among people. Whereas feminists in the 1970s developed the term "gender" to distinguish the socially constructed differences between men and women from biological sex differences, a parallel term has not been invented to pinpoint or highlight the imaginary from the biological in terms of "race." So, whereas, gender always implies social relations between men and women, "race" signifies groupings of people perceived as being "naturally" different from each other. "Gender" is a term that actually pinpoints the social relation between two groups of people, but the term "race" doesn't have that connotation; this is problematic. Using quotation marks around "race" is a good start, but there is a need for us to invent a new language, indeed, for us to imagine ourselves beyond the category of "race" developed by our oppressors to divide us and to keep us from discovering the common conditions of our lives.

Second, racial differences are not the only or primary differentiation among people at any given time. Within any racial grouping, gender, age, class, and ability are among other relations that distinguish people from one another. So, for example, relations between people of different ages and genders serve to mark the internal differentiation within any given group. People's different relations then serve to differentiate them in a class society. For an immigrant woman, gender, race, ethnicity and class are simultaneous properties that produce her as different and inferior.[2] Thus, we need to develop ways of thinking and acting that enable us to work with and across these axes of differences simultaneously.

On the basis of the preceding arguments, my third point is that apart from its most general characteristic, that of producing a hierarchical ordering of people for the purpose of establishing dominant-subordinate relations, racism takes different forms across time and space in relation to groups of people. So, for example, the subordination of the aboriginal people in North America during the fur trade was undertaken to supply markets in Europe. This form of racism was different in character and effect from the period of colonization when aboriginal peoples were forcibly confined to reserves during the development and expansion of markets within Canada itself. This form of racism was different yet from the importation of South Asian and Chinese men as indentured labourers or the internment of Japanese Canadians during World War II. I want to use a lot of aboriginal and Asian examples because British Columbia is the province marked by its racism against these two groups of people. Now that I live in Ontario it is very hard for Ontarians to understand these forms of racism; people always tell me, "Oh there's no racism towards the Chinese, they're rich." I will return to this perception toward the end of my presentation.

So, in every specific instance, we have to interrogate how racism actually operates and what kinds of divisions it creates. As well, we have to examine how it intersects with other axes of power and difference. It is all the more important for us to examine the changing contours and effects of racism and sexism in the current period of globalization, because work-restructuring, which is concomitant with the advance of globalization, is creating new forms of marginalization and differentiation in Canada as well as around the world. In my recent research on the garment industry and the condition of garment workers, many of whom are immigrant women from Asia, I argue that immigrant women are undergoing a process of recolonization. This time, colonization is not occurring in the geographical boundaries of their home country; it takes place inside the nation to which they have migrated in order to seek better employment or to avoid warfare and other forms of violence (see Ng 1998). That is, with the re-structuring of the garment industry, women who were working in factories with unionized wages and relatively decent working conditions have been displaced. This does not mean they lost their jobs altogether. It means they are now sewing at home as piece work with little job security (see Ng 1999). Although these women might have enjoyed an improvement of their living standards, this is temporary as global competition affects the economies of the North and South equally.

As for aboriginal peoples, I would argue that they have never been decolonized in Canada or elsewhere despite token gestures extended by the Canadian government in the form of promises of self-government and land-claims. However, the situation of aboriginal communities varies greatly across the country. The continuing effect of colonization needs to be made a matter for concrete empirical investigation. I emphasize here that this era of globalization signals a stage in capitalist development in which capital has developed the capacity to move across national boundaries in search of cheap and flexible labour pools and of markets for profit augmentation. Jeannette already touched on this point. Although in some social situations it isn't fashionable anymore to talk about capitalism, especially in light of the dissolution of the socialist bloc, I want to preserve an understanding of capitalism, not just as an economic system, but as a mode of production and reproduction. A mode of production refers to the ways in which people produce and reproduce their livelihood under concrete material conditions that go beyond the economy. Capitalism is a dynamic process that transforms and reorganizes our livelihoods according to the requirements of capital accumulation. Capitalism is characterized not only by money as the universal medium of exchange and accumulation but also by the subordination of masses of people as wage labourers. This is the kind of exploitation that Jeannette talked about. But there is something peculiar about this form of exploitation and subordination. These relations appear to represent individual choices and freedom. People are supposedly free to sell their labour power in a free market in exchange for money to sustain their livelihood. In reality, especially as the world economy is increasingly integrated, many people have little choice but to work as wage labourers. Furthermore, the nature of wage labour is also changing in this period of globalization: the changing conditions of immigrant garment workers from factory to home-based workers signals yet another phase in economic and social relations, one in which people are considered to be self-employed. In fact, this form of work organization (class relation) deepens the vulnerability of racial minority women, making them more susceptible to exploitation. It is in this and other ways that women's lives are transformed by work restructuring. In the case of garment workers in Canada, we see that gender, race, class are the essential, though not by any means the exclusive, ingredients in this process of transformation. These relations are interwoven; they work in complicated ways to give shape and contours to people's everyday lives. By examining the changing conditions of garment production, we see concrete ways in which sexism, racism, and class exploitation intertwine and intersect to keep minority women workers captive.[3]

Indeed, what we have been witnessing in the last thirty to forty years is the growing gap between the rich and the poor divided along racial and gender lines. This has created common conditions among larger and larger segments of the world's population regardless of their actual geographical locations in the economic North or South. In other words, the present stage of capitalism we call economic globalization has also opened up spaces for people previously deemed different to attempt to work across these differences by forging coalitions and alliances. The anti-globalization movement, expressed as the anti-sweat movement in the garment sector, is an example of how people from different localities and social positions can join forces to help ameliorate the detrimental effects of globalization on garment workers. However, to mount successful resistance against global capitalism, of which racism and sexism are essential elements, I argue that an anti-racist, feminist, and anti-colonial perspective is necessary. Thus, I will end this talk by exploring what it may mean to incorporate an integrative anti-racist approach into our thinking and acting.

First, I need to make a distinction between what I call non-racism and anti-racism. Here, I'm relying on the work of Linda Briskin on feminist pedagogy, and her distinction between non-sexism and anti-sexism

(Briskin 1990). Non-racism is an approach that suggests that racism can be made irrelevant by focusing on the notion that all people are equal and that we should all be treated equally. It is an individualistic approach that attempts to rid individuals of racist attitudes without attending to the systemic operation of racism in our lives. Here's a quote from Terri Wolverton. This is what she said when she discovered the difference between non-racism and anti-racism in one of her consciousness-raising groups: "I had confused the act of trying to appear not to be racist with actively working to eliminate racism. Trying to appear not racist had made me deny my racism and therefore exclude the possibility of change" (Wolverton quoted in Briskin 1990, 14–15).

An integrative anti-racist approach would acknowledge explicitly that we are all gendered, racialized, and differently constructed subjects who do not participate as equals in interactional settings. It recognizes that racism as well as sexism and other forms of oppression are systemic and that we therefore cannot cleanse ourselves of racism through good will. Eliminating racism is a collective, not an individual project. This does not mean that we shouldn't reflect on how we unwittingly participate in courses of action that implicate us in the perpetuation of racism. When I say that racism is systemic, I mean that certain ways of doing things have become normalized or naturalized to the point that they become considered common sense; they are taken for granted and therefore not open to interrogation. The confinement of the aboriginal peoples to reserves and the internment of Japanese Canadians during World War II were based on what was common-sense reasoning at those historical moments. New forms of common-sense racism are emerging all the time. So, for example, I return to my earlier example. In a series of events that occurred in my own institution lately it was reported to me that even among anti-racist educators there is the belief that Asians, especially Chinese, don't count as people of colour because they have lots of money, they live in monster homes, and their kids do well in school. The B.C. press have reported on these phenomena, too – during the 1990s leading up to the return of Hong Kong to China, newspapers were full of stories about rich Chinese immigrants buying up Vancouver. In reality, at the height of this period business class immigrants from Hong Kong constituted about 2 per cent of the total number of immigrants coming into Canada annually (Man 1996). In this instance, stereotyping Chinese immigrants as rich and therefore irrelevant in anti-racism work is a form of racism where class and race are conflated, and where the privilege of a small minority stands in for an entire population. An integrative anti-racist approach would require that we analyse how racialization and class articulate[4] with each other under what conditions to produce particular forms of racism.

I suggest that we need to question how the kind of thinking about Chinese and other groups arises and becomes common sense for ordinary people and anti-racist educators alike. Rupturing what we take for granted and interrogating what we know to be "true" is the first step in embodying anti-racism. We need to be cognizant and vigilant about how racism and other forms of marginalization operate in everyday settings to divide us, especially in this era of globalization when the cross-boundary movement of people, not to mention the movement of capital, is so much more frequent. But as I said earlier, this period also holds unique opportunities for us to work across boundaries of race, gender, ability, nation, and so forth, because one of the effects of globalization is to homogenize us – we share common conditions arising out of the transformations of our livelihood across the spatial divide of the North and the South and across the regional divides within Canada. These common conditions, rather than our socially constructed, so-called natural characteristics, can become focal points for building alliances.

JEANNETTE ARMSTRONG AND ROXANA NG IN DIALOGUE

JA: I guess what I was thinking about when you were talking is the construct of "race" as it occurs today. And I was thinking about the fact that within the apparatus of globalization, one of the parts of the construct, for me at least, that I think really needs to be deconstructed is the idea of accepting the way the world economic situation dictates the racial construct to us. And the reason I say that is when we think about globalization, what's at the centre of it is the need for creating competition – competitive economies and competition are at the source of mobilizing capital to countries where people can produce something more competitively, in other words cheaper. You can employ people more cheaply where there are no laws governing labour and rights of women and children and no laws regarding our other relatives on the land in the form of environmental controls. So, as there is increased mobilization of capital, there's also increased marginalization of peoples in terms of that competition and increased pressures in terms of producing things cheaper and cheaper. When you look at that model one of the things that it postulates is that it's guaranteed to create and construct tensions where there were no tensions before. Where local economies had built up systems in which cooperation and competitiveness were balanced in terms of the return and the benefit to the members of those local economies, there was less racial tension among people from different background, which suggest that tensions are constructed through economic competition. When there's higher competition, more and more people want and need those jobs to feed their children. The construction of race and the construction of oppression intensify. As the jobless rate and the homeless rate increase, and the safety net disappears, because the state has privatized services that were formerly the government's responsibility, the people's citizenship rights become commodified; health, education, and welfare disappear for the poor, and only the wealthy can afford them. Increasingly, there's competition for those few jobs that are offered to people in return for being part of this great country. One of the things you see is that racial constructs start to emerge as a result of increased competition, and as a result, for example, right here in this province there has been a rise in hostile sentiment toward the treaty-making process with aboriginal people pitted against non-aboriginal people for control of a diminishing resource base. Even in that construct, there's an inherent racism saying, "This is the way you have to do your treaty with me." The construction of racist attitudes that comes with the loss of jobs and the loss of opportunities is a necessary consequence of our present economic conditions. The construction of racist ideas is a central issue, and it's really good to hear you putting into words some of the ways in which we might approach dismantling these ideas.

RN: What I was interested in, and I thought your work provided a different kind of model for us to start to work with, is the concept *Enowkin*, because usually when we talk about difference it is thought of as divisive. You put forward a way of seeing difference as something that needs to be recognized to form a common ground. Your conceptualization provides a different way of thinking about difference that is not in the current discourse around "race" and racism. This is a really interesting notion to explore, and I hope that it will be taken up. What I'm finding increasingly frustrating too is that we have been unable, with no additional tools, to imagine a different world apart from the one we live in. Thank goodness we do have other cultural forms to turn to. For example, I have returned to some of the ideas in Daoism, while recognizing that it was a patriarchal and very traditional system. I want to retrieve things that we can use to remake, to help us think through, the kind of fixes that we are in. Like aboriginal cultures and principles, Daoism as a system of thought gives us a different way of beginning to deconstruct the problems in which we are caught and which we think are inevitable.

JA: I think that's really an interesting point because the whole question of biodiversity leads us to think about human diversity as one of the totally necessary ingredients for our survival as humankind, and yet it's almost, I think, put in terms of the negative when you think about difference. When you're enjoying, embracing, and acknowledging difference, it is really important to understand how difference has been used and constructed to racialize, to oppress, to create pain, and to create the kinds of conditions that exist worldwide through what's called racism. I think that's really an important place to begin and I really appreciate sharing this podium with you.

POSTSCRIPT BY ROXANA NG

As the editors prepared this manuscript to go to press, I was asked whether I could re-work my section of the dialogue in light of post-colonial and post-modern literature on race. I want to preserve the piece with Jeannette as a dialogue as much as possible; therefore I have only made minor changes and additions, such as references, to the main text. My reasons for not addressing post-colonial study directly has to do with my discomfort with the term "post-colonialism," given the continuing colonization of the aboriginal peoples in Canada (e.g., Adams 1999) and worldwide (e.g., Smith 1999), and with what I have named the recolonization of people of colour occurring right now.

In this postscript, I would like to discuss further the key concepts I mentioned in my presentation. While some of these concepts and theoretical formulations appear in the post-colonial and post-modern literature, they come from other theoretical traditions, which have been incorporated into the "post-" literature with little acknowledgement of their origins.

The concepts I want to clarify are *racialization* and *racism*. Racialization refers to the process whereby groups of people are reified as different "races" based on their biological and phenotypical characteristics. The concept was first used by Fanon (1963) when he discussed the difficulties facing decolonized intellectuals (see Miles 1989 Chapter 3 for details). Racialization is a process of classification, representation, and signification used by various groups to distinguish themselves from the "other" (see Omi & Winnart 1986, Miles 1989). Racialization can lead to *racism*, which refers to a process of inferiorization, exclusion, and marginalization of the other. For analytical purposes, it is important to distinguish between these two terms, because racialization does not always lead to racism. In his classic *Racism*, for example, sociologist Robert Miles points out that during the Greco-Roman empire, although Africans were seen to be different from Europeans, there was no sustained negative stereotype or discrimination against them. European superiority did not cohere until around the fifteenth century, when European nation states began to expand their political and material boundaries through a system of international trade. This was the beginning of European colonization (Miles 1989, Chapter 1). Based on his historical examination, Miles refers to racism simply as an ideology, and provides a detailed discussion on the criteria for determining racist ideology vis-à-vis other forms of discrimination and exclusion (Chapter 3).

I tend to use the term more broadly to refer to both the ideology *and* practice of inferiorizing and excluding groups of people by virtue of their "race," bearing in mind that racial differences are socially constructed. For me, what is most insidious is that although the process of inferiorizing certain groups may begin with those with power, for example with the colonizers, once "races" are reified as real differences among and between individuals, these differences become naturalized and normalized (see Foucault 1978 on normalization). To use Italian communist Antonio Gramsci's formulation, once a ruling idea (ideology) is normalized, it becomes common sense (as opposed to good sense), and is held, not only by the oppressors, but also by the mass of population (Gramsci 1971). *This* is hegemony. The concept "hegemony" stresses the incorporation and transformation of ideas and practices into the common sense thinking and practices of the masses, although these ideas may have originated from the dominant classes. Once an idea becomes hegemonic, it is taken for granted and not open for examination. Applying this Gramscian understanding to race and racism, British anti-racist sociologist Stuart Hall (1996) asserts that labour cannot be treated as a homogenous entity; it is differentiated by cultural specificity. Thus, he furthers the notion that in order to understand how racism operates in advanced capitalist societies, we need to pinpoint precisely how racial differences articulate with class formation (for a discussion of these various positions see Loomba 1998). He also discusses the role of anti-racist educators, including the ongoing need for critical reflection on the part of anti-racist activists and intellectuals.

The above discussion provides the theoretical background to my presentation and dialogue with Jeannette back in 1998. I maintain that the theoretical formulations I advanced then are no less relevant today, especially in light of world events following from the 11 September 2001 attacks on the United States. What we are witnessing right now is renewed racialization of those seen as "Muslims" and racism directed toward them in the name of the war against terror (see, for example, Jiwani's essay in this volume). As in earlier periods of colonization, this form of racism is enacted by extreme acts of aggression and violence. At the present historical conjuncture, we see clearly how sexism, racism, and religious and class oppression are effected simultaneously to facilitate the expansion of capitalism as a global system. This expansion is carried out through two major means: trade and war. It is made possible, not only by U.S. dominance and aggression, but also by the complicity of other nation states in support of transnational corporations. As anti-racist intellectuals and activists, therefore, it is all the more important for us to pinpoint ways in which racism, sexism; and economic and military processes operate to produce specific divisions. We also need to identify spaces for alliances and to develop an anti-racism politics that is capable of addressing multiple forms of oppression simultaneously that serves to unite rather than to divide us.

NOTES

1 I have written about these experiences of how sexism and racism operate in tandem elsewhere. See Ng (1993a and 1995).
2 I have developed this point elsewhere. See Ng (1993b).
3 Terminologies such as majority, minority, North and South, are always problematic when used to reference reality. While recognizing their problematical character, I will simply state here that when using these terms I am always cognizant that they designate unequal power relations. So, when I call women of colour minority women, I know that numerically they are the majority, but in power terms they are the minority.
4 See Hall (1980) and Miles (1989, 1993) for the concept of articulation.

REFERENCES

Adams, H. 1999. *Tortured People: The Politics of Colonization*. Penticton, BC: Theytus Books Ltd. (revised edition).

Briskin, L. 1990. *Feminist Pedagogy: Teaching and Learning Liberation*. Ottawa: The Canadian Research Institute for the Advancement of Women.

Fanon, F. 1963. *The Wretched of the Earth*. New York: Grove Press.

Foucault, M. 1978. *The History of Sexuality: An Introduction, Volume 1*. New York: Vintage Books Edition, 1990.

Gramsci, A. 1971. *Selections from the Prison Notebooks*. New York: International Publishers.

Hall, S. 1980. "Race, Articulation and Societies Structured in Dominance." In *Sociological Theories, Race and Colonialism*, 305–45. Paris: UNESCO.

– 1996. "Gramsci's Relevance for the Study of Race and Ethnicity." In *Stuart Hall, Critical Dialogues in Cultural Studies*, eds. D. Morley and K.H. Chen, 131–50. London & New York: Routledge.

Loomba, A. 1998. *Colonialism/Postcolonialism*. London and New York: Routledge.

Man, G. 1996. *The Experience of Hong Kong Chinese Immigrant Women in Canada*. Ph.D. Dissertation, Department of Sociology and Equity Studies, The Ontario Institute for Studies in Education, University of Toronto.

Miles, R. 1989. *Racism*. London and New York: Routledge.
- 1993. *Racism after "Race Relations."* London and New York: Routledge.
Ng, Roxana. 1993a. "A Woman out of Control: Deconstructing Sexism and Racism in the University." *Canadian Journal of Education* 18, no. 3 Summer: 139–205.
- 1993b. "Racism, Sexism, and Nation Building in Canada." In *Race, Identity and Representation in Education*, eds. C. McCarthy and W. Crichlow, 50–9. New York: Routledge.
- 1995. "Teaching against the Grain: Contradictions and Possibilities." In *Anti-Racism, Feminism, and Critical Approaches to Education*, eds. R. Ng, P. Staton, and J. Scane, 129–52. Westport: Greenwood Publishers Inc.
- 1998. "Work Restructuring and Recolonizing Third World Women: An Example from the Garment Industry in Toronto." *Canadian Woman Studies* 18, no. 1 Spring: 21–25.
- 1999. "Homeworking: Dream Realized or Freedom Constrained? The Globalized Reality of Immigrant Garment Workers." *Canadian Woman Studies* 19, no. 3 November: 110–114.
Omi, M., and Winant, H. 1986. *Racial Formation in the United States: From the 1960s to the 1980s*. New York: Routledge.
Smith, L.T. 1999. *Decolonizing Methodologies: Research and Indigenous Peoples*. Dunedin, New Zealand: University of Otago Press & Zed Books Ltd.

ALI RATTANSI

On Being and Not Being Brown/Black-British: Racism, Class, Sexuality, and Ethnicity in Post-Imperial Britain

(with Postscript 2004: The Politics of Longing and (Un)Belonging, Fear, and Loathing)

THE QUESTION OF HYPHENATED IDENTITIES

Hyphenated identities are obviously here to stay.[1] And nowhere does this seem more true than in North America. Here a particular multiethnicity, produced by a series of inward flows of migrants appears to have given a legitimacy and stability, especially in the wake of post-1960s struggles for group recognition and redistribution, to identities such as African-American, Native-American, Asian- or Japanese- or Chinese-Canadian and so forth. Nevertheless, it would obviously be mistaken to assume too much homogeneity and stability to these identities, however easily they may slip off the tongue in public discourse. The 1980s and 1990s saw fierce struggles around the essentialisms that such hyphenated identities have often implied, repressing gender and class inequalities in their headlong rush to finally fracture America's and Canada's official identities of white ethnicity. The cross-currents of cultural, political, and economic conflict and debate unleashed by the rise of identity politics and issues of multiculturalism, affirmative action, and so-called political correctness in North America should serve to reinforce the argument of more post-structuralist and "post-modern" authors that the closure around identities is always provisional. Decentring and de-essentializing forces are constantly at work, and the relative stability of hyphenated identities is always a precarious achievement, stabilized only in particular contexts.

If *North American* hyphenated identities have to be regarded as chronically riven with internal conflict and obviously the subject of backlash in the form of the political correctness debate, how much more difficult might it be to establish the legitimacy of such forms of official and self-identification in Britain – a nation that has prided itself on a history supposedly free of the kinds of major internal convulsions and external invasions that have wracked its European neighbours and indeed its former colonies, and of the massive immigration flows that have characterized Canada and the United States?

It is the purpose of this essay to begin the difficult task of unravelling just these complexities for a period in which Britain, too, has had to confront its mythical "white island race" self-image.

IS THERE BLACK OR BROWN IN THE UNION JACK NOW?

In Britain 1998 was the year of the Windrush celebrations. The year marked the fiftieth anniversary of the fateful arrival of 492 Jamaicans aboard the *S S Empire Windrush*, an event that heralded the beginning of the post-war immigration of black and Asian colonial and post-colonial subjects to the "mother country." Many of the new arrivals were not new. Some had served in the British armed forces during the war and had already spent brief periods in Britain. The anniversary of the event was marked, particularly on television, by high profile documentaries and discussion programs. Although punctuated by references to urban riots and the nasty faces of British racism, the overall note was one of complacency and even muted celebration of narratives of integration, multiculturalism, and notable cases of immigrant success, including elevation to the House of Lords. The British, it seemed, could generally be satisfied that their self-conception as a tolerant nation committed to fair play had survived the era of black and Asian immigration relatively untarnished.

The public narratives, although not entirely devoid of justification, serve to hide darker, more complex pictures of the intervening fifty years. It is clear from a wide variety of research studies, some of which are referred to later, that a majority of immigrants and their descendents do not feel entirely at home in Britain. Feelings of rejection or grudging and conditional acceptance abound, sometimes captured in the view that while black and Asian people can be *British*, lack of *whiteness* poses insuperable barriers to being English, Scottish, or Welsh. It is not even easy to be black/British or Asian/British, as the title of a set of essays puts it (Modood 1992). Moreover, survey after survey records high degrees of prejudice against blacks and Asians among the white population of the U.K. (see Alibhai-Brown 1999), with no linear change in one direction or another over this period.

Why, after fifty years of a growing and significant black and Asian presence in Britain is it still so difficult to be black or Asian and British (to focus on these broader conjunctions)? This has obviously been a period of rapid transformation in which new so-called hybrid identities have mushroomed and older ones have been strained almost to crisis point, and these changes have a dynamic of considerable significance. This essay, drawing upon a large variety of research and also a distinctive theoretical perspective which I have called the "post-modern frame" (Rattansi 1994, 1995a) attempts to tease out some of the key processes involved in the insertion of a chronic set of centrifugal forces which continually threaten the stability of identificatory couplets such as black-English and Asian-English, and more broadly, black British/Asian British. The title of this essay uses "Brown" instead of Asian, serving to throw into sharp relief the inconsistencies – one based on colour, the other on geographical origin – in the more usual labelling of *black* and *Asian* which is otherwise used throughout the essay.

As we shall see, the story is not the same old one of an intransigent racism against which visible minorities have heroically battled in desperate attempts to plant solid roots in Britain. Yet there remains enough truth in that narrative to require close attention. Moreover, class, "race," and sexuality have been almost inextricably interconnected in creating the particular, shifting cultural mix of ethnic and national identities in Britain in the past sixty years.

RUSHING TO HALT THE WINDRUSH – AND AFTER

While official discourses have portrayed the agencies of the British state as swayed this way and that by the contradictory pressures of post-war labour shortages and racist rejection of black and Asian workers, the early phase of post world war immigration was one in which most state apparatuses more or less consistently sought to prevent the arrival of black and Asian immigrants, labour shortages or no labour shortages. This much is now clearly revealed by the official papers from the 1950s that have had to be placed in the Public Records Office and elsewhere. To put it differently, *the British state has from the start created wedges between Britishness and blackness/Asianness which have continued to have profound repercussions* (although these were not necessarily the categories used at the time, the white/coloured dichotomy being generally more prevalent in official and popular discourse). A very important effect of this reluctance to accept blacks and Asians has been the continuing institutional racism of many parts of the national and local state apparatus, extensively documented in research studies (for example, Braham, Rattansi, and Skellington 1992), which in turn has affected the dynamics of minority and majority ethnic identity formation.

As against conventional liberal and Marxist narratives of post-war immigration, which have always suggested that an initial phase of welcoming and indeed recruiting black and Asian workers to fill labour shortages was followed in the 1960s by sometimes reluctant British governments bowing to popular white pressures to curtail immigration by way of a series of Immigration Acts beginning in 1962, it is now emerging that even *before* the Windrush set sail, panic had gripped Attlee's Labour government at the prospect of this influx of "undesirable elements" as Attlee himself immediately labelled the potential Jamaican immigrants (Dean 1987, 317; Rattansi 1995a, 27; 2002a). Until then, labour shortages had been quietly dealt with by recruiting white workers, mainly from Eastern Europe.

Frantic backstage attempts were made to prevent the *S S Empire Windrush* from leaving at all. When these failed, Attlee suggested that the ship might be diverted to East Africa, so that the Jamaicans could be employed in what turned out to be a disastrous groundnut scheme. But even the British government realized the folly of that manoeuvre. So, finally, plans were laid to make the migrants feel as uncomfortable and unwelcome as possible by giving them temporary accommodation in a reopened war-time shelter at Clapham North underground station, where they were told that very soon they would have to move out and find their own housing (Rattansi 1995a, 27–28).

To prevent any more *Windrushes* from setting sail Colonial Office functionaries were despatched to lobby administrations in the West Indies and India and every attempt was made to convince potential migrants that the availability of jobs in Britain was a myth. Not surprisingly, there was considerable annoyance in government circles when some within the Ministry of Health and London Transport broke ranks and initiated recruiting campaigns in just those places.

Official discussions at the time in the Home Office, Ministry of Labour, and other state agencies reveal the strong hold of colonial stereotypes which underpinned the almost instinctive reaction that blacks and Asians were undesirables. They were regarded as, variously, innately lazy, quarrelsome, disorderly, and prone to criminality. Certainly not suitable material for good workers, to put it mildly. One report even claimed that black men had chests that were too weak for the British winter and were too delicate to cope with work in the heat of British factories and coal mines (Harris 1993, 32; Rattansi 1995a, 28).

The racism that permeated these discussions was thoroughly *sexualized*. Fears were expressed in committees about the degenerative consequences of miscegenation and about what was regarded as a potentially explosive sexual mix of black men and white women, especially working class white women. The extent to which these fears were a legacy of conflicts regarding black U.S. servicemen is not clear. The anxieties certainly fed upon stories of young white women queuing up on the dance floors to partner the black men because of their "natural sense of rhythm," as one report put it, as well as reports that predicted that Liverpool, for example, could turn into a "new Harlem"– again, a term actually used – characterized by black pimps and white prostitutes, and high crime rates (Carter, Harris, and Joshi 1993, 64; Dean 1987, 308, 311; Rattansi 1995a, 29).

But what of the real need for extra workers, especially as the supply of displaced Eastern Europeans had all but dried up? In fact different departments of the state were rarely in agreement as to the amount of extra labour required and at what level of skill. Some even argued by the early 1950s that there was actually a danger of surplus labour and overmanning. Generally, black and Asian workers were consistently routed away from skilled jobs and training schemes, even if this meant that skilled jobs were left unfilled. In other words, there was no consensus then and no "objective" evidence even now about the precise extent of post-war labour shortages and, *pace* Marxist arguments (e.g., Sivanandan 1978), no real knowledge about the needs of capital that the state was supposedly serving by controlling labour flows.

Restrictive Immigration Acts began in 1962, officially justified by the need to restrict numbers to ensure good race relations and the goals of integration. Of course, they had some quite contrary effects, by highlighting blacks and Asians as "problems" that needed state management. The racism of various white British populations, key players in the Notting Hill "riots" of 1957 and other incidents remained, in large part, unrecognized and unchallenged.

Without delving more deeply into subsequent developments, three points are worth drawing out from this revised narrative of early post-war black and Asian immigration into Britain. First, it is arguable that various sexualized racisms appear to have been as important as the perceived needs of British industrial capital in influencing the state's contradictory initiatives in relation to black/Asian immigration. Second, class seems to have figured in highly complex ways, one of the most important being in terms of the fear of white working class women's sexuality. One implication of the above two points, as I have argued elsewhere (Rattansi 1995a), is that the narrative of post-1945 black and Asian immigration is much more plausibly recounted with Foucaldian thematics regarding bio-politics and the state's management of national populations together with various other elements of what I have called a "post-modern" frame (Rattansi 1994) than with Marxist or Weberian analyses.

Finally, the above account suggests that within state apparatuses the idea of black and Asian Britishness was always rejected, from the start of the post-war migrations onwards. The very notion seemed as preposterous during the period of emergent post-coloniality as in the heyday of colonialism. Racism, the state, class, nationality, and sexuality criss-crossed in myriad ways to prevent staining the Union Jack with black or brown.

The more recent release of official documents connected to the attempts to block the arrival of British passport-holding Asians from Kenya in the wake of policies of Africanization in the former colony serve to confirm even more starkly how thoroughly un-British it is to have "coloured" skins. The Commonwealth Immigrants Bill of 1968 was specifically framed to keep out entrants of Asian origin, rather than any whites who might also be leaving in the wake of Africanization. And this, despite full awareness in the Labour Government's cabinet discussions that the proposed legislation would actually contravene the European Convention on Human Rights, in addition to the explicit acknowledgement of the small matter of reneging on the public undertakings given to Kenyan Asians at the time of Kenya's independence in 1963 (Lattimer 1999). Asians from Uganda, expelled by Amin in 1972, were admitted in the wake of public campaigns and finally a decision by the Conservative Heath government to honour earlier promises of rights of entry and residence to East African Asians with British passports.

ETHNIC MINORITY LOCATIONS: FIFTY YEARS ON

Did the *Empire Windrush* celebrations really have anything to celebrate? Fifty years after the arrival of the *Windrush*, Darcus Howe, a black radical journalist well known over the years for editing the militant (and now defunct) *Race Today* and for many high profile anti-racist campaigns, declared in the centre-left weekly, *The New Statesman*, that racism was "on its last legs in Britain" and that a majority of blacks agreed with him (13 November 1998, 24). In addition to a few personal anecdotes, Howe relied on a survey conducted by the London *Evening Standard* which purported to show that most black and Asian Londoners believed that race relations had improved in the past ten years and would continue to improve. For good measure Howe prefaced his comments on the survey by suggesting, "It seems to me that those who live by race are determined not to recognise the devastating blows that we have wielded against this dangerous social phenomenon." However, only two months before, a report commissioned by Operation Black Vote and carried out by the University of Warwick's Centre for Research in Ethnic Relations in a range of British inner cities claimed that large sections of the black and Asian communities were pessimistic about the future of racism in Britain, a belief particularly concentrated among the young. In the age group eighteen to twenty-four, 79 per cent of blacks, 50 per cent of Asians and 38 per cent of whites predicted that race relations would worsen over the next five years. With a slight exaggeration, the respected broadsheet *The Independent* headlined its gloss on the findings:

Britain is failing us, say blacks.
(9 September 1998)

Of course, the stark discrepancy could conceivably be explained by the peculiarities of London. But this would be too simple. The weight of evidence is that racist discrimination and the disadvantages of ethnic minorities are alive and well and thriving in a whole variety of key British institutions, although *in some contexts* it may be that overt racism may be more muted than before. However, here some instances of persistent racism and inequality will have to suffice as indications of the continuing significance of Howe's "dangerous social phenomenon." Racism in the police force, criminal justice system, armed forces, legal profession, civil service, Local Authorities, schools, National Health Service; in mental health procedures; in obtaining bank loans; and on the streets has been consistently documented in the 1990s, with the high profile of the inquiries into the lack of prosecution of the murderers of the young, black Stephen Lawrence, being a particularly tragic point of condensation for discussions of the state of racism in Britain (see, among many others, Braham, Rattansi, and Skellington 1992; Runnymede Trust October 1998).

This is not to underplay the significant socio-economic advances registered by some members of the ethnic minorities. The latest in a series of national surveys carried out by the Policy Studies Institute (Modood et al. 1997) reports that African Asians and Chinese have an economic profile very similar to that of whites. Indian and Caribbean-descended male employees' average earnings have not caught up with those of white men, but the gap has narrowed and the average earnings of British Caribbean women appear to be slightly higher than those of white women. On the other hand, a substantial proportion of people of Pakistani and Bangladeshi origin are living in serious poverty and unemployment rates among most ethnic minorities are substantially higher than those among whites. Moreover, men from all ethnic minorities are seriously under-represented as managers and employers in large establishments. Even the best-off minorities are only half as likely to hold these top jobs as white men.

In other words, in terms of social class, while there is no homogeneous concentration in the shrinking manual working class, the few Asian and black millionaires cannot hide the continuing concentration of ethnic minorities in the lower reaches of the class structure. Arguably, the advances that have been registered are as much products of dogged tenacity in obtaining educational qualifications and establishing niche businesses serving ethnic minority markets than of significant reductions in racial discrimination.

SOCIAL LOCATIONS AND ETHNIC IDENTITIES

Ethnic identities, while hardly free-floating, cannot be read off from historical placements and socio-economic transformations. Whatever else may be disputed about identity formation, this much may safely be assumed to have been established in recent discussions of class, racialization, gender, and ethnicity (Hall 1992; Hall and Du Gay 1996; Laclau 1994; Rattansi 1994, among innumerable others). Moreover, as discussions by Laclau, Hall, and others have suggested, what is true of ethnic identities may be said to be true of identities and subject formation in general. My own investigations of racialized and ethnic identities have supported the general proposition that identities are riven by contradictions, ambivalences, situational and contextual variations, and unpredictable individual and group alliances (Rattansi 1992; 1994; 1995b). They remain provisional and unfinished. Closures are temporally and spatially contexted, involve varying degrees of emotional attachment, and there is a continual switching, making, and remaking of identifications. Moreover, this process of subject formation and re-formation has to be understood as operating in social fields that are themselves relatively open and shifting in structurations around various nodal points, to borrow the suggestive theorization of the "social" from Laclau (1990; see Rattansi 1994, 31).

This is not the occasion for rehearsing the theorizations and evidence which underlie such a conception of identity-formation. Rather, the intention here is to take this form of "post-modern framing" for granted and focus on the variety of social currents which create the chronic instability in the black British and Asian British identificatory couplings. Why is it not easy to be black or Asian and British? In addition to the operation of state policies already discussed, a range of ethnographic accounts can be read with and against the grain to provide some insight into the particularities and peculiarities of the processes that may be at work.

However, at this stage it is important to confront a possible argument which could undermine the whole exercise undertaken in this essay. If, as argued above, all identities are decentred and riven by contradiction, ambiguity, ambivalence, and so forth, what is the point in exposing and exploring the instabilities of black and Asian British identities? Are they not bound to be unstable and shifting anyway? What is so special about these or indeed any other particular forms of identification?

The answer is to be found in the way I have posed the last part of this problem. There may not be any identities, individual and collective, that are not de-centred, but this still requires that the particularities and peculiarities of any unique identificatory configuration need to be carefully plotted and narrated precisely because of the complex historical and contextual features which condition the formation and reformation of all identities. Moreover, as I have pointed out in criticism of a certain kind of vulgar postmodernism, identities have to be regarded as having relative stabilities as well as instabilities (Rattansi 1994, 71–72). Some configurations may be more strongly embedded in individual psyches and collective cultures and institutions than others at specific historical periods and in particular locales. The special fragilities and vulnerabilities of some identities makes the albeit provisional, and temporally and spatially bounded project undertaken here, possible and necessary, just as it makes the projects of mapping and narrating other identificatory processes also necessary.

BLACK AND BRITISH: TO BE OR NOT TO BE?

Take the ethnic and racial identifications of young British people of African Caribbean descent. It must be accepted at the outset, of course, that all generalizations about such a disparate group have to be made with extreme circumspection. There is no essential black British "youthness." Nevertheless, it has become clearer in recent research (Alexander 1996, 60; Modood, Beishon, and Virdee 1994, 82–83;) that whatever the differences among such black youth, the salience of their West Indian islands of origin is far weaker than for older generations. Loyalties to different British locales may now play a more important role as young blacks, in some contexts, see themselves as coming from particular parts of London or Birmingham and draw distinct black British boundaries (Alexander 1996, 61–62). This makes it a little easier now to speak more generally of young black British people in general, as Stuart Hall does, than ever before (Hall 1998).

This has not, however, necessarily strengthened the coupling of black with British. Rather, the emphasis appears to have shifted to differential commitments to "blackness," which mediate the formation of black Britishness. Class plays an important role, although in a perhaps surprising guise, with language forms becoming symbolically crucial. Aspirations to *middle-classness* are often seen as heralding a weakening of commitment to *blackness*, and the use of patois and standard English serve as markers for both types of identification (Alexander 1996, 58). The perceived feeling that career and economic success could only be achieved by compromising with "white" norms (ibid, 92–99), and that this would in some way imply a betrayal of the black community, intersects with and reinforces the oppositions and ambivalences that chronically destabilize the conjunction of blackness and Britishness.

In other words, there exists a set of processes whereby the experience of racism and lack of perceived acceptance by white society, which make it difficult for young blacks to identify themselves as British are buttressed by the emergence of defensive resistances from below; these have become imbricated with considerations of social class to create unstable and shifting boundaries and identities around race, class, community, and national belonging. The significance for these issues of the fact that 20 per cent of those described as "Caribbean" in British surveys have a white partner and that 40 per cent of children described in this way have a white parent obviously requires urgent investigation (see Ahmed 1997; Ifekwunigwe 1997; Tizard and Phoenix 1993).[2]

At this point it is worth pursuing the issue of class. One other way in which middle-class and working-class dynamics affect processes of identification among young black people is through the various forms of interaction that working-class black youth have with white middle-class figures of authority. The routine generational conflict with white teachers, social workers, and youth workers is exacerbated by race and class, adding to young black people's alienation from a sense of belonging and "Britishness" (see, for example, Wright 1995, 49–51 on primary schools). Friendship patterns at school and outside, where it is noticeable that an informal polarization between black and white occurs, have the consequence of foregrounding "blackness" rather than other forms of belonging (Alexander 1996, 52; Phoenix 1998, 89–93).

To a considerable extent, despite the syncretisms which I shall remark upon later, strong identities of "blackness" appear to be sustained by continuing attempts by young black men, especially, to differentiate themselves stylistically from their white counterparts. Some young black people are determined to prevent a co-optation of their distinctive cultures by constantly inventing new clothes or dance styles to stay ahead of and different from whites (Phoenix 1998, 89–90). The young black men in Alexander's study gave her what one might call a rough guide to some of the outward trappings of being black:

> drink Canei wine or Tennants lager, because these were black man's drink; blast your music very loud when driving and nod your head to the beat; never listen to Radio One or Capital Radio, because these catered for white people; never buy your music from HMV ... The basic tenet of this identity was solidarity to each other as individuals and to the idea of "the community," and was primarily oppositional in nature. The identification of and with "blackness" were acted upon by a show of verbal and non-verbal "respect" for other black people, especially in white-dominated public spaces (Alexander 1996, 50-51).

Of course, the ways of staying "black" mentioned to Alexander, apart from seeming tongue in cheek, are contingent and contextual. Another group of black youths at a different location or the same group at some other time could point to other markers of differentiation, keeping ahead of any changes in white youth styles.

It would be seriously misleading to assume from the account provided so far that aspirations to middle-class status are absent from black youth cultures or that middle-class conceptions of "blackness" are not developing. The emergence of the "buppie" (black yuppie) phenomenon, trivialized by these labels, is real enough. There is after all a growing black middle class in Britain, reflected in the growing numbers of professionals and successful entrepreneurs. The extent to which such groups aspire to a certain differentiation from the white middle class, either by force of design, or both, may in part be gauged by the arrival of magazines that cater for and help create precisely this type of blackness. The recently started glossy, *Untold,* carrying subtitles such as "Making a Difference" and "Black Male Lifestyle" may be a significant marker. The magazine's third issue, for October/November 1998, carried a feature entitled "Cool Aid" and described its contents thus: "What's the difference between black and white cool? The great debate starts here." Paul Mackenzie, author of the feature, gives a resounding *yes* to the question, "Are blacks cooler than whites?" and an equally emphatic *no* to the idea of white cool ever being a match. On the other hand, his pessimism about blacks ever having equal treatment in relation to whites speaks volumes.

A particularly interesting aspect of the issue of *Untold* I have been discussing is its front cover. It carries a glamorous shot of Ian Wright, the well-known black footballer. *Untold's* choice of image is revealing. Apart from the obvious arena of music and entertainment, it is in sports (especially football and boxing, and to some extent in cricket) and athletics that black men, and women too, have achieved spectacular prominence. Despite the pride so often expressed by these black men and women in representing and winning for Britain or, in the case of football, England, there is little doubt about the ambivalence with which these achievements are viewed by many white Britons. In turn, this constitutes one further force for disrupting the establishment of a more solid bond between blackness and Britishness.

The destabilization takes generally crude forms. There are the racist chants that are regularly hurled at black footballers, which have led to the development of various campaigns to "Kick Racism out of Football," as one of them has appropriately titled itself. In cricket, it was quite recently that *Wisden*, the most established publication on the sport, published "reflections" that non-white players were likely not to give their best for England as they could not be expected to have the same commitment as full-blooded white Englishmen. And it is in this context of sports and athletics, where questions of black and white *bodies* are paramount that sexualized racism figures again in a predictable manner. A revealing instance is the treatment of the champion black British sprinter, Linford Christie. After Christie's spectacular gold medal at the Barcelona Olympic games in 1992, the British tabloid *The Sun* immediately turned its attention, and that of the nation, away from the sporting achievement to the sexual potential of this black body. What *The Sun* referred to as Christie's "Lunch Box" and its supposed prodigious size became an obsession. This is how the tabloid posed the question:

Linford Christie is way out in front in every department and we don't just mean the way he stormed to victory in the 100 metres. His skin tight lycra shorts hide little as he pounds down the track and his Olympic-sized talents are a source of delight to women around the world. But the mystery remains -just what does Linford, 32, pack in that famous lunchbox? (*The Sun*, 6th August 1992)

This is a classic playing out of the recurrent treatment of the black male as sexual Other – source of attraction to white women and threat to the white male. A similar fear, although usually without the saucy humour and the implicit admission of a non-racialized woman figure, had earlier animated the reluctance to recruit blacks as workers, as I have documented in the first part of this paper. The ambivalent pulls of fear and desire that are evident here go back to the earliest encounters between black and white (see, among many others, Rattansi 1994, 43–46; Rattansi 1997; and especially, of course, Fanon's 1986 *Black Skins White Masks*).

Much more could be said here about how these ambivalences are constructed in various forms of British popular culture, especially the media. However, the central point in this context is that for as long as the black male continues to be regarded, in one of his guises, as a sexual, alien threat, the conjunction of black and British is bound to find itself also chronically threatened. The fact that black women are also often burdened with assumptions of an abnormally powerful and deviant sexuality, a cultural staple in cinema, for example (Young 1996), only serves to reinforce the argument I am making.

At this stage, two last points on being and not being black and British. First, Hall is undoubtedly right in acknowledging a shift away from Africa and the Caribbean to African-American culture as a constitutive current in the identifications of young British blacks, thus further complicating the black British conjunction (Hall 1998), although it may be of more than passing interest that the black journalist from *Untold* is adamant that black British cool still owes more to the Caribbean than to Afro-America. Second, and crucially, there appears simply not to be enough systematic research and knowledge about young black *women's* identifications, although Phoenix's investigation suggests that black young women, although inclined to regard Englishness as exclusively white, nevertheless would prefer to have black partners (Phoenix 1995). This is perhaps part of a wider set of anxieties, preferences and choices about racial embodiment – skin colour, hair texture, facial characteristics, and body shape – as revealed in Weekes's research into the ambivalences of black British young women faced with the pressures of mainstream white norms of beauty and sexual attractiveness as well as the ambiguities of mixed race embodiment (Weekes 1997). It may be significant that in schooling and qualifications young black women are outperforming young black men (see Rattansi 1992, 20, for a discussion of earlier research), already giving rise to a media discourse of the black superwoman (Reynolds 1997). There may soon be growing discrepancies in the incomes and employment prospects of the women, which in turn are complexly imbricated with and have unpredictable consequences for black British masculinity (on blackness, masculinity and British schools see Sewell 1997).

In itself, this raises the whole vexed question of black masculinities in Britain, which is not a subject that can be pursued here in any detail. But there is a related terrain that requires some consideration. That is, the development of a linguistic and cultural crossover, documented particularly in London, resulting in the use, in certain parts of the metropolis, of a black-dominated mixture of cockney and patois, resulting in expressions such as "na mean" (you know what I mean), "safe" (good, OK, certain), "innit" (isn't it) and "wicked" (really good), the last two also being particularly widespread among working class Asians (and used to produce a "wicked" send up of British Asian-ness in a recent set of sketches by British Asian comedians on BBC TV, entitled "Goodness Gracious Me" (another play on Indians caricatured in a famous British comedy film of the late 1960s).

Back, in a brilliant ethnography of cultural practices in working class South London, has pointed out that these and other linguistic forms should be seen not as a mixing of heritages, but as the creation of a potential new heritage (Back 1996, 52; see also, Hewitt 1986 and Rampton 1995). The extent to which this represents the formation of a set of resources for non-racist and anti-racist meanings and practices is a difficult question. For the present it is worth noting that, in their intertwining with syncretic musical and other expressive cultures, these linguistic styles are undoubtedly giving birth to genuinely new ways of being black/Asian/British which, in some locales at least, is going to have a profound significance on what "Britishness" is going to mean, from both above and below. The recent campaign to give part of London's East End the label Banglatown is perhaps indicative of some of the transformations to come, and of the complex imbrications between community-based movements and the local state.

The use of this emergent creole is by no means restricted to young men, with both black and white young women being involved in its creation and development, although Alexander acknowledges its seminal significance as a symbol of masculinity among black young men (1996, 57). However, white women have to be particularly tactful in their display of their facility with the new language forms because of the possible perception, particularly acute among young black women, that the displays could be part of attempts to go out with black men (Hewitt 1986, 155–6). Another gendered aspect of these new dialects is their connection with often racialized "wind ups" between young white and black men (Back 1996, 85–90). Various codes of masculinity come into play in such interactions.

It is precisely in this context that the ambiguities of local and national "belonging" are played out. As the ethnographic accounts suggest, these new linguistic cultural crossovers are not necessarily "neutral," de-racialized and de-ethnicized social fields. The racist name-calling and other put-downs which are part of the masculine "wind ups" reveal a shifting set of meanings around the issue of who really belongs and whether colour matters and how. It is not merely that the Vietnamese, for example, can become treated by both black and white as those who are not "us," as Back's study suggests, but that the wider significance of whether this new syncretism allows a consolidation of the black-British coupling remains an open issue, subject to a range of contextual variations. In other words, the new cultural forms themselves are no guarantee of a firm and unshakeable new youth identity in which cultures of origin and colour vanish to leave behind a non-racist, colour-blind British identity. There is a need to treat the new crossovers with some caution when it comes to deciding their potential for black Britishness.

BRITISH ASIAN: WHAT'S IN A NAME?

Nothing and everything, one is tempted to say. Rather like the various Trinidadians, Jamaicans, and other Caribbeans who discovered that they were "West Indian" and even black, rather than just members of the "mother land," only after they arrived in Britain, so it was that most of those of Indian, Pakistani, Bangladeshi, and Sri Lankan origin were forced to recognize their "Asian-ness" – and, more rudely and abusively – their "Paki-ness," only after their arrival in Britain. Those arriving from East and Central Asia had had to get used to the appellation, which the British colonial authorities had used to differentiate them from those of African origin (or "natives"), but for the rest it was a puzzling and only gradual "realization" and, eventually, contextual acceptance, of a unified identification (Modood, Beishon, and Virdee 1994, 93–94).

The point is that the label hides an extraordinary and, to even the most knowledgeable, bewildering variety of labyrinthine cultural differentiations. The more recent, post-colonial divisions of nation and geographical origin have been superimposed on dense interwoven patterns of identities based on religion; caste, sub-caste, and various other kinds of descent groups; and rural/urban and regional differences which have made generalizations about "Asians" an extremely hazardous exercise. As the editor of a recent collection on "The South Asian Presence in Britain" argues about the essays written by his contributors, "What every ... chapter serves to emphasise is not only how much each community differs from the next, but also that each is following its own distinctive dynamic ... The result is both steady progress and ever-growing diversity ... to talk of an 'Asian' community – or even of 'Indian,' 'Pakistani' or 'Bangladeshi' ones – is often to reinforce a fiction" (Ballard 1994, 29).

Despite the effects of homogenizing forces such as the experience of racism, cultural differentiations continue in forms that make generalizations about "British Asians" a foolhardy project except at a highly abstract level. As with British "blackness," de-essentialization is crucial for any discussion. On the other hand, to resist *any* form of generalization is to fall into the opposite, vulgar, post-modernist trap of complete disaggregation and discursive and practical paralysis. Some tentative generalizations may be advanced in the patterns that may be discerned around the conjunction of "British" and "Asian."

There is acute sensitivity among "Asians" living in Britain regarding the cultural violence that is done to them by that very label. This is revealed in much of the research conducted among these "communities" (Baumann 1996, 154; Gillespie 1995, 140–1; Modood, Beishon, and Virdee 1994, 91–4). The commonalities, however, are recognized more readily in their juxtaposition with those regarded as even more Other than the other folk from India, Pakistan, and Bangladesh; that is, in relation to those of African Caribbean descent and whites, although not without recognition of the commonalities of the racism faced by black and brown (Baumann 1996, 155; Modood, Beishon, and Virdee 1994, 95–96).

Of course, the most fashionable tropes in academic discourses on ethnic minority youth in general, and Asian youth in particular, are hybridity and syncretism as suggested by my own earlier usage. But there is now something of a reaction against the simplifications that even these concepts are prone to (Caglar 1997; Sharma 1996. See Young 1995 for a critique framed rather differently); despite their attempts to point precisely to the de-centredness and multiplicity of black and Asian youth identities.

For now, two propositions may be ventured. The explosion of new "Asian" dance musics and expressive cultures that is now being documented (Sharma 1996) points to a huge process of transformation of the identities of second, third, and subsequent generations whose origins lie in India, Pakistan, and Bangladesh. It is important to recognize that the extraordinary mix of musical styles, cultural borrowings from black and white youth sub-cultures, contingently and contextually de-centred identities, variety of gender and other politics, internal conflicts, and ever-growing diversity are only at the beginning of an unpredictable set of journeys that will constantly have to be re-narrated. There is obviously no singular description or analysis that can capture this vibrant phenomenon in some clever discursive totalization – witness the failure of suggestions that a specifically British Asian youth identity was finally coalescing around the culture of *bhangra* music as suggested by Gillespie (1995) and Baumann (1996) and comprehensively contested by Sharma and his co-authors (1996). Little wonder that concepts such as hybridity encounter severe limitations so soon after their celebration in cultural studies.

There is another consideration that appears to be highlighted in research on British Asians of all generations. Whatever the degree of tenacity with which they wish to assert their rights to citizenship and cultural belonging to a multicultural nation, there seems to be a pervasive sense that a majority of the white British population will never accept "Asians" as full, legitimate members of the nation and that as a result they will continually have to negotiate a particular set of multiplicities of ethnic and national belonging which will always make their experience of Britishness different from that of whites, and closer to that of British people of African, African Caribbean, and other "visible" (read: nonwhite) minority origin (Eade 1997; Gardner and Shukur 1994; Gillespie 1995, 101–103; Modood, Beishon, and Virdee 1994, 96–100, among many others). These are not merely the forced manoeuvres of thwarted individuals and communities desperate for inclusion in the British nation-state at any price. All evidence points to the desire on the part of young Asians to retain a variety of vestiges of their cultures of origin as a positive mark of difference, a refusal never to attempt to merge invisibly into a nebulous blob of ill-defined Britishness, and certainly not *Englishness,* which is definitely seen as forever a "white thing."

If anything gives a lie to earlier notions that young Asians were suffering from the pathology of "culture clash" and "identity crisis" it is the skilfulness with which they are juggling a whole spectrum of identities and bringing off brilliantly staged performative acts, the sheer variety of which will continue to defy easy description (see the range of identificatory labels and reflexivity about their meaning in the studies by Afshar 1994; Baumann 1996; Brah 1996; Gardner and Shukur 1994; Gillespie 1995; Modood et al. 1994, and in Eade's research on "Educated Young Bangladeshis in East London," 1997). The idea of the local/global nexus may have become something of a cliché, but it nevertheless serves as a useful way of indexing the extraordinarily complex identificatory nexus that is developing among British Asians between locales in British regions, towns, and cities – from London's East End, or Leicester, and Glasgow and Scotland – and within Britain as a whole, and a plethora of other imagined homelands, ranging from Sylhet or Calcutta to the whole Indian sub-continent, which are transforming Britain's Asian populations into a cosmopolitan, culturally polygot, and increasingly diverse set of groups and networks which have no linear cultural, economic, or political trajectory.

What is true in this general sense is equally true of a much commented-upon phenomenon – the supposed emergence of an Islamic/Muslim identity in Britain, as a result of the global resurgence of Islam and galvanizing events such as the Rushdie affair and the Gulf wars. Arguably, something that might be labelled "Islamophobia" exists in

Britain. There is certainly no shortage of derogatory comments about Islam and British Muslims by influential public figures in the U.K., as the Runnymede Trust's consultation paper on the subject fully documents (1997). Such attitudes rarely recognize that there is no singular "Muslim" identity in Britain. The general, historically constituted divisions in global Islam are not only reproduced in Britain – for example between Shias and Sunnis – but are imbricated with a host of other differentiations, reworked in the migrations and settlements over time, deriving from Indian and Pakistani regional, caste, and descent group affiliations, and further reconfigured by growing changes in class location, generation, and a complexity in relation to contemporary global Islamic politics (Lewis 1994a, 1994b; Shaw 1994). This without taking into account the diversities generated by the existence of British North African and Arab populations with few direct links to Muslims of Indian, Pakistani, or Bangladeshi origin. A small group influenced by Louis Farrakhan's Nation of Islam has recently attempted to make inroads into British public life, as yet with minimal impact.

THE UNBEARABLE WEIGHT OF BEING ENGLISH AND BRITISH: A NEW WHITE MAN'S BURDEN?

The racism that disfigures the lives of brown and black Britons and contributes so much to the chronic instability of the black/Asian-British configuration is itself ruptured and interrupted by a series of ambivalences. Longstanding in origin, they are constantly reworked, renewed, and added to. Most recently, the revelations of the degree of police racism documented in the inquiry into the death of the black South London teenager Stephen Lawrence (Cluny 1999) has led to a flurry of governmental pronouncements regarding the need to change not only the racist culture of the police, but to strengthen anti-racist measures more generally, for example by extending the scope of the existing Race Relations Act of 1976.

It is clear that this is a reaction to a particular set of revelations that simply cannot be ignored by the Blair Labour government. The same government, when setting out its manifesto committments, gave little indication that "race" was anything more than an issue of keeping the black and Asian vote with Labour (see Alibhai-Brown 1999). In office, as Keith Vaz, one of the Asian Members of Parliament has pointed out in his report, the Blair government made no more than a token attempt at including blacks and Asians in senior appointments (Vaz 1998), although, perhaps as a result of his report, Vaz became the first Asian minister in Blair's government. He represents the Lord Chancellor's Department in the House of Commons.

On the campaign trail, both Labour and Conservative parties vied for the Asian vote in particular, by visiting temples and lauding Asian values of family and hard work, which, magically, were also the very British virtues that both parties were promoting. The fact that Asian gays and feminists, and a much wider range of Asians did not fit this characterization in a wholly credible way serves only to reinforce the argument that inclusion is conditional and selective. Stereotyping continued and in its usual ambivalent fashion split off the good Asians from the unsuccessful bad ones, for example the long-term unemployed, the pathologized sufferers of identity crises, the otherwise demonized Muslim women-oppressors, the fundamentalists, the warring Sikh and Muslim gangs, the Pakistani drug barons – the list could go on and on.

And yet there may be a sting in this tale. For it is arguable that in some ways, while new generations of black and Asian young people become adept at code and identity switching, combining various forms of Asianness and Britishness with other elements, and *as they become more at home with not being at home,* as they become the classic well-adjusted figures in the Kleinian sense of being able to survive ambiguity, uncertainty, fragmentation, and the uneasiness of being, it may be the English, and in particular, white working males, who will bear the brunt of a series of shattering identity shocks (although the attempts of some of them to defend an imagined "old England" are likely to get the moral and intellectual support of elements of the *Daily Telegraph*-reading middle and upper classes, if their outraged responses to accusations of racism against the police are anything to go by; see Toynbee's analysis (1999) of that newspaper's coverage of the Stephen Lawrence Inquiry. See also Henry and Tator's essay in this volume.)

The marginalization and poverty of an increasing number of white working-class young males, their plight sanitized by the label of the Social Exclusion Unit set up by the Blair government, may be the harbinger of a crisis of the working class English, as Scotland and Wales develop stronger cultural identifications in the wake of political devolution and as the middle-class English, already Europeanized with their holidays and villas in Provence and Tuscany, their children's increasing facility with European languages, and their business and professional links with the United States, manage to develop a more cosmopolitan set of identities. The collapse of older trade-union – engendered solidarities and the break up of communities, documented for example by Bea Campbell (1993) and Nick Davies (1997), may place an unbearable burden on the young English working-class males, outperformed at school by their female counterparts. Arguably, it is from these sections of the working class that complaints of second-class status "in their own country," a discourse consistently documented in research (Back 1998; Cohen 1989, 1992; Hewitt 1997), are particularly popular. They are part of a culture of resentment and anger so many of whose victims are the black and brown people who almost inevitably personify for these marginalized English the causes of their social exclusion.

Paradoxically, it may be the emasculation of working-class men that follows from the disappearance of the heavy industrial work that sustained a sense of "hardness," self-esteem and masculinized racism (as documented in Willis 1978) that will, in displaced form, continually renew a violent racism that has already claimed a large number of victims. Arguably, the threatened masculinity is also expressed in acts like joy-riding in cars in suburban working class estates (Campbell 1993; Cohen 1997). These, indeed, may be some of the most depressing and perverse ways in which the long night of the crisis of English national identity will play itself out, the consequence of a growing social configuration produced by the imbrication of changing patterns of social class, gender – especially an incipient crisis of white working-class masculinity – and ethnicity in an era that, for England especially, combines the legacies of imperialism with a new, de-industrializing globalization of capitalism and the destabilization of older political settlements.

POSTCRIPT 2004: THE POLITICS OF LONGING AND (UN)BELONGING, FEAR, AND LOATHING

Reflecting on developments since completing the earlier version of the chapter, I have some foreboding about the fate of brown and black Britishness. For the time being, at least. Not that I was brimful of optimism when composing what you have just read, but a series of events since then suggest a straining of already vulnerable conjunctions of identities. Of course, signs of hope can always be found. In any case, the burden of my argument has been the injunction to eschew conceptions of linear movement in any particular direction. Multiplicity, differentiation, fragmentation, reconfiguration, new unities and conjunctions, new kaleidoscopic shapes are what we should continue to expect. But none of this can hide the fact that the politics of belonging in Britain has taken on a nastier, harsher edge. We are in altogether more dangerous and hostile terrain. More benign differences in visions of the future ("multicultural") shape of the polity have given way to sharper polarizations as questions of national identity and cultural pluralism have moved to centre stage in a new mood of fear, deeply coloured by a longing among many sections of the nation for simpler and more secure times past, both real and imagined. What I referred to as the long night of the crisis of British national identity has got darker still.

As I write, this nation, like many others, is convulsed by a media-driven panic about supposedly bogus asylum seekers, refugees, illegal immigrants, and potentially millions of *legal* "invaders" from the new members of the European Union drawn from the Eastern European states of the former Soviet bloc. Fears are particularly being focused on the spectre of hordes of "gypsies" – Roma, more properly called – poised to "flood" into the country to live off the British welfare state. The role of the media in fuelling these panics of suspicion, fear, and hatred has been well documented (Buchanan, Grillo, Article 19, and Threadgold 2003). The government has now given in to the media pressure and is announcing a series of measures which will renege on previous commitments to allow free entry to the new Europeans.

Only a few weeks previously, large sections of the popular press – and a substantial but difficult-to-estimate proportion of the "nation" – were enraged that the BBC had suspended a long-running breakfast television show after its host, one Robert Kilroy-Silk, a former Labour MP, published a singularly vitriolic attack on "Arabs," claiming that they had made no contribution to civilization, their only "achievement" being the creation of a culture of "limb amputators," "women oppressors," and, of course, "terrorists" (Kilroy-Silk, 2004). This, in the wake of numerous statements by prominent British politicians, including the Home Secretary, David Blunkett, that British Asians, and British Muslims in particular, had to choose between allegiance to Britain and other cultural and national loyalties. So much for hyphenated identities.

Several sets of currents have converged to create a particular crisis around the legitimacy of British Asian-ness in general and British Muslim-ness in particular, and I shall devote much of my postscript to delineating these destabilizing forces. In the process, the black British couplet will receive less treatment than it would in a longer addendum.

The most obvious and alarming destablizing force is the current unleashed by 9/11 and its aftermath. Apart from the general effects felt by the global "war on terrorism," the participation of a tiny number of British Muslims in Al-Qaeda-related groups and the war in Aghanistan, and the role of a notorious cleric, Abu Hamza, in recruiting members of his mosque in Finsbury Park in north London for various anti-Western jihads has led to opprobrium and harassment against Asian and other Muslims out of all proportion to the numbers involved and in the face of repeated condemnations of terrorism by the major Muslim organizations in the country.

Add to this an intermittent British phenomenon, youth "race" riots, this time by British Asians, Muslims in the main, in the so-called "Mill-towns" of the north – Bradford, Oldham and Burnley in particular – in the summer of 2001, immediately preceding 9/11. The towns have been devastated by de-industrialization, particularly in textiles, but affecting other manufacturing sectors as well. The parts of the towns affected are among the 20 per cent most deprived in the country. Some areas of Oldham and Burnley rank in the most deprived 1 per cent, miring both white and ethnic minority populations in severe poverty. Violence between white and Asian youth in these areas has been a regular occurrence, but this time the disorders were particularly large scale and intense. Cars and buildings were set alight and there were violent confrontations with police. The immediate trigger for this round of disorder appears to have been the activity of far-right groups and protest marches by Asians and anti-racist campaigners.

Several days of confrontation and violence were followed by another regular British phenomenon after "race riots": the instigation of several official inquiries. The reports that resulted from the investigations documented the appalling deprivation suffered by both white and Asian populations, the role of the local and national media in exacerbating tensions by exaggerating the grants and help provided to Asians, and the role of the extreme-right British National Party (BNP) in further fanning the flames of violent tension (Cantle 2001; Clarke 2001; Ouseley 2001; Ritchie 2001).

Particularly relevant to the fate of the British-Asian-Muslim conjunctions was the argument of the reports that in these northern cities the Asians and the whites were living "parallel lives." That is, most schools and neighbourhoods were now either almost wholly Asian or white. Moreover, Asians were rarely seen in town centres and were under-represented in employment in key public services where they might otherwise have interacted with white fellow townspeople. The reports concluded that this mutual isolation provided fertile ground for misleading rumours and media scare stories about the supposedly preferential treatment of Asians by local authorities. Given the genuine deprivation of the white population it was not surprising that resentment among them ran high, with the BNP playing its predictably pernicious part.

But no one could have anticipated the extraordinary intervention of the Home Secretary on the eve of the publication of the government's own findings. David Blunkett interpreted "parallel lives" to mean a failure on the part of Asians to integrate properly into British national culture. "They" were resisting learning the language, were preventing "their" women from participating in education and employment and were practising forced marriages and female genital mutilation. He identified an urgent need for "citizenship" classes, a program of induction into "the British way of life" and suggested that no immigrant should henceforth be granted nationality without passing a "Britishness" test (details of which have yet to be finally agreed).

I was not alone in pointing out that the young British Asian men involved in confrontations with the BNP, police and others were hardly ignorant women oppressors, mired in pre-modern Asian/Muslim cultures. They were thoroughly local, born in the towns where they lived, spoke in the dialects of the Lancashire towns where they had gone to school, and were demanding citizen rights and inclusion in the mainstream opportunities of the nation (Rattansi 2002b). Moreover, it was not difficult to point out that forced marriages and clitoredectomies were abhorred by all but a small minority. Research also showed that estate agents ("realtors" in Canada and the United States) had played a part in the creation of separate neighbourhoods by creating panics that Asian arrival in locales would result in a collapse in prices, thus encouraging "white flight." In addition, Asians had been routed away from more desirable public housing (Harrison and Phillips 2003).

Blunkett's intervention mischievously conflated second and third generation minorities with new immigrants from diverse regions of the globe and varying degrees of familiarity with Western and British norms. In effect, British Asians and Muslims have been lumped into one category, and insufficiently differentiated from small numbers of radical Islamicists, many of North African origin, and myriad groups of refugees and asylum seekers. The "mistake" has allowed the government to continue with forms of racism in its new immigration proposals (Solomos and Schuster 2004; Schuster 2003). It also dovetails with what some of us have called New Labour's turn to a "new assimilationism," away from a (usually lukewarm) endorsement of multiculturalism (Back et al. 2002; Rattansi 2002b; Rattansi 2003).

Inevitably, in the process, "brown British" identities are experiencing considerable strain if not outright crisis. Influential voices have joined a bandwagon warning of the dangers of a "too diverse" nation that endangers cherished institutions such as the welfare state, as taxpayers supposedly become unwilling to fund services for those whose cultures are too "alien" to British values and indeed threaten civilization itself (Goodhart 2004). The chair of the Commission for Racial Equality, Trevor Phillips, has dubbed the "too diverse" argument a "genteel xenophobia" and a form of "liberal Powellism." And he concurs with my view that the sub-text is strongly anti-Muslim (Phillips 2004; Rattansi 2002b, 102–103; see also Alexander 2002, 564; for my response to Goodhart, who cites me in his "Too Diverse" piece, see Rattansi 2004a).

Is this part of the Islamophobia identified by the Runnymede Report and referred to in my chapter? Indeed, does Islamophobia really exist? And is it a form of racism? Halliday (1999) has argued, rightly, that the concept homogenizes diverse anti-Muslim discourses and practices from the Crusades to the present period. Moreover, in his view it introduces a misleading confusion between attacks on Muslims and critiques of Islam. However, Miles and Brown have pointed out in response (2003, 165–8) that hostility in the West is usually targeted against both Muslims and Islam and that it is difficult to see how Islam can exist without Muslims. For Miles and Brown, discrimination against Muslims on the grounds that their religion is inferior and incompatible with Western culture reproduces elements that may properly be labelled racist. I would add that there is also a tendency to conflate the Islam-Muslim couplet with membership of supposed ethno-racial types such as "Arab" – as in the piece by Kilroy-Silk which led to his suspension from the BBC – and, particularly in Britain, the ethno-racial-national category of "Paki" (an abusive shortening of "Pakistani," beloved of British racists who include people of any shade of brown in the insult). In other words, it is indeed arguable that a new form of racism, specifically directed at British and other Muslims has indeed taken shape in the U.K., one which allows the formation of a malleable discourse to include terrorism, patriarchy, rural pre-modernity and other elements, depending on the context and strategic need. Especially, it allows British Muslims and sometimes British Asians and occasionally all brown Britishers to be positioned as "the enemy within." The participation of British Muslims in the mass demonstrations against the war in Iraq has provided further resources for the representation of Muslims as potential and actual fifth columnists.

Moral panics over the development of "Asian gangs" have allowed another strand to be added to the unfolding narrative of brown Britishness and British Muslims (Alexander 2000). While the vocabulary of "race and ethnic relations" in British social science had seen "Asians" as having "culture" and blacks as having "problems" (Benson 1996), Alexander has remarked on the manner in which the emergence of the "Asian gang," its associations with an Asian "underclass," its partial identification with young Muslims (and therefore also its articulation with fears over the radical Islamicization of Bangladeshi and Pakistani youth) has allowed a coalescence in public discourse whereby both black *and* brown youth now have "problems," although culture now is also the problem (Alexander, 2002).

This coincides and intersects with a renewed fear over black gang culture, its growing links with Jamaican "Yardies" and international drug trafficking, and an apparent rise in gangland shoot outs in inner-city areas in London, Birmingham, and Manchester. Interesting gender dynamics have emerged within the black populations of these cities and in black popular culture. Black women are beginning to play an important role in combatting what is called "black on black violence" – curious since, no category of "white on white" violence has figured in public discourses. The rap artist "Miss Dynamite," rather unfortunately named given the role she has now adopted, has made a number of high-profile interventions to challenge the hyper-masculinity that appears to be involved in black gang culture. Meanwhile, a debate continues about a "culture of failure," under-achievement, drug abuse, expulsion from schooling, and general criminalization that is the experience of young black men in Britain's inner cities. Diana Abbot, a prominent black Member of Parliament, has hosted a conference on what is widely perceived to be a crisis for young black British men. Commentators such as Tony Sewell, whose book on black masculinity and schooling I have referred to in the chapter, have joined a wider chorus of opinion in the popular media around the supposed "failure of fatherhood," damaging peer group pressures deriving from a nihilistic street culture, and the absence of inspiring role models in explaining what is undoubtedly a depressing narrative for some young black British men.

Interestingly, so far this has not spilled over into a more generalized panic over the "unbelonging" and un-Britishness of black British populations. For the present, this type of discourse is overwhelmingly directed at British Asians and British Muslims in particular, although there is a permanent undercurrent of such sentiment which can be mobilized in particular circumstances against black British populations.

Also, and again for the time being, middle-class Asians of Indian and especially East African origin continue to be represented as models of enterprise, "family values," and professional advancement, and together with British-born Chinese continue to outperform their white counterparts in the education system. But as I have remarked earlier, this is a selective take, simply disavowing those who fail at school, are unemployed, have got involved in crime and drug abuse, are beginning to experience high rates of divorce, and are ever more prominently gay and lesbian. Equally unremarked upon so far is the role of the British Indians in funding Hindu fundamentalist movements in India (Mukta and Bhatt 2000). It would not, however, be surprising if Hindu fundamentalism became included in a national rogue's gallery and the image of the model "community" were tarnished if events impinge in some way on the British polity.

Meanwhile, the persistence of institutional racism in the police, the National Health Service, employment, the immigration service, the Crown Prosecution service and other spheres is continually and sometimes dramatically exposed despite the injunctions and policies that followed the Macpherson Inquiry into the racist murder of Stephen Lawrence and the role of police racism in undermining the subsequent criminal investigation. For instance, an undercover TV journalist filmed new police recruits openly espousing extreme-right views in a chilling BBC national broadcast, while absurd internal charges against Asian policemen have dramatically collapsed at trial and large compensations have had to be paid. Chronic centrifugal pressure from above on hyphenated-identities, in other words, seems to show no real signs of easing off.

Somewhat alarmingly, the British National Party has now established a foothold in local government in Burnley and may succeed in sending an MEP to the European Parliament in upcoming elections. Predictably, white working-class resentment and BNP success has been reinforced rather than challenged by the Home Secretary and New Labour's strategy of confirming both their analysis of the Asians' "lack of integration" and a general hostility to refugees and asylum seekers, while still trying somehow to meet the acute shortage of labour that afflicts various sectors and regions of the country (Rattansi 2003). The problems besetting young white working-class men show no signs of abating (Frosh, Phoenix, and Pattman 2002; O'Donnell and Sharpe 2000) and will continue to provide fertile ground for racism and more generalized social disaffection. The government has responded in ever more authoritarian manner, introducing increasingly draconian "antisocial behaviour" measures. The depressing cycle of deprivation, disaffection, felt emasculation, and heavy-handed state intervention looks set to be a semi-permanent feature of the social landscape in the de-industrialized zones of Britain.

This chapter began by documenting how the first post-Second World War Labour government tried frantically to prevent the famous *SS Windrush* with its cargo of Jamaicans from setting sail. It ends as the country is entering another phase of keeping out would-be immigrants before they reach its shores, with proposals to set up processing centres in mainland Europe. The period in between has seen dramatic changes as black and brown Britishers have attempted to put down roots while bringing new meanings to what it means to be British. A meandering multiculturalism that allowed new forms of Britishness to emerge is now giving way to a phase in which "immigrant" has yet again become an insult. In the battle between "cosmopolitans" and "locals" in an emergent post-national age (Rattansi 2004b), the former are on the "back foot," to use a cricketing metaphor beloved of British public discourse.

Being brown/black British has always been a perilous adventure. The journey continues to be fraught with tensions and dangers. The politics of longing, fear, loathing, belonging, and un-belonging plays out now in a national and international climate that stretches out the hyphens to make them longer still. But the elastic will not snap. Black/brown British cultures are now too deeply embedded, whatever the misgivings and regrets on the part of populations of all hues and cultures. There is no going back to imagined homelands and purities.

It may be that in the future, new progressive projects will ground themselves more on notions of human rights and conceptions of post-national citizenship than on visions of multiculturalism. We shall have to see whether this is indeed the case and whether the effect will be to open up spaces for a greater variety and more secure forms of brown and black Britishness.

NOTES

1 An earlier, shorter version of this chapter, without the Postscript, has been published in *Interventions: the Journal of Postcolonial Studies* 2, no. 1 (2000).
2 Lack of space prevents me from pursuing this issue further. For recent research into "mixed-race" British identities, see Alibhai-Brown (2001) and Ali (2003). See also Parker and Song (2001).

REFERENCES

Afshar, H. 1994. "Muslim Women in West Yorkshire: Growing up with Real and Imaginary Values amidst Conflicting Views of Self and Society." In *The Dynamics of "Race" and Gender: Some Feminist Interventions*, eds. H. Afshar and M. Maynard. London: Taylor and Francis.

Ahmed, S. 1997. "It's a sun-tan, isn't it?: Auto-biography as an Identificatory Practice." In *Black British Feminism*, ed. H.S. Mirza. London: Routledge.

Alexander, C. 1996. *The Art of Being Black*. Oxford: Oxford University Press.

– 2000. *The Asian Gang: Ethnicity, Identity, Masculinity*. Oxford: Berg.

– 2002. "Beyond Black: Re-thinking the Colour/Culture Divide." *Ethnic and Racial Studies* 25, no. 4.

Ali, S. 2003. *Mixed-Race, Post-Race: Gender, New Ethnicities and Cultural Practices*. Oxford: Berg.

Alibhai-Brown, Y. 1999. *True Colours: Public Attitudes to Multiculturalism and the Role of the Government*. London: Institute of Public Policy Research.

– (2001) *Mixed Feelings: The Complex Lives of Mixed-Race Britons*, London: The Women's Press.

Back, L. 1996. *New Ethnicities and Urban Culture: Racisms and Multiculture in Young Lives*. London: University College Press.

– 1998. "Inside Out: Racism, Class and Masculinity in the 'Inner City' and the English suburbs." *New Formations*, no 33 Spring.

Back, L., Keith, M., Khan, A., Shukra, K., and Solomos, J. 2002. "New Labour's White Heart: Politics, Multiculturalism and the Return of Assimilation." *Political Quarterly* 73, no 4.

Ballard, R., ed. 1994. *Desh Pardesh: The South Asian Presence in Britain.* London: Hurst.

Baumann, G. 1996. *Contesting Culture: Discourses of Identity in Multi-Ethnic London.* Cambridge: Cambridge University Press.

Benson, S. 1996. "Asians Have Culture, West Indians Have Problems." In *Culture, Identity and Politics,* eds. T. Ranger, Y. Samad, and S. Stuart. Aldershot: Avebury.

Brah, A. 1996. *Cartographies of Diaspora: Contesting Identities.* London: Routledge.

Braham, P., Rattansi, A., and Skellington, R. 1992. *Racism and Antiracism: Inequalities, Opportunities and Policies.* London: Sage.

Buchanan, S., Grillo, B., Article 19, and Threadgold, T. 2003. *What's The Story? Results from Research into Media Coverage of Refugees and Asylum Seekers in the UK.* London: ARTICLE 19.

Caglar, A.S. 1997. "Hyphenated Identities and the Limits of 'Culture'." In *The Politics of Multiculturalism in the New Europe: Racism, Identity and Community,* eds. T. Modood and P. Werbner. London: Zed Books.

Campbell, B. 1993. *Goliath: Britain's Dangerous Places.* London: Methuen.

Cantle, T. 2001. *Community Cohesion: A Report of the Independent Review Team.* London: The Home Office.

Carter, B., Harris, C., and Joshi, S. 1993. "The 1951–55 Conservative Government and the Racialisation of Black Immigration." In *Inside Babylon: The Caribbean Diaspora in Britain,* eds. W. James and C. Harris. London: Verso.

Clarke, T. 2001. *Report of the Burnley Task Force.* Burnley: Burnley Council.

Cluny. 1999. *The Stephen Lawrence Inquiry: Report of an Inquiry by Sir William Macpherson of Cluny.* London: The Stationary Office.

Cohen, P. 1989. *The Cultural Geography of Adolescent Racism.* London: Institute of Education.

– 1992. "'It's racism what dunnit'; Hidden Narratives in Theories of Racism." In *"Race," Culture and Difference,* eds. J. Donald and A. Rattansi. London: Sage.

– 1997. "Labouring under Whiteness." In *Displacing Whiteness,* ed. R. Frankenberg. Durham and London: Duke University Press.

Davies, N. 1997. *Dark Heart: The Shocking Truth About Hidden Britain.* London: Chatto & Windus.

Dean, D. 1987. "Coping with Colonial Immigration, the Cold War and Colonial Policy: The Labour Government and Black Communities in Great Britain." *Immigrants and Minorities* 6: 145–51.

Eade, J. 1997. "Identity, Nation and Religion: Educated Young Bangladeshis in London's East End." In *Living in the Global City: Globalisation as a Local Process,* ed. J. Eade. London: Routledge.

Fanon, F. 1986. *Black Skins, White Masks.* London: Pluto Press (originally published in 1952).

Frosh, S., Phoenix, A., and Pattman, R. 2002. *Young Masculinities*. London: Palgrave.

Gardner, K., and Shukur, A. 1994. "'I'm Bengali, I'm Asian and I'm living here': The Changing Identity of British Bengalis." In *Desh Pardesh: The South Asian Presence in Britain*, ed. R. Ballard. London: Hurst.

Gillespie, M. 1995. *Television, Ethnicity and Cultural Change*. London: Routledge.

Goodhart, D. 2004. "Too Diverse?" *Prospect*, February.

Hall, S. 1992. "The Question of Cultural Identity." In *Modernity and Its Futures*, eds. S. Hall, D. Held, and A. McGrew. Cambridge: Polity Press.

— 1998. "Aspiration and Attitude ... Reflections on Black Britain in the Nineties." *New Formations*, no. 33 Spring.

Hall, S., and Du Gay, eds. 1996. *Questions of Cultural Identity*. London: Sage.

Halliday, F. 1999. "'Islamophobia' Reconsidered." *Ethnic and Racial Studies* 22, no. 5.

Harris, C. 1993. "Post-war Migration and the Industrial Reserve Army." In *Inside Babylon: The Caribbean Diaspora in Britain*, eds. W. James and C. Harris. London: Verso.

Harrison, M., and Phillips, D. 2003. *Housing and Black and Minority Ethnic Communities*. London: Office of the Deputy Prime Minister.

Hewitt, R. 1986. *White Talk Black Talk: Inter-racial Friendship and Communication amongst Adolescents*. Cambridge: Cambridge University Press.

— 1997. *Routes to Racism: The Social Basis of Racist Action*. Stoke on Trent: Trentham Books.

Ifekwunigwe, J. 1997. "Diaspora's Daughters, Africa's Orphans?: On Lineage, Authenticity and 'Mixed Race' Identity." In *Black British Feminism*, ed. H.S. Mirza. London: Routledge.

Kilroy-Silk, R. 2004. "We Owe Arabs Nothing." London: *The Daily Express*, January 4.

Laclau, E. 1990. *New Reflections on the Revolutions of Our Time*. London: Verso.

Laclau, E., ed. 1994. *The Making of Political Identities*. London: Verso.

Lattimer, M. 1999. "When Labour Played the Racist Card." *New Statesman*, 22 January.

Lewis, P. 1994a. *Islamic Britain: Religion, Poltics and Identity among British Muslims*. London: I.B. Taurus.

— 1994b. "Being Musim and Being British: The Dynamics of Islamic Reconstruction in Bradford." In *Desh Pardesh: The South Asian Presence in Britain*, ed. R. Ballard. London: Hurst.

Miles, R., and Brown, M. 2003. *Racism*, 2nd ed. London: Routledge.

Modood, T. 1992. *Not Easy Being British*. Stoke on Trent: Trentham Books.

Modood, T., Beishon, S., and Virdee, S. 1994. *Changing Ethnic Identities*. London: Policy Studies Institute.

Modood, T. et al. 1997. *Ethnic Minorities in Britain: Diversity and Disadvantage*. London: Policy Studies Institute.
Mukta, P., and Bhatt, C., eds. 2000. *Hindutva Movements in the West: Resurgent Hinduism and the Politics of Diaspora*. Special Issue of *Ethnic and Racial Studies* 23, no. 3.
O'Donnell, M., and Sharpe, S. 2000. *Uncertain Masculinities: Youth, Ethnicity and Class in Contemporary Britain*. London: Routledge.
Ouseley, H. 2001. *Community Pride not Prejudice: Making Diversity Work in Bradford*. Bradford: Bradford Vision.
Parker, D., and Song, M., eds. 2001. *Rethinking "Mixed Race."* London: Pluto Press.
Phillips, T. 2004. "Genteel Xenophobia Is as Bad as Any Other." *The Guardian*, February 16.
Phoenix, A. 1995. "Young People: Nationalism, Racism and Gender." In *Crossfires: Nationalism, Racism and Gender in Europe*, eds. H. Lutz, A. Phoenix, and N. Yuval-Davis. London: Pluto Press.
– 1998. "'Multiculture,' 'Multiracisms' and Young People: Contradictory Legacies of Windrush." *Soundings*, no. 10 Autumn.
Rampton, B. 1995. *Crossing: Language and Ethnicity Among Adolescents*. London: Longman.
Rattansi, A. 1992. "Changing the Subject? Racism, Culture and Education." In *"Race," Culture and Difference*, eds. J. Donald and A. Rattansi. London: Sage.
– 1994. "'Western' Racisms, Ethnicities and Identities in a Postmodern Frame." In *Racism, Modernity and Identity: On the Western Front*, eds. A. Rattansi and S. Westwood. Cambridge: Polity Press.
– 1995a. "Race, Class and the State: From Marxism to Postmodernism." *Labour History Review*, Winter.
– 1995b. "Just Framing: Racism and Ethnicity in a 'Postmodern' Framework." In *Social Postmodernism: Beyond Identity Politics*, eds. L. Nicholson and S. Seidman. New York: Cambridge University Press.
– 1997. "Postcolonialism and its Discontents." *Economy and Society* 26, no. 4.
– 2002a. "Sexuality, Racism and Political Economy: Marxism/Postmodernism/ Foucault." In *Ethnicity and Economy: "Race and Class" Revisited*, eds. S. Fenton and H. Bradley. Basingstoke: Palgrave-Macmillan.
– 2002b. "Who's British? *Prospect* and the New Assimilationism." In *Cohesion, Community and Citizenship*, ed. R. Berkeley. London: The Runnymede Trust.
– 2003. "The End of Multiculturalism? New Labour, Race and the Nation." In *Society Matters*, no. 6, ed. R. Skellington. Milton Keynes: The Open University.
– 2004a. "A False Dilemma." *http//:Guardian Unlimited.co.uk*.
– 2004b. "Dialogues on Difference: Cosmopolitans, Locals and 'Others' in a Post-National Age." *Sociology* 38 (in press).

Reynolds, T. 1997. "(Mis)representing the Black (Super)woman." In *Black British Feminism*, ed. H. Mirza. London: Routledge.

Ritchie, D. 2001. *Oldham Independent Review: One Oldham One Future*. Manchester: Government Office for the North West.

Runnymede Trust. March 1997. *Islamophobia: A Consultative Document*. London: The Runnymede Trust.

– October 1998. *The Runnymede Bulletin*. London: The Runnymede Trust.

Schuster, L. 2003. "Common Sense or Racism? The Treatment of Asylum-seekers in Europe." *Patterns of Prejudice* 37, no. 3.

Schuster, L., and Solomos, J. 2004. "Race, Immigration and Asylum: New Labour's Agenda and its Consequences." *Ethnic and Racial Studies* (in press).

Sewell, T. 1997. *Black Masculinities and Schooling: How Black Boys Survive Modern Schooling*. Stoke on Trent: Trentham Books.

Sharma, A. 1996. "Sounds Oriental: The Impossibility of Theorising Asian Musical Cultures." In *Dis-Orienting Rhythms: The Politics of the New Asian Dance Music*, eds. S. Sharma, J. Hutnyk, and A. Sharma. London: Zed Books.

Shaw, A. 1994. "The Pakistani Community in Oxford." In *Desh Pardesh: The South Asian Presence in Britain*, ed. R. Ballard. London: Hurst.

Sivanandan, A. 1978. *Race, Class and the State: The Black Experience in Britain*. London: Institute of Race Relations. Also in *Race and Class* 17, 1976.

Tizard, B., and Phoenix, A. 1993. *Black, White or Mixed Race? Race and Racism in the Lives of Young People of Mixed Parentage*. London: Routledge.

Toynbee, P. 1999. "The White Backlash." *The Guardian*, March 3, p. 20.

Vaz, K. 1998. *Whitehall Remaining White*. London: The House of Commons.

Weekes, D. 1997. "Shades of Blackness: Young Black Female Constructions of Beauty." In *Black British Feminism*, ed. H.S. Mirza. London: Routledge.

Willis, P. 1978. *Learning To Labour: How Working Class Boys Get Working Class Jobs*. Farnborough: Saxon House.

Wright, C. 1995. "Ethnic Relations in the Primary Classroom." In *Ethnic Relations and Schooling*, eds. S. Tomlinson and M. Craft. London: Athlone Press.

Young, L. 1996. *Fear of the Dark: "Race," Gender and Sexuality in the Cinema*. London: Routledge.

Young, R.J.C. 1995. *Colonial Desire: Hybridity in Theory, Culture and Race*. London: Routledge.

MINELLE MAHTANI

Mixed Metaphors: Positioning "Mixed Race" Identity

In the last twenty years, we have witnessed an explosion in scholarship and popular media accounts about the experience of "mixed race" identity (O'Hearn 1998; Parker and Song 2001; Spickard 2001). Much of the historical literature about "mixed race" people reflects a pervasive psychopathologizing, where "mixed race" individuals are positioned as "out of place" on the social landscape. There have been several metaphors employed to describe the "mixed race" experience. Researchers have noted that animal (zebra, mulatto) and food metaphors (bananas, Heinz-57, oreos, coconuts, bounty bars[1]) have been derogatorily employed to describe the experience of multiraciality (see Ali 2003; Root 1996). I suggest that these metaphors continue to characterize the multiracial experience in ways that maintain racialized hierarchies. In this chapter, I explore some of the metaphors employed by "mixed race" people to describe their own experiences of racialization. I draw on the particular metaphors of spies, tricksters, ambassadors, and interpreters in order to consider other models to describe the multifaceted experience of "mixed race" identity.

METAPHORS EMPLOYED TO DESCRIBE THE "MIXED RACE" EXPERIENCE

The public imaginary surrounding the "mixed race" person has traditionally been marked by a relentless negativity. The popular discourse is made up of a series of myths which explicitly pronounce the "mixed race" individual as "out of place" or having "no place to call home" (Root 1992; Tizard and Phoenix 1993). As the work of Maria Root and other "mixed race" researchers aptly demonstrates, the "mixed race" person has historically been stigmatized as torn and confused about her racial identity (Ifekwunigwe 1999; Nakashima 1996). This stereotype has been further compounded by gender, whereby "mixed race" women have been positioned as flighty, exotic, erotic, dangerous, oversexed, tormented and even pathetic through various mainstream fictional literatures (see Nakashima 1992). It has also been argued that the "mixed race" individual has the solution for the world's racist problems in a vacant celebration of cultural hybridity (Ifekwunigwe 1999; Mahtani 2001; Parker and Song 2001). The notion of cultural hybridity has particularly problematic personal and political connotations for the "mixed race" individual, who herself can be envisioned as the very emblem of hybridity given her "mixed race" status. To celebrate the existence of the "mixed race" individual as "hybrid" without problematizing the very real shifting configurations of power surrounding how she is simultaneously both raced and gendered can be superficial. While the literature on hybridity provides a marked contrast with the previous work in critical race theory by presenting identity in a very optimistic and upbeat way, providing a much less sombre exploration of race than has been previously available, I am afraid that its agenda is not quite as politically progressive as had been intended (see Ifekwunigwe 1999; Mitchell 1997; Young 1995). Both these discourses effectively fractionalize the "mixed race" person's identity. By imposing dis-order upon the "mixed race" person, these categories are more than simply a means of asserting intellectual hierarchies – they also exert political power laden with the privileging of partriarchal discourses.

Theories of race have always reflected beliefs about the sanctity of so-called racial purity, allowing these powerful social constructions have become fully embedded in social relations, political interactions, and economic structures (Omi and Winant 1994). The mere presence of "mixed race" people challenges mainstream racial categories constructed precisely to police boundaries that are already heavy with classed and gendered meanings. This tendency to focus upon the "mixed race" people's problematic nature, through the use of phrases like "marginal," "groupless," or "not fitting in" derives from ideas about people's attachments to their ethnic community. It presumes that people of the same ancestry necessarily share a common bond. Reducing individuals to their ethnic identity effectively denies or devalues other social axes of difference. Clearly, "mixed race" people have been made intelligible in ways that maintain racial hierarchies. Those who see themselves (and are seen) as neither black nor white, yet sometimes both simultaneously, are therefore effectively erased on the racialized terrain. Although the "out of place" metaphor is a tired one, it still fuels the dichotomous and divisive understandings of the "mixed race" experience. As the cultural geographer Tim Cresswell points out, the metaphor of "out of place" brings to mind images of isolation, fear, dread, terror, loneliness, or despair (Cresswell 1996). This chapter challenges this dominant popular imaginary by unveiling sharper explorations of the "mixed race" experience. I explore the ways that some "mixed race" women contemplate their relationship to their ethnic and racial identity by asking how they imagine themselves, and examining the metaphors they themselves employ to describe their experiences.

Before embarking upon a discussion of my methodological approach, I want to clarify the differences between the notions of "race" and "ethnicity." These two terms are often confused, and one reason for the proliferation of racial categories is the conflation of the terms "ethnicity" and "race." Ethnicity is a term that is widely applied, but it is difficult to define its differences from the notion of "race." It remains that biological associations with both ethnicity and race continue to proliferate with a tenacity which is staggering, where the expectation is that "cultural differences are founded in natural ones" (Baumann 1996, 16). Obviously, people identified as being of the same racial background may belong to a vast array of ethnic groups. I believe that the concept of ethnicity must be unpacked and unveiled as a complex social construction and interpreted within particular socio-spatial contexts as many writers have suggested (Root 1992; Zack 1995). In this chapter, I focus on the process of racialization, rather than race classification. To this end, I have been greatly influenced by the work of Robert Miles (1989). Miles proposes the notion of racialization to refer to the process of being racially marked, and argues that it must be understood in its geographical and historical specificity:

Racialization is a political or ideological process by which particular populations are identified by direct or indirect reference to their real or imagined phenotypical characteristics in such a way as to suggest that populations can only be understood as a supposed biological unity (Miles 1989, 12).

METHODOLOGY

This research draws from twenty-four qualitative, open-ended interviews with women of "mixed race" living in Toronto, Canada. This study recruited women who chose to identify as (or multiracial, biracial, or racially mixed). As a self-identified "mixed race" woman of Canadian, South-East Indian, and Iranian descent, I was interested in examining how other self-identified women of "mixed race" contemplate this politicized category of identity. Researchers exploring "mixed race" identity in the last ten years have focused upon specific ethnic compositions of biraciality, such as Japanese-European (King and DaCosta 1996), Korean-European (Standen 1996), and African-American-Jewish (Azoulay 1997). Recent work in the field of critical "mixed race" theory has suggested the importance of analysing the experiences of those whose identity includes the awareness, acknowledgment, and affirmation of several threads of racial, cultural, and ethnic backgrounds (Mahtani and Moreno 2001). Following these calls, this study gave women the space to define their "mix." Several women interviewed were not just of "white" and "black" descent. They clarified in rich detail their multiple lines of ancestry (for example, one grandparent Irish, one grandparent "First Nations" Native, one grandparent Iranian, and one grandparent Polynesian). Although I used the term "mixed race" to recruit the population I interviewed, the women interviewed did not limit themselves to the use of the phrase "mixed race" to describe their racialized identities. Indeed, they also explained that on some days they might also see themselves as biracial or multiracial, among a wide array of options (Song 2001; Waters 1990). If they chose to identify themselves in these ways, I was curious as to when and where they would use these designations.

All names that follow are pseudonyms to protect the participants' privacy. The majority of participants were recruited through word of mouth and through the posting of signs. The women were between the ages of 17 and 55. The age range of participants is significant, as it plays a role in the shifting ways that "mixed race" women choose to identify racially (for a lengthy discussion on this topic, see Mahtani 2002b). It is imperative to note that although the class categories in which these women defined themselves meant different things in different contexts, the majority of the women saw themselves as being part of the "middle to upper class" segment of society. Although I did try to recruit women of various class backgrounds, I discovered that low to lower-middle class "mixed race" women's experiences of racialization were structured differently from the population I interviewed, because of their constrained financial situations. The majority of the women interviewed in this study had access to a university education, through which many of them began to learn a language by which to define themselves outside of restraining racial labels. Their education affected how they "read their race," reflecting the complex ways race and class are co-constructed. The very distinctive educational, socio-economic, and cultural privileges of participants cannot be overlooked. The majority of women who were interviewed are members of a distinctive socio-economic service class. These professional and academic experiences may make them more confident and assertive, thus they are more able to challenge identifications than other "mixed race" women who

may be economically disadvantaged, for example. The lively de
that ensued about the contestation of the "mixed race" label is
specific to this particular population who had studied at university. We
require more research about the different ways "mixed race" women's
identities are dependent upon class dynamics.

The interviews were carried out in Toronto, Canada, between 1996
and 1997. The very experience of living in Canada has a significant impact upon these women's choices to identify as "mixed race." Canada
is the only country in the world to implement a state-legislated form of
multiculturalism, through government policy instituted in 1971 (see
Kobayashi 1993). I have suggested in other work that this framework
produces particular discursive and material social spaces within which
"mixed race" women may choose to identify as "mixed race" (author,
forthcoming). Multicultural policy, according to which ethnic identities
are celebrated as a backdrop for Canadian identity, often ensures that
forms of institutionalized racism are rendered invisible (see Kobayashi
1993; Kymlicka 1995). As a result, the concept of racialized ethnicities
(as opposed to "race") has figured largely in questions of identity for
visible minority Canadians (Bannerji 2000). This has an impact on the
ways women in this study identified. I have prefaced each quote with a
brief introduction to each woman – including her age at the time of the
interview, her job, and how *she* defined her ethnic background in order
to avoid defining her readings of her ethnic identity myself.

In other work I document the relationship between "mixed race"
identity and performativity in more detail (see Mahtani 2002a). In this
particular chapter, I am interested in the ways that some women in this
study shared stories about the names they use to identify themselves. Not
all the women interviewed identified themselves as "ambassadors" or
"tricksters" – but a large enough number of participants did discuss their
use of these metaphors with me to warrant a more thorough discussion.
It is also important to note that the interviewees are multiply situated. At
times and in various places, they chose to privilege identifying themselves
as "mixed race" over "black" or "white," but these choices did not necessarily depend on their personal identification options. Much depended
on the ways that these women's phenotypes were perceived by others
– again, this is an issue I discuss more fully in Mahtani (2002a). Finally, I
am aware of the tensions involved in employing the phrase "mixed race"
to describe participants in this study. I fear that the term reiterates the
idea that racial categories are static or impenetrable. However, I chose to
use the phrase to describe interviewees because "mixed race" is more
part of common-day parlance as a personal identification label, whereas
"multiracial," "biracial," or "mixed ethnicity" have yet to catch on or
take on political clout outside the academic realm.

TRICKSTERS: LIMINALITY AND DUALITY

The notion of the "trickster" has been subject to significant scrutiny in cultural studies (Haraway 1991; Landay 1998;[2] Scott 1990; Young 1995) and literature (Beer 1998). Geographers have also alluded to the trickster in relation to the development of an "un-naturalized discourse" where "practices that would in the past [have] ... been designated as ... witchcraft or voodoo ... [might] be seen as a means of bringing about social change" (Kobayashi and Peake 1994, 238). Indeed, appearing on the academic horizon is now something called "trickster studies" (Landay 1998, 27). Folklorists and anthropologists have described tricksters as cultural figures whose attributes of liminality, duality, and irony challenge and often subvert the boundaries of social regulation. As Lori Landay argues, however, scholars have presumed the trickster to be a male figure, or, at best, a genderless figure. Although tricksters are known for switching genders, implicit in these definitions are "the criterion of masculinity and the privilege of autonomy and mobility with which masculinity is synonymous" (Landay 1998, 2). What is the role of women in cultural acts of duplicity and subversion? Gender is a previously neglected yet important aspect of trickster studies (Landay 1998, 27) whereby by female tricksters can articulate the paradox of femininity and autonomy ... by transgressing the cultural delimiters of "women's sphere ... female tricksters violate [gendered] boundaries" (Landay 1998, 26). In the genre of the passing novel, "mixed race" women are often characterized as possessing what is deemed the trickster tactic of deception and boundary crossing. On the whole, these experiences of being a trickster tend to be tragic ones (Landay 1998, 19). However, the following narrative explores the potential for agency employed in identifying as a trickster.

One of the participants in my study, Zillah, introduced the notion of the trickster as a way to describe herself in the midst of a discussion about her latest film project which follows the story of an animal trickster in Northern Ontario. Zillah is a twenty-nine-year-old filmmaker who told me her mother was "Asian" from Hong Kong and her father of "German ancestry" who grew up in a small farming community in northern Ontario. While describing the film to me, Zillah abruptly stopped and said,

I love being a trickster.
Minelle: A what?
Zillah: A trickster. I really like the whole notion of the trickster pretending. In the traditional trickster fashion, the trickster always being someone who's de-

fined by difference ... And I see myself as a trickster. So what I'm doing right now is masquerading as white but that's just so I can get off the ground ... I'm putting on the guise of a white human whenever I want. So that I can push my own ends and help save the animal community which is the people who aren't in the privileged group. And I think I see that as what my role is. Turning things a little upside down, changing people's expectations, surprising them. I think being mixed heritage works to my benefit in that I find myself in situations like this where I can protect the interests of Asian people in situations where people are not anticipating me to be Asian.

Zillah reveals the destabilizing potential of the managed self and acknowledges her capacity to infiltrate racist spaces unnoticed, without the blink of an eye. By operating through spaces where she is read as white, while at the same time being the Other set against whiteness, Zillah readily admits that she can "masquerade" as white which allows her the opportunity to enjoy the privileges that attend white skin. At the same time, however, Zillah insists that she has the ability to challenge the construction and encoding of spaces by occupying these spaces simultaneously. Zillah imagines that she is able to perform acts of resistance in a veiled fashion. At the same time, Zillah also must manoeuvre through other people's perception of her racialized self. The only stability in others' perception of her racialized self is that it is constantly shifting and changing. By deeming herself a trickster, Zillah is producing "a skill ceaselessly recreating opacities and ambiguities – spaces of darkness and trickery – in the universe of technocratic transparency, a skill that disappears into them and reappears again, taking no responsibility for the administration of a totality" (de Certeau 1985, 18). Zillah acknowledges her privilege by being able to masquerade as a "white person" and doubles that privilege by demonstrating how she can move in and out of particular spaces to "speak up" for marginalized groups.

The trickster character is often explored as an ambiguous and equivocal mediator of contradiction. I suggest that the use of the trickster metaphor tells a story about racial hierarchies. Historically, the trickster earns success not by physical prowess or strength, but instead by wit and cunning. He snakes through treacherous spaces where enemies reside, seeking to defeat him, and yet, in principle, he is unable to win any direct confrontation as he is smaller and weaker than his antagonists. Only by knowing the habits of his enemies does the trickster manage to escape their clutches and subsequently win victories (Scott 1990). The motif of the trickster has been considered a comic trope, a creative production, and an imaginative liberation in comic narratives:

"the trickster is postmodern" (Vizenor 1989, 9). "Mixed race" researcher Jayne Ifekwunigwe (1999) uses the term *metis(se)* to describe individuals who have British or European mothers and continental African or African Caribbean fathers (Ifekwunigwe 1997, 147) and I juxtapose that against the definition of metis defined by Detienne and Vernant, who investigate its (one of many potential) origins[3] as understood by the Ancient Greeks: "[Metis means to combine] flair, wisdom, forethought, subtlety of mind, deception, resourcefulness, vigilance, opportunism, various skills and experience acquired over the years. It is applied to situations which are transient, shifting, disconcerting, and ambiguous, situations which do not lend themselves to precise measurement, exact calculation, or rigorous logic" (Detienne and Vernant 1978, 3–4).[4]

Clearly this is the case for Zillah, who reads her own racialized identity as a way of employing these specific strategies in order to achieve her own ends. Instead of being sighted and re-sited, an experience which is constantly being reinterpreted on various terrains when you are "mixed race," Zillah asserts her ability to site her audience – to manipulate those who have so often manipulated and positioned her own identity. Ideas about female trickery in particular can underscore issues of women's exercise of covert power (Landay 1998), challenging ideals of femininity against which female tricksters rebel. It might be suggested that some participants, like Zillah, imagine themselves as double tricksters in that they regularly contest both gendered and racialized representations.

The results of identifying as a trickster, among other metaphors, are not clear. The stories I heard from participants reveal that the results range from being indeterminate, contradictory and sometimes even revolutionary. I suggest that these forms of struggle are by no means always coherent nor progressive. In the next narrative, I hope to illustrate how one such incident could be read as a way to maintain control of a particular situation. Not all trickster behaviours can be seen as acts of resistance. In the presence of the powerful, individuals are often obliged to adopt strategic stances (Scott 1990).

Acts of deliberate covertness are employed for a range of reasons. Often, they signify exhaustion with the question, "Where are you from?" and offer a detraction from invasive or probing questions. They can provide opportunities to shock or surprise people who make racist comments, silencing them from further questioning. However, strategies of covertness can also be employed at times – a necessary tactic due to vulnerability to racist attacks, often compounded by the variable of gender, which rarely permits the luxury of direct confrontation.

There are times when some participants actively or passively veil or conceal their ethnicity for safety's sake, where covertness is enacted primarily as a survival strategy. I want to illustrate some of these covert strategies by discussing how some participants often presented anonymous stances in the face of oppressive situations, or adopted the role of the "spy" or "trickster" to define their movement in particular places.

Some participants explained how they adopted an anonymous stance in order to protect themselves from racist attacks, employing covertness by not saying anything about their ethnicity when it was assumed for them by others. Clearly, there are times – and spaces – when it is advantageous to conceal your multiethnic background. Maribel explains how she obscures her ethnic identities in order to sidestep a potentially threatening situation. Maribel is a twenty-five-year-old graduate student who identified as "a child of a mixed marriage between a Swedish mother and a Bangladeshi father." In the following narrative, Maribel tells me how keeping quiet offered her an opportunity to escape potential persecution:

I was in the subway [in New York City] stupidly at 2.00 in the morning with my friend Julie. And this guy was really harassing Julie about her ethnicity. She's black. To me, she's obviously black. But she's dyed her hair. Actually what he first said was, "You're black, aren't you?" And Julie said, "No" because she didn't want this guy to … well, it was just weird. And finally she said, "Yes, I'm black." And he said, "GOOD!" And then he flashes this gun. On the side of his hip. (chuckle) And he goes, "Because us black people," and he looks at me, "and us Puerto Ricans, we gotta stick together." So I was thinking, "I'll happily be Puerto Rican for you today!" (laughter) No problem!

While Maribel's omission to pipe up: "Well, no, actually, I am mixed" reflects her tentativeness to identify herself as "mixed race" in this particular arena (earlier in the interview, she insisted that she defines herself as "mixed race" in most social spheres), any open resistance in this situation might have resulted in instant retaliation. She explains how the situation was fraught with tension, where any misspoken word could have meant disastrous consequences. Resistant political subjectivities are constituted through positions in relation to authority which can often leave people in awkward, contradictory, and dangerous places. As Shrage reminds us, "there are contexts in which downplaying one's assigned racial or sex identity might be a good thing to do and contexts in which playing it up may be good" (Shrage 1997, 188). Clearly, racism has an uncanny ability to adopt new stances in different times and places, as Stoler's chapter in this book attests.

SPIES: OVERTURNING THE MARGINALIZATION ASSOCIATED WITH COVERTNESS

Participants also explained that they employed particular furtive and covert strategies in order to move through spaces which might not be accessible to them if they proclaimed their ethnic allegiances aloud. These "spies" are often offered entree to particular spaces which are traditionally restricted to those of a particular phenotype and they are thus able to transgress certain racialized boundaries. In the following narrative, Zillah explains how she and her friend Katya identify as "spies," subverting and revitalizing inversions of official discourses. Zillah told me about a conversation she shared with Katya, a thirty-year-old filmmaker in Toronto, whose father is "black from the West Indies" and whose mother is "white from Ireland."

We were talking about how we would both make great spies cause we don't look like we're people in the context that we're in when we're transplanted into that culture ... there's been instances where people have said things where I think they just don't realize what they're saying and I will correct them on it. And then they always do a double take and they look at me closer. I think if I had an affinity for languages I would make a perfect spy because I can transcend those borders. I would be able to enter all those communities without them realizing that I'm nowhere near where those communities are.

By passing as "white," Zillah suggests that she has the potential to shake the foundations of naturalized racial categories. At times, she chooses to uncloak her identity in order to shock people out of their stereotypes. Zillah expresses a desire to destabilize racialized spaces, whereby the link between racialized meanings and identities is unsettled and the slipperiness of naturalized racial categories can be revealed.

Envisioning oneself as a spy was a common thread in many narratives. At the end of our interview, Maiko, one of the youngest women I interviewed, abruptly stopped me and told me there was something she forgot to talk about. Maiko is seventeen and explained to me that her mother "is from Hong Kong," and her Dad is "white white white from New York." Unprompted by a question, she began:

Oh actually there's one more thing I wanted to say, and it's not exactly about people questioning my race, [it's more about me feeling] like a spy? There's this one memory I have, basically in grade seven, the first dance I was at, at school. And I was talking to two girls, and they were talking about which boys they wanted to dance with. And these are girls that I had just met, like I had just got to that junior high school. And they were discussing, they were both discussing.

And then they said, "Well what are you going to do if a Chinese boy asks you?" And they were like, "I don't want to dance if a Chinese boy asks me, they're too short." And they said this like, like, I mean, I was so shocked that they were saying this in front of me? Like because I can't believe that they're saying this, they, then I realized that they didn't realize that I was Chinese as well? They were saying such offensive things, right when I was RIGHT THERE. There were the three of us. And that was a big shocker. And I just said to her, I just said, "I'm half Chinese. Why don't you want to dance with a Chinese boy?" I mean, they were just talking about Chinese people with such disdain! You know? And then I sorta realized, and we just changed the subject, or whatever. But that was just like, first I thought they were doing it just to get me going. To get me, to get some sort of response from me. To isolate me, to show me that they didn't like me. But then I realized that they didn't even know? And then I just felt, like I felt like I was, like that part of me was invisible? Sort of? And that I had all these powers, so I made up this fantasy in my mind, like of being to infiltrate all these racist groups, of people, and then go, "HA!" or whatever.

There are several tangled threads in the above narrative. A preliminary reading indicates that Maiko initially read the girl's decision to speak disparagingly about the Chinese boys as a slight against Maiko herself, indicated by Maiko's statement, "I thought they were doing it just to ... isolate me, to show me that they didn't like me." She is surprised to discover that the girls had not associated her as being Chinese at all. When she discovers this, Maiko chooses to expose the girls' racist practices. With me, she expresses glee and amusement about her potential to undermine ethnic stereotypes in the future, where she acknowledges the destabilizing potential to infiltrate racist spaces.

There are glimpses of similarity between these two narratives and the management of lesbian identities in everyday spaces, as discussed by geographers David Bell and Gill Valentine (1995), whereby, in different environments, gay women may adopt a short-term or strategic approach by "waiting to see how the land lies before 'coming out'" (Bell and Valentine 1995, 148). Maiko and Zillah both focus upon the process of "coming out," albeit in a drastically different way than is explored in Bell and Valentine's account. Maiko chose in this particular situation to declare her ethnicity to those who made the racial remark. She envisaged her declaration as a strategy of resistance in order to attack and expose racism. She indicates to me that she looks forward to a time when such an encounter would become a source of discomfort and momentarily a crisis of racial meaning where she could pose a threat to boundaries and hierarchies by creating cultural anxiety.

By no means am I suggesting that the moment at the dance was not fraught with feelings of exclusion or unhappiness. However, in telling the story to me, Maiko chose to focus upon the post-productive readings of the incident. This was not an uncommon tendency among the women I interviewed. In most narratives, participants chose to emphasize the positive aspects of their racialized identities.[5] Undoubtedly, my own identification as a woman of "mixed race" may well mean that I privileged these stories in order to challenge socially constructed myths about "mixed race" individuals. However, upon reflection, I believe these particular anecdotes were revealed to counter particular socially constructed impressions of multiethnic women as either marginal or as "out of place." I suggest participants recognize the need for alliances in struggle – where "the space of separatism in these discussions, then, is also a space of interrelations ... a paradox" (Rose 1993, 153). Identifying as "mixed race" is seen not as necessarily oppressive, but rather as occupying a place where difference is envisioned as a strength. This was abundantly clear in my interview with Katya.

INTERPRETER AND AMBASSADOR: NEGOTIATING RACIALIZED SPACES

Katya specifically employed the terms "interpreter," "ambassador," and "translator" to describe how she feels about her racialized identity:

> [I think I can look] at things from both sides. In acting like an ambassador. Which is something I recognized, I think, for many years, but didn't realize what it was that I was doing. And trying to explain one side to the other. I act as a translator. Interpreter. And I think that I do that, I feel that is one of my roles. Not necessarily something that I asked to take. But I felt some sort of duty that I did not want black people to be misunderstood. And I didn't want white people to be misunderstood. Or I didn't want black people to misunderstand white people. And [I am able] to move between, move across a spectrum, being able to be the ambassador, to present different sides, to represent the other in both circumstances. To come from an informed position on both sides. So a knowledge, a partnership. And I don't necessarily think that someone that was here or (points across) here would be able to give that much information.

I am particularly struck by Katya's implicit refusal to read her "mixed race" status as a problem: instead, she sees it as part of a potential solution in dealing with conflict. I think the use of multiple metaphors here – interpreters, ambassadors, and translators – is important. I am fascinated by the mobility in the use of these phrases. Katya explains that she can simultaneously act as an interpreter, translator, and ambassador between groups, roles which have been traditionally read as those of a negotiator. Katya sees herself as being able to interact with many groups, fostering communication and understanding. Stuart Hall has made allusion to this tendency, stating that "the future role of mixed people may be that of negotiators. Since they belong to many groups, they will be seen as insiders, with vested interests in making plans work for all sides" (Hall 1992, 328–9). Katya explores the construction of a different kind of space where women need not be victims (Rose 1993, 159). She locates a place that articulates a troubled relation to the hegemonic discourse of the "mixed race" woman. Instead, Katya emphasized that she deliberately practises crossing boundaries to increase communication across groups.

Marical echoed many of Katya's sentiments. Marical is a twenty-eight-year-old writer. Her father is "Albino from South Africa," and her mother is "European, but from New Zealand." When I asked her whether she feels that her "mixed race" identity has given her a certain kind of perspective on the way she looks at race, she responded:

Oh yeah, I think I'm a genius! (laughter) I think it's great, definitely. Just because I always feel like I'm a fly on the wall, I feel kind of like I've been privy to certain ideas and I seem to spend a lot of my life explaining ... black people to white people and white people to black people, just explaining. I've decided that I'm special. And I think that gives you a lot of freedom. I don't feel like I have a lot of things that contain me. Because I've broken most of the rules already, just by existing. So I feel like I have unlimited potential, to a large degree? You know? And I think that that's a really good thing.

Much like Katya, Marical explained that she can act as a translator within groups by virtue of ability to take on a fly-on-the-wall role of observer. I do not want to dismiss the fact that at times, the "mixed race" woman does in fact experience alienation as a result of society's rigid rules about racialization. However, alternate readings of the experience of marginalization are turn suggested by Marical. She deliberately decides that she is "special" and although she recognizes that she is seen as different in many ways, she also feels she has unlimited potential, thus turning her marginality into a productive site.

CONCLUSION:
MOVING BEYOND MIXED METAPHORS

This paper has attempted to examine the multifaceted metaphors employed by some "mixed race" women to consider questions of racialized identity. Women in this study suggested that occupying a space at the threshold of the margin can provide a perspective from which to consider the complexities of difference. The metaphors employed (ambassador, fly on the wall, spy) suggest that individuals who are traditionally positioned at the margins may read their marginality as a positive, or even superior, stance from which to forge new alliances. Some participants even credited their "mixed race" status with ability to understand marginality. Thus, they expressed to me that they often occupy spaces at both the centre and the margins. Many women interviewed offered me opportunities to see them outside the pervasive "out of place" paradigm where they occupied distinct spaces that are not inferior to other so-called "pure" spaces. These spaces are obviously privileged places for these women, who can often manoeuvre through this racialized landscape in powerful ways. I would suggest that these women's choice of metaphors to describe their racialized experiences reflects a form of feminized resistance. For these women, naming is more than simply a discursive act – it is also necessarily embodied.

These narratives tell us multiple tales about the momentary and multi-textured configurations of power and resistance that take place during the process of naming. The narratives suggest the importance of reconceptualizing resistance beyond a definition of an encounter between the powerful and the weak. This notion locks resistance into a binary characterization which is hardly productive. Interventions made on one level can be compromised by reinscriptions of power at another (Kondo 1997). It is more helpful to ask how various positionalities highlight what kinds of power relations are being understood and explored among participants during encounters in particular sites. For these women, senses of identity were not described as rootless or homeless. Instead, they referred to their identities in terms of moving through categories, and of developing scattered senses of belonging with a diverse range of collectives.

ACKNOWLEDGMENTS

I would like to thank Jo-Anne Lee for her useful editorial comments on this piece. I am also grateful to Michael Keith, who encouraged me to explore the relationship between "trickster" identity and critical "mixed race" theory. Finally, I wish to acknowledge the pioneering research of fellow "mixed race" writer Jayne O. Ifekwunigwe. Both her research and her emotional support have been pivotal to my personal and professional development.

NOTES

1 The terms "coconut" and "bounty bars" have also been employed in the U.K. to describe black children raised by white, middle-class families or in what have been deemed transracial adoption placements (see Ali 2003).
2 For a detailed exploration of the female trickster in popular American culture, see Landay (1998), whose focus on the recurring figure of the female

trickster in the developing mass consumer market serves as a way of adding gender to current discussions about consumption.
3 The notion of the "trickster" is drawn from many cultures, including, but certainly not limited to, indigenous cultures – in Canada and South America.
4 Again, it is crucial to note that "Metis" as an identity has many meanings for various cultural groups, including people of mixed indigenous and European descent in Canada, as well as someone who, "by virtue of parentage, embodies two or more world views." See Ifekwunigwe 1999, 18–22, for an insightful discussion on the myriad connotations of this term.
5 However, it is crucial to note that this was not always the case. One of the participants in this study revealed some painful memories related to her experience of "mixed race" and said that she felt pity whenever she saw a black baby in a stroller being pushed by a white woman. As we were packing up after the interview, Chantal, a woman who identified her mother as "British" and her father as "Trinidadian," expressed concern that she would "throw off" my data by confessing that being mixed had caused her considerable emotional trauma (this was of interest to me as I was very careful not to celebrate the experience of multiraciality with her during my interview or during my pre-interview discussions with her). She noted grimly that her insights might disrupt readings of the experience of "mixed race" that I had already garnered from previous responses – and that I might want to drop this particular interview from my case study. I feel this comment should not be overlooked. Chantal is pointing out to me the very real paradox of "mixed race," emphasizing that not all "mixed race" people share similar experiences of either absolute oppression or complete freedom. Instead, she stressed how physical appearance is a strong factor in the conflation of genotype and phenotype (an issue I explore in more detail in Mahtani 2002a).

REFERENCES

Ali, S. 2003. *Mixed-Race, Post-Race: Gender, New Ethnicities, and Cultural Practices.* Oxford: Berg.
Azoulay, K.G. 1997. *Black, Jewish and Interracial: It's Not the Color of Your Skin, but the Race of Your Kin, and Other Myths of Identity.* Durham and London: Duke University Press.
Bannerji, H. 2000. *The Dark Side of the Nation: Essays on Multiculturalism, Nationalism and Gender.* Toronto: Canadian Scholar's Press.
Baumann, G. 1996. *Contesting Culture: Discourses of Identity in Multi-Ethnic London.* Cambridge: Cambridge University Press.
Beer, J. 1998. "Doing it with Mirrors: History and Cultural Identity from *The Diviners* to *The Robber Bride.*" Paper presented at the British Association for Canadian Studies Conference, 6 April 1998.

Bell, D. and Valentine, G. 1995. "The Sexed Self: Strategies of Performance, Sites of Resistance." In *Mapping the Subject: Geographies of Cultural Transformation*, eds. S. Pile and N. Thrift, 143–158. London: Routledge.

Cresswell, T. 1996. *In Place/Out of Place*. Minneapolis: University of Minnesota Press.

de Certeau, M. 1985. *The Practice of Everyday Life*. Berkeley: University of California Press.

Detienne, M., and Vernant, J.P. 1978. *Cunning Intelligence in Greek Culture and Society*. Trans. J. Lloyd. Atlantic Highlands: Humanities Press.

Hall, S. 1992. "Cultural Studies and Its Theoretical Legacies." In *Cultural Studies*, eds. L. Grossberg, C. Nelson, P.A. Treichler, 328–45. New York: Routledge.

Haraway, D. 1991. *Simians, Cyborgs and Women: The Reinvention of Nature*. London: Free Association Press.

Ifekwunigwe, J.O. 1997. "Diaspora's Daughters, Africa's Orphans? On Lineage, Authenticity and 'Mixed Race' Identity." In *Black British Feminism*, ed. H. Mirza, 127–53. London: Routledge.

– 1999. *Scattered Belongings: Cultural Paradoxes of Race, Culture and Nation*. London: Routledge.

King, R., and DaCosta, K. 1996. "Changing Face, Changing Race: The Remaking of Race in the Japanese American and African American Communities." In *The Multiracial Experience*, ed. M.P.P. Root, 227–45. London: Sage.

Kobayashi, A. 1993. "Multiculturalism: Representing a Canadian Institution." In *Place/Culture/Representation*, eds. J. Duncan and D. Ley, 205–31. London: Routledge.

Kobayashi, A., and Peake, L. 1994. "Un-natural Discourse: 'Race' and Gender in Geography." In *Gender, Place and Culture* 1, 3: 225–43.

Kondo, D. 1997. *About Face*. London: Routledge.

Kymlicka, W. 1995. *Multicultural Citizenship: A Liberal Theory of Minority Rights*. Oxford: Clarendon Press.

Landay, L. 1998. *Madcaps, Screwballs and Con Women: The Female Trickster in American Culture*. Philadelphia: University of Pennsylvania Press.

Mahtani, M. 2001. "I'm a Blonde-Haired, Blue-Eyed Black Girl: Mapping Mobile Paradoxical Spaces Among Multiethnic Women in Toronto, Canada." In *Rethinking "Mixed Race,"* eds. D. Parker and M. Song, 173–191. London: Pluto Press.

– 2002a. "Tricking the Border Guards: Performing Race." In *Environment and Planning D: Society and Space*: 425–40.

– 2002b. "What's in a Name?: Exploring the Employment of 'Mixed Race' as an Ethno-Racial Identification." In *Ethnicities* 2, 4: 469–90.

Mahtani, M., and Moreno, A. 2001. "Same Difference: Towards a More Unified Discourse in 'Mixed Race' Theory." In *Rethinking "Mixed Race,"* eds. D. Parker and M. Song, 76–99. London: Pluto Press.

Miles, R. 1989. *Racism*. London: Routledge.

Mitchell, K. 1997. "Different Diasporas and the Hype of Hybridity." In *Environment and Planning D: Society and Space*, 15: 533–53.

Nakashima, C. 1992. "An Invisible Monster: The Creation and Denial of Mixed-Race People in America." In *Racially Mixed People in America*, ed. M.P.P. Root, 162–81. London: Sage.

– 1996. "Voices from the Movement: Approaches to Multiraciality." In *The Multiracial Experience*, ed. M. Root, 79–101. London: Sage.

O'Hearn, C., ed. 1998. *Half and Half: Writers on Growing Up Biracial and Bicultural*. New York: Pantheon Press.

Omi, M., and Winant, H. 1994. *Racial Formation in the United States*. London: Routledge.

Parker, D., and Song, M., eds. 2001. *Rethinking "Mixed Race."* London: Pluto Press.

Root, M.P.P., ed. 1992. *Racially Mixed People in America*. London: Sage

Root, M.P.P. 1996. "The Multiracial Experience: Racial Borders as a Significant Frontier in Race Relations." In *The Multiracial Experience*, ed. M.P.P. Root, xiii-15. London: Sage

Rose, G. 1993. *Feminism and Geography*. London: Polity.

Scott, J.C. 1990. *Domination and the Arts of Resistance: Hidden Transcripts*. New Haven: Yale University Press.

Shrage, L. 1997. "Passing Beyond the Other Race or Sex." In *Race/Sex*, ed. N. Zack, 183–91. London: Routledge.

Spickard, P. 2001. "The Subject Is Mixed Race: The Boom in Biracial Biography." In *Rethinking "Mixed Race,"* eds. D. Parker and M. Song, 76–99. London: Pluto Press.

Standen, B. 1996. "Without a Template: The Biracial Korean/White Experience." In *The Multiracial Experience*, ed. M.P.P. Root, 245–63. London: Sage.

Tizard, B., and Phoenix, A. 1993. *Black, White or Mixed Race?* London: Routledge.

Vizenor, G. 1989. *Narrative Chance*. Norman and London: University of Oklahoma Press.

Waters, M. 1990. *Ethnic Options: Choosing Identities in America*. Berkeley: University of California Press.

Young, R. 1995. *Colonial Desire*. London: Routledge.

Zack, N., ed. 1995. *American Mixed Race*. London: Rowman and Littlefield Publishers.

ROY MIKI

Turning In, Turning Out: The Shifting Formations of "Japanese Canadian" from Uprooting to Redress

> Everything on earth has its moment of testimony:
> its valorous presence as a witness to mutability.
>
> (Kiyooka, 389)

Gazing into the crystal ball of shifting formations has never been a straightforward procedure. In these times of intense skepticism and uncertainty, as familiar national boundaries – real and symbolic – dissolve under the pressure of global drifts, the prospect of identifying something so seemingly isolate as "Japanese Canadian"[1] is anxiety producing. I discovered this while preparing this chapter and becoming conscious of a constructed "I" who performs the critical function of the gaze. Isn't there, I or "he" asked himself, the risk of a tautological folly, as one who is already presented as a "Japanese Canadian," a curious creature of history and imagination, gazes at "Japanese Canadian" as a shifting formation?

I begin with this qualifying question, not as an excuse for what may turn out to be folly, but to acknowledge that attempts to address "Japanese Canadian" from a subject positioning tied to personal investments may tempt the conceptual closures I set out to open. This identity formation, of course, has preoccupied me for decades in all the most immediate ways imaginable from the personal and familial to the social and historical. Yet even if "Japanese Canadian" (JC) has been a given – or what has been given me – for more years than memory can safely retrieve, it has never remained static and autonomous; rather it has been contingent and mobile, producing in its mediated relationships a network of signifying effects – effects that have been unpredictable, sometimes turbulent, sometimes imprisoning, sometimes liberating, and sometimes dumbfounding.

But here I was troubled by a dilemma: How to speculate on the historical production of "Japanese Canadian," its context-specific configurations, variations, and significances, without falling back on a fixed point of reference, some origin that it stands for? I didn't want in any way to diminish a "life lived" or the "lives lived" in all their minute and quotidian particularities over many decades under its name. But at the same time I wanted to avoid some unquestioned assumptions – aware that doing so entailed accepting other assumptions. In other words, however normalized the designation appears to be, the reach of the representational boundaries of "Japanese Canadian" should never be taken for granted. For me, it is the very unpredictability of its movements that calls for critical reflection, particularly in relation to the ways it has been inhabited, shaped, and resisted by those social subjects who have fallen under its spell (pun intended). This self-reflexive exercise, it seems to me, has taken on some urgency at this moment when its 20th century formations, forged as they were in the crucible of race constructs and the Canadian nation state, appear so much less tangible in the blurred border zones of global flows.

On this occasion, then, I want to turn to the boundaries of "Japanese Canadian" in order to nudge them towards a provisional, and I hope malleable, opening to whatever future awaits their arrival in yet to be articulated transformations. In doing so I necessarily implicate the historical limits of my own formation, one that has been coloured by the fortunes and misfortunes – the gifts and burdens – of becoming such a subject in the process. (Turning in, turning out, so a voice whispers.)

Given the critical scope of this presentation – on "Japanese identities" – and given the current porosity of the borderline between "Japanese" and "Canadian" under the influence of transnational processes, I want to begin by returning to a moment – an anecdotal one – when these two formations found themselves, not negotiating, but clashing with each other in a much younger consciousness.

It was the summer of 1970. It was the year of Expo70 in Osaka. I was sauntering along in Asakusa, in Tokyo. I was drawn to the insistent rhythm of a barker's voice. A tightly knit crowd had cohered around him. Entering that circle my imagination suddenly shuttled back and forth, from the voice to the site of the Royal American Show in Winnipeg. There, at least for a "normal" JC kid, the barkers were mesmerizing for the uncanny ability they had to perform a stream of constant talk. I fantasized that, one day, I too might be able to perform so fluidly in the English language. But it wasn't only the voice, more its discursive calling into appearance the object of its gaze – the so-called "freak" show.

Here were men and women doing wondrous feats, such as swallowing a sword or breathing fire, but alongside them were others whose bodies were the spectacle, the object displayed for its divergences from the normative gaze: the fattest person in the world, the tallest, the bearded woman, twins whose bodies were joined, the limbless body. In the crowd at Asakusa, among the normative bodies there, my own invisibility took on some uncanny effects. Without thought, I found myself slipping into the barker's world: anticipating the gaze, enticed by the sample others – so familiar from childhood memory yet so alien in Japanese bodies – displayed on a make-shift stage beside him.

Those bodies, acting as the retrieval cue,[2] struck a deep chord of an estrangement located in the memory of my body. It was the ease with which, sixteen months after moving to Tokyo, I could enter the language and "pass" in a critical space that began to warp in my imagination. Against the Japanese-identified body that made the kid growing up in Winnipeg visible, I was transparent in the Asakusa crowd; but instead of feeling relaxed by the ability to comprehend – after all, I had been studying Japanese – the act of slipping into the barker's voice suddenly made me conscious of my own displacement in the crowd. The translation process that allowed the barker's voice to be folded into the remembered childhood moment disrupted my consciousness of the scene, exposing what might be called (in Roland Bleiker's provocative terms) a "discursive void, the space where ... multiple and overlapping discourses clash, where silent and sometimes not so silent arguments are exchanged, where boundaries are drawn and redrawn" (Bleiker 2000, 189). As the barker's voice trailed on, there I was, on a warm and pleasant Saturday afternoon, utterly immersed in the memory of a racialized, hence "freakish" as well, body that haunted my childhood in Winnipeg.

In what was then a largely unconscious move to redraw boundaries, I decided to return to Canada, convinced that the "I" in the crowd at Asakusa would never be "Japanese," whatever that term might have meant at the time. Read as a conventional autobiographic moment, this revelation was an individual crisis of identity that led the subject to alter the course of his life. But for a Japanese Canadian – one born into the aftermath of uprooting and cultural deracination – the same moment initiated a turn away from Japan as a point of origin and towards Canada as the site of future critical work.

The social and cultural spaces of the nation that I re-entered were themselves undergoing a turn – coincidence or not, who can tell?

The historically constituted nation state, which was constructed on the discursive pillars of the so-called "founding" groups, the English and the French, was in the throes of confronting the disenchanted voices of the Others of European background, the so-called "ethnic" voices who were engaged in a "politics of recognition" (Charles

Taylor's phrase, 1994). Alongside these voices, or perhaps more metaphorically appropriate, on the back burner, were the "other others" (Wayde Compton's phrase in *49th Parallel Psalm*, 1999, 169). These were the social subjects whose own claims emerged out of a largely unspoken racialization of cultural hierarchies, including the not-white groups variously identified as "Asian," "black," and "Indian." But even here, perhaps affected by the civil rights movement, or by demographic shifts, or by a nascent identity politics, or by a combination of these and other variables, there arose the signs of cultural capital attached to those – the faces of the multicultural – who were being constructed as the Other vis à vis the founding groups.

Strangely, then, my own realization that "Japanese" could not provide an origin for subjectivities produced in the historical contexts of the Canadian nation state was countered by an emergent identity politics. It was based on efforts to make visible previously covered-over histories and to appropriate the narrative of the nation to construct ethnic variations on the dominant narrative of settlement and nation-building.

With all the attendant ironies, and in a climate in which the state generated a language of multiculturalism to contain, or otherwise mediate, the growing internal challenges to Anglo-dominant liberal discourses, even Japanese Canadians, a relatively small group who had had no real public voice since the 1940s, found themselves awakening to transformed social spaces. As if the process were alchemical, lo and behold, the modifier "Japanese," once anathema to transcending the gate of assimilation, was accruing cultural value as an ethnicity that should be recognized and preserved.[3]

One telling sign of the shifting valence of Japanese Canadian came in the form of capital support for a project – the only national one – that had been languishing for years. Back in the late 1950s Ken Adachi had been awarded the contract from the National Japanese Canadian Citizens' Association (which became the National Association of Japanese Canadians in 1980) to write the official history of Japanese Canadians. Here it was, some fifteen years later, and the book had yet to reach a state of publication, though the manuscript had apparently been completed. In one of its first projects the newly created Multicultural Directorate planned to commission a series of ethnic histories, and hearing about Adachi's manuscript, approached the NJCCA to offer direct financial support for publication. What better way to inaugurate the "multicultural" series than with the history of Japanese Canadians, a model minority in the government's eyes? Thus *The Enemy That Never Was* was published in 1976 by McClelland and Stewart "in association with Supply and Services."[4] The timing could not be more fitting. The following year would be the celebration of the Japanese Canadian Centennial, a constructed event which received substantial government funding and through which "Japanese Canadian" was re-invented as a hyphenated or multicultural identity[5] – in other words, as a sign of arrival in the narrative of the nation. This was despite the racialization implicit in the model minority identity that transformed the Japanese Canadian subject from the "enemy alien" to the "friendly Canadianized alien."

The adoption of the narrative of the nation[6] – a narrative that, in fact, constituted the formation of the Canadian nation out of the violence of colonial invasion and territorialization – was indeed a dramatic turn for the JCs whose memories were still tied closely to the trauma of mass uprooting and dispossession of the 1940s. The irony (which I will return to) was that the turn would be enacted through the discursive frameworks of nation-building – frameworks that had once excluded JCs as Japanese or "Asiatic" and deemed "undesirable" or "unsuitable" in the language of the Immigration Act.

Worth mentioning here are three projects that emerged in the 1970s and subsequently served critical pedagogical functions during the redress movement of the 1980s:

(1) In the mid-1970s, Ann Sunahara, benefiting from the influence of well-known nisei, Tom Shoyama, then Deputy Minister of Finance, was the first researcher to access the federal government files on the mass uprooting. Her research would uncover material evidence to show what Japanese Canadians knew but could not prove, namely that the mass uprooting was not a military necessity but a political move made possible through the intense racialization of Japanese Canadians. The results of her work were circulating in the late 1970s; her book would be published in 1981 with the telling title, *The Politics of Racism: The Uprooting of Japanese Canadians During World War Two.*

(2) Around the same time as Sunahara was carrying out her research in Ottawa, in the same city Joy Kogawa had herself uncovered the archive of nisei writer and community activist, Muriel Kitagawa, whose voice, particularly in the letters she wrote to her brother Wes Fujiwara in Toronto amidst the turmoil of the uprooting, would infuse the writing of *Obasan*. Kogawa's novel would be published, first by Lester and Orpen Dennys in 1981, and then in its more familiar Penguin edition in 1983. It was immediately acclaimed as a novel that brought Japanese Canadian internment to a contemporary Canadian generation that was apparently receptive to a tale of injustice in the nation. The front cover blurb of the Penguin edition announced it as "A moving novel of a time and a suffering we have tried to forget."

(3) Simultaneous with Sunahara's and Kogawa's writing, a small group of community activists in Vancouver, myself included – mostly sansei and young nisei, collaborating with young shin-issei – consti-

tuted themselves as the Japanese Canadian Centennial Project (JCCP) and decided, as a collective voice, to write and produce the official history project for the 1977 centennial celebrations, *A Dream of Riches: Japanese Canadians 1877–1977* (1978). This photo-history with commentaries in English, French, and Japanese would open in Ottawa and subsequently tour several Japanese Canadian centres. A core of this group later formed the JCCP Redress Committee and brought the issue of redress to public attention.

In short, during the 1970s the production of identity was at a high pitch. As if overnight it was not only acceptable but even good to be Japanese Canadian. The tenacity of those so named to read themselves into the nation's narration demonstrated their incredible resourcefulness in negotiating with a formation that had written them out. Yet despite this recognition, "Japanese Canadian" would remain implicated in the racialized history out of which it has arisen. Unable, finally, to stand alone as "Canadian" or as "Japanese" this identity formation, even in its positive incarnation, could not extricate itself from the history that it embodied. This critical perspective did not arrive after, in a belated fashion, but was concurrent with anti-colonial critiques of the Canadian nation state emerging on the critical edges of identity politics in the 1970s. The conjunction of race and the nation, in this framework, allowed for – and allows for here – a reconsideration of the negative production of "Japanese Canadian," the memory of which, no doubt for many, tempered and made much more resonant the sense of pride that surfaced in the 1970s.

We need to constantly remind ourselves of the scene of arrival for the Japanese issei who were the first to cross the territorial border of the twentieth-century Canadian nation state in the making. From the moment they entered its racialized borders they had to engage in a process of negotiations with a powerful network of social, political, and cultural formations already premised on their "alien" status. Though they carried in their cultural and psychological baggage a complicated network of their own subjective identifications and references, the real and symbolic territories they came into were laced with legal and ideological determinants that interpreted their bodies according to the prevalent orientalism, especially virulent on the B.C. coast, the site-specific "contact zone"[7] of their arrival. Positioned as a minority according to the colonializing codes of nation-making at the time, they had to contend with a barrage of constraints, legal or otherwise, that conspired to restrict their entry, and once admitted, to contain and manage them as the perpetual "alien" – equivalent to a figurative contaminant that constantly threatens a fantasized racial purity and thus necessitates regulatory mechanisms to protect and police its borders.

Much has been written about the history of the Canadian nation in its formative moments in the late nineteenth and early twentieth century but less so on the instrumental role the discursive frames of the "alien-Asian" played in forging the modern nation-state out of the violence of colonial invasion, territorialization, and settlement. Within this frame were to be scripted the "Japanese," the "Chinamen," and the "Hindu," the names of imposed identities who became the "strangers within our gates," to invoke the title of J.S. Woodsworth's 1909 book that addressed the coming of Asians into Canada. These "strangers" became the constitutive outside of a white-identified nation, and in the logic of its making "they" had to be written out of its legal and symbolic boundaries as the disenfranchised – as they, along with "Indians," were excluded in the language of the Provincial Elections Act of B.C.: "No Chinaman, Japanese or Indian [Hindu would be included] shall have his name placed on the Register of Voters for any Electoral District, or be entitled to vote in any election."[8] This simple but starkly discriminating piece of legislation would remain in effect until the late 1940s, well after the nation state known as Canada had established the precedents for the "alien-Asian" within as the exterior limit of its Westernized (read white-dominant) identity formation.

In "Strange Encounters," a study of the figure of the stranger in the theoretical approaches to nation formation – approaches compatible with Canadian conditions – Sara Ahmed proposes that those demarked as strangers inhabit an "abject" body. This body occupies an exteriorizing zone that functions to solidify and authenticate the dominant subjects whose bodies, largely produced as white, male, and heterosexual, signify the constituted norm. What remains important, though, is to recognize that the exclusionary effects of abjection "involve prior acts of incorporation" (Ahmed 2000, 52), so that the figure of the "outsider" is the obverse of an "insider" who has been named as the different – colloquially a social freak – against which the same assumes its normalized or goes-without-saying position. In this social and political configuration, the very possibility of "home," or "at-home-ness," comes to be governed by internal borders that allow certain subjects to take ownership of the geocultural spaces of the nation, but not the others who remain strangers. This, then, accounts for the pervasive thematic of the unhomely in Asian Canadian cultural work, an affect familiar to those who, racialized as strangers, have appeared in the nation as spectral, aberrant, monstrous in their "foreignicity" (to borrow from Fred Wah in *Diamond Grill*, 1996, 69). But their status as outsiders, as Ahmed carefully reminds us, has been bound into a social and political system that produces them as such in the interests of its national agendas: "The strange body can only become a material 'thing' that touches the body-at-home, or a figure that can be faced in the street, through a radical forgetting of the histories of labour and production that allow such a body to appear in the present" (Ahmed 2000, 53–4).

The violent implications of naming hit home for Japanese Canadians with a vengeance in the most traumatic turn of events that would subsequently underwrite their subjectivities: their mass uprooting and dispossession, carried out under the Canadian state's War Measures Act and enabled through what I would call a discursive sleight-of-hand. I hardly have the time to retell this most painful period, except to rearticulate the shifty and deceptive power of the state-produced language of racialization that permitted the gross violation of rights in a supposedly liberal democratic regime. Of course, Japanese Canadians, such as nisei writer Muriel Kitagawa, were not at all fooled by the effects of the legislation that converted her, a citizen by birth, into the "Jap," the "enemy alien." As she wrote to her brother Wes Fujiwara, on 4 March 1942, the day she found out that even the Canadian-born would be subject to mass expulsion from their homes, "Oh we are fair prey for the wolves in democratic clothing" (Kitagawa 1985, 91). Then again in a letter written two days later: "Lord, if this was Germany you can expect such things as the normal way, but this is Canada, a Democracy! And the Nisei, repudiated by the only land they know, no redress anywhere" (Kitagawa 1985, 93).

What a difference discourse can make. In Naomi's reported words of Aunt Emily in *Obasan* on the abjection of Japanese Canadians: "None of us," she said, "escaped the naming. We were defined and identified by the way we were seen. A newspaper in B.C. headlined, 'They are a stench in the nostrils of the people of Canada.' There was a tidy mind somewhere" (Kogawa 1983, 118). The process of symbolic identification as a "stench" in the nation that had to be corralled, contained, and dispelled was preceded by a literal process of registration the year before, when all Japanese Canadians were fingerprinted, "duly registered in compliance with the provisions of Order-in-Council P.C. 117," and required to carry a registration card with their photograph and "specimen of signature."[9] The stage, then, had already been set for the federal government to mobilize the language of racialization to transform the Japanese Canadian subject from "citizen" to "enemy alien." Thus there was first the more routine Order-in-Council PC 365 (16 January 1942) to remove male "Enemy Aliens" (of all national backgrounds, including Japanese nationals) from the coast for security purposes. This regulation paved the way for Order-in-Council 1486 (24 February 1942), under the signature of Minister of Justice, Louis St. Laurent, in which the discourse of race took the place of nationality.

Between those two dates, only a month apart, the federal government had decided, against the advice of the RCMP and the military, as Sunahara documents, to carry out the mass removal of all Japanese Canadians. In the notice directed to them they are henceforth to be named and identified and therefore discursively contained through the prepositional phrase "of the Japanese race." That simple epithet would prove to be the most powerful weapon in the government's arsenal to completely ignore the very liberal discourse of rights they were supposedly defending in their war efforts.[10]

While some progressive efforts were made by idealistic nisei in the 1930s to eliminate the barriers to the franchise, all of these were erased by the seemingly monolithic language that produced them in the crucible of the mass displacement as the face "of the Japanese race" in Canada which, in turn, would brand them as the "enemy alien," a script so powerful it would be internalized by those who were subjected to its relentless application. Consider, for instance, the consequences for the members of the Nisei Mass Evacuation Group who protested the family break-up policy of the B.C. Security Commission, which they rightfully argued served no purpose, especially because Japanese Canadians had agreed to cooperate with the government's supposed security measures. In other words, they were not the enemy. They were Canadians, as they said forcefully in their cogent letter to the B.C. Security Commission rejecting the break-up of families:

When we say "NO" at this point, we request you to remember that we are British subjects by birth, that we are no less loyal to Canada than any other Canadian, that we have done nothing to deserve the break-up of our families, that we are law-abiding Canadian citizens, and that we are willing to accept suspension of our civil rights. (Quoted in Miki and Kobayashi 1991, 37)

The request was flatly turned down, and when they continued to mount their protest movement, they were taken into custody by the RCMP, placed in the Immigration Hall, and sent to barbed wire prisoner-of-war camps, first at Petawawa and then at Angler, both in Ontario. Many languished in a discursive limbo, erroneously re-scripted as prisoners-of-war under the jurisdiction of the military.

The reduction of a once highly differentiated collective to the one-dimensional category – "of the Japanese race" – would be followed by another re-inscription as the war drew to a close. Once the language of security threat was no longer tenable, other means were needed to disallow Japanese Canadians from returning to the B.C. coast. After all, in the logic of racialization giving coherence to Prime Minister Mackenzie King's address to the House of Commons on 4 August 1944, it was their very visibility as a "group" that accounted for the racism directed against them. Therefore, for their own good – in a move that replayed the protective custody myth used to uproot them – the prime minister announced to all the MPs, none of whom challenged him: "The sound policy and the best policy for the Japanese Canadians themselves is to distribute their numbers as widely as possible throughout the country where they will not create feelings of racial hostility" (Quoted in Adachi 1976, 433).

The policy Mackenzie King had in mind would, in fact, be two-pronged, and it would reach the still confined Japanese Canadians in the form of two notices posted, or otherwise distributed, side by side.

I'm referring, of course, to the infamous notices with two new terms that would once again determine the futures of the subjects under their jurisdiction. These were "repatriation" (to Japan) or "dispersal" ("east of the Rockies," i.e., out of B.C.). The subjects were offered a choice that was no choice; in other words, the federal scriptwriters had devised yet another language trap. First off, there was no option to remain in B.C. Then again, the vast majority of those who were asked to consider "repatriation" had "Canada" as their "patria," hence could not by definition be "repatriated." The brutal reality was that they were being asked to consider their own "deportation" or "exile" from the country of their birth. Finally, the connotations of "dispersal" were ominous and threatening, implying both that "repatriation" would signify loyalty to Japan and that rejection of "dispersal" would signify disloyalty to Canada. Listen closely to the language used in this notice:

Japanese Canadians who want to remain in Canada should now re-establish themselves East of the Rockies as the best evidence of their intentions to co-operate with the Government policy of dispersal.

Failure to accept employment east of the Rockies may be regarded at a later date as lack of co-operation with the Canadian Government in carrying out its policy of dispersal.

Those who do not take advantage of present opportunities for employment and settlement outside British Columbia at this time, while employment opportunities are favourable, will find conditions of employment and settlement considerably more difficult at a later date and may seriously prejudice their own future by delay.

The repatriation and dispersal policies caused untold grief and anxiety, often tearing apart friendships and families, forced as Japanese Canadians were to demonstrate their loyalty to a country that had violated their rights, dispossessed them, and cast them as enemies of the state. In the end, as the records show, some 4,000 were shipped to war-torn

Japan. "The main casualties," Ken Adachi writes, "were the Canadian-born, who comprised over half of the repatriates, 33% of whom were dependent children under 16 years of age" (Adachi 1976, 318).

By the time the war ended, the Japanese Canadian presence on the west coast had been erased, and the robust collective that was uprooted en masse in 1942 had become a tattered remnant of the complex fabric of the identity formations – of, for instance, geographic location, employment, class, religion, political stance, and region (or "ken") of origin in Japan – that once constituted their social and culture relations. Now undifferentiated in the raced language of federal policies, as merely a "person of the Japanese race," they found themselves reduced to a fixed identity, at least in the language through which their movements were policed and monitored.

With the war's end, the more explicit discourse of racialization mobilized by the government was no longer as transparent as before. In his speech in the House of Commons, King is thus conscious of avoiding any accusations of racism by distancing his policy from the "hateful doctrine of racialism which is the basis of the Nazi system everywhere."[11] What is also striking in the rhetoric of his articulation of the so-called "Japanese problem" is his use of the identity formation "Japanese Canadian." In King's language the persons "of Japanese race" who have been uprooted and dispossessed are now more benignly designated as "Japanese Canadians." The shift in terms is certainly neither an accident nor a reflection of enlightenment on King's part, and instead conforms to the intent of the government's dispersal program. The addition of "Canadian" in this instance may have softened overt racism, but it manifested a strategy of Canadianization that amounted to forced assimilation. Now you see them, now you don't.

The public effect of King's speech was to construct the figure of a Japanese Canadian subject who, once incorporated into the postwar nation, was expected to be not seen, and certainly not heard as a collective of individuals – citizens even – who had been betrayed by the very democratic system that should have protected them. The absorption of the supposedly rehabilitated "Japanese" into "Japanese Canadian" functioned – in a forgetting process that liberalism itself fosters – to cover over the violence of the mass uprooting. But for the JCs who emerged from the war years and turned into a model minority, often more Canadian than other Canadians, the legacy of the trauma would linger on, sometimes in self-imposed silences and other times in whispered exchanges among friends, relatives, and in the enclave of family narratives.

It was not so much a simple repression of memory but more what I would call a disarticulated history of loss and displacement that marked the 1950s and early 1960s – even in the face of upward social mobility – a displacement whose unresolved tensions would filter through the margins of my own formative years in Winnipeg. Remember the mantra of the times: Education, education, and more education. Enter the professions. Gain proficiency in English. Don't speak Japanese. And, of course, don't think of yourself as "Japanese." But as a kid growing up in a white-identified city, it was difficult not to be tagged with a connection to Japanese, especially when the childhood "I" was usually the only identifiable "Jap" in sight. Remember all those war movies when the demonic "Japs" get it in the end? Well, those scenes were played out on the neighbourhood streets too. Internal resistances to that childhood interpellation process came much later, and – to make a long story short – would eventually open the speculation that perhaps the secret to identity could be found in that other place – that place where my grandparents came from. Little did I know then that other sansei, as we began to identify ourselves more collectively, were also aroused by a curiosity about our so-called "roots." (Here my own generational roots are showing!) Hence the search for origins in Japan, a search that dead-ended, for me, that day in Asakusa. In returning to Canada, in an act that uncannily remembered my own grandparents' entry, I got involved in a process of "claiming"[12] the nation that marked the 1970s for Japanese Canadians and others whose histories had not been voiced in the dominant narratives of Canadian history.

I am reminded of Judith Butler's statement in *Excitable Speech* on the disjunctures that distance social naming from personal naming. "The time of discourse," she says, "is not the time of the subject" (Butler 1997, 31). The subject who left in search of "Japanese" and came back in search of "Canadian" re-entered a nation-state space in which the "Japanese" of "Japanese Canadian" was undergoing a complex reinvention process of its own. No longer necessarily attached to the abjection of the alien, it appeared to have flipped over to become a sign of a multicultural discourse in an expanding liberalism. Yet the obvious fact that Japanese Canadian subjects could not stand alone as Canadians, that the modification of "Japanese" was still necessary, belied a continuing racialization in a nation state that was itself adjusting to centrifugal forces altering its hegemonic structures.

Nevertheless, from this turn in the shifting fortunes of "Japanese Canadian" we can draw at least one salutary conclusion. The agency exercised by JCs in the 1970s – and then taken in unprecedented directions through the redress movement in the 1980s – shows that processes of racialization are never simply one-way and imposed, but are dynamic and folded into specific limits. The contingencies that made the power of racism indeterminate could then become the nexus of a subject-oriented discourse of identity-making, resistance, and opposition. The complication, of course, is that this nexus of social agency is also contingent on the "contact zone" between "them" and the "nation" in which they have already been named or identified.

The stage was set for a much more compelling question: If we can read ourselves into the narrative of the nation, as evident, for instance, in the production of *A Dream of Riches*, then should not this nation acknowledge *Democracy Betrayed*? I am here referring to the title of the redress brief issued by the National Association of Japanese Canadians in November 1984, an event that marked the entrance of "redress for Japanese Canadians" into mainstream public spheres.

The logic of the shift from identity-making in the 1970s to social justice in the 1980s in one sense appears inevitable from the subjective perspective of JCs. The process of reclaiming history could only expose the blank spaces – the unspoken lack – left in the persistent memories of the wartime trauma. Without an official acknowledgement that Japanese Canadians had been the victims of a "democracy betrayed" by a systemic capitulation to racialized policies, they would remain "enemy aliens."

The language of redress located its impetus in a deep-seated grievance that called out for resolution, most urgently because of the age of those affected. Redress as a discourse took on a tangible existence, functioning as a medium through which "Japanese Canadian" as an identity formation could be aligned with social justice, anti-racism, participatory democracy, and human rights – all issues that became central to the social and cultural activism of the 1980s. In the wider social contexts, at times distant from the inside turmoil and confusion that infiltrated the nooks and crannies of local JC communities, the formerly uprooted and dispossessed Japanese Canadians began to make visible the contradictions of the liberal democratic assumptions that were built into the Canadian nation state. How then to account for the legacy of racism and injustice in its own backyard? Think now of the intense politics surrounding the patriation of the Canadian constitution; the constitutional hearings which attracted considerable press coverage, and to which Japanese Canadians were even invited to present the story of their mass uprooting; the passage of the Charter of Rights and Freedoms, a document that – so Canadians had been told – would prevent any minority group from being abused in the ways Japanese Canadians had been in the 1940s; and the fanfare surrounding the publication of the all-party *Equality Now!* report on recommendations to enable so-called "visible minorities" to overcome racist barriers in Canada, including one supporting redress for Japanese Canadians.

These were only a handful of the sign-posts for the contexts in which the redress movement – a movement that mobilized Japanese Canadians to assume an unprecedented social visibility – found itself incorporated into the unravelling nationalist politics of the time.

In speculating on the relationship between the redress movement and the shifting formation of "Japanese Canadian," I want to fast forward to a reading of the redress settlement of 22 September 1988. I recall how struck I was by a question posed to Art Miki, the President of the National Association of Japanese Canadians, at the press conference following the official signing. Miki was asked about accepting the agreement: "Do you think you're being used at all for political purposes and does that bother you?" In hesitating to answer, I sensed that my brother was momentarily a bit dumbfounded, as I was, at what seemed pretty obvious, but perhaps we were missing something. We thought it was quite clear that redress was undertaken as a social justice movement whose goal was political, despite the diverse subjectivities of the JCs involved. More, in negotiating the agreement the NAJC had engaged in a political exchange. The questions of "being used" and "bother," on the other hand, could be explained through a misalignment – between the political discourse out of which the reporter's question arose and the time of the traumatic uprooting and dispossession out of which the redressed subjects had come to represent themselves.

It seemed to me that the reporter was speaking from – in a systemic more than conscious mode – a social discourse that identified the Japanese Canadians named in the agreement as the model minority who were being "used" by the political system. But hadn't JCs, through the NAJC, in effect used the political system to negotiate a redress agreement? Since the press conference did not allow for follow up reflections, the ramifications of the question disappeared as quickly as it took for another question to be asked. What the moment exposed, however, was what Katherine Verdery has referred to as the "nation as a construct, whose meaning is never stable but shifts with the changing balance of social forces" (Verdery 1996, 230). As such the nation is necessarily plural in the field of meanings it generates – in that case for the reporter and for Miki as the voice of JCs – and so takes on different formations depending on subject positioning and relations of privilege and disadvantage to its dominant representations. To take this one step further, we can then posit that the nation performing the acknowledgement of injustices for Japanese Canadians was not the same as the nation that was officially redeemed by the actions of the prime minister in the House of Commons – even though the event itself, the redress settlement, constituted itself as a resolutionary act that produced a new substance, in this case a nation state that sought to renew itself through the reification of its citizenship.

What was uncanny then seems today much more understandable, given the dispersal of the nation as a centralizing discourse in the face of the ubiquitous discourses of globalization. At the time of the settlement, in September 1988, the most heated social and political issue was the Free Trade Agreement (FTA) followed by the North American Free Trade Agreement (NAFTA). While the moment of redress may appear to bear no relationship to these tangible signs of the end of Cold War era – the Berlin Wall would come down a year later to provide a more global sign – their conjunction marked a turn in the Canadian nation away from cultural nationalism towards the market agendas of transnational corporations with its neoliberal values that encourage self-serving individualism and unfettered consumerism.

Against the global politics that has come to dominate the post-redress era, it may be possible to read the settlement back into the underlying crisis of the nation, circa 1988, hence the sign of an attempt to reinvoke a post-war identity formation that had itself lost its efficacious hold on the body politic. For Japanese Canadians, on the other hand, the moment of the redress settlement in the House of Commons, as ephemeral as it was, was bound to the history of attempts to negotiate with the Canadian nation, most unsuccessfully in the 1940s, but extending back in a chain of moments – back, for instance, to 19 October 1900, when Tomey Homma applied to have his name placed on the voters' list because, as a naturalized Canadian, he was not the "Japanese" identified in Section 8 of the Provincial Elections Act (Adachi 1976, 53). He was refused. Homma's follow-up court challenge was endorsed by the provincial and federal courts, but then was flatly denied, in England, by the House of Lords. Had he won, it remains fascinating to speculate, the course of Japanese Canadian history could have taken very different turns in the decades ahead. The mass uprooting might have been averted, or at least have been challenged through the same legal machinery that justified the abrogation of rights.

The branding as an "enemy alien," as the alien "Jap" figure contained through racialization, struck to the core of Japanese Canadians, and it was this haunted identity formation – the unredressed "citizen" of injustice – that was released from its historical confinement in the moment of the settlement. But paradoxically, and here the complexity for JCs comes "home" to roost, this unprecedented shift from an unredressed state – a state of speaking through a "wounded identity" – to a redressed state came to constitute a resolution that simultaneously – and inevitably – announced the passing of that identity.

It is in this passing that an identity formation so closely bound to the trauma of uprooting and dispossession was itself dispersed in what came to be a "post-redress" time. In one sense "Japanese Canadian" was liberated to become a floating sign with the potential to take on an unpredictable range of alternate significations. If anything the redress movement demonstrated that identities need to be approached as always in movement. There is no "where" for them prior to their enactments. They become representations that subjects perform and these are always shaped by the specific positions out of which they are produced. As fixed and pre-determining points of origin they can only re-produce the model of control that interned a group of innocent people on the basis of racialization.

Given the dramatic upheavals that have marked our social lives since the end of the Cold War era, and even more urgently since 9/11, the critical tasks now – at least from the perspective of this essay – are to expose the danger of forming identities through processes of inclusion and exclusion and to forge creative discourses that can address the uneven network of interdependencies and power relations that implicate all of us in the future of the planet. Where we are going from here then becomes an ethical question – of what kinds of critical concepts and practices can help us, however modestly, to negotiate those formations that move us towards the seemingly impossible but necessarily hopeful cultual conditions that can transform the legacy of violence and trauma that marked world history in the twentieth century.

NOTES

1 As many cultural theorists have cautioned, naming is always a situated act with differential consequences depending on who is doing the naming, who is being named, and what the name signifies in its social, political, and cultural effects. As a naming of a group of Canadian subjects, "Japanese Canadian" needs to be approached as a construct that has never been stable in its referential reach, and yet has also been historically attached to those who have both identified themselves and have been identified through its circulation. For the purpose of talking about its shifting formations from the position of one whose own subjectivity has been directly inflected by these formations, in some instances I resort to "JC" when alluding to the more familiar situation of actual life histories and experiences. In adopting this practice for this talk, I am aware that it opens a discursive gap between assumptions and what is written but I do it to respect and honour the quotidian events making up the fabric of particular lives lived out in the heat of historical conditions. When I address the term "Japanese Canadian" more strictly as a discursive entity I use quotation marks, but even in the absence of these marks readers should imagine their traces.

2 Here I am taking this term from Daniel L. Schacter (1996), in *Searching for Memory*, who distinguishes it from the "engram (the stored fragments of an episode" (70) as a crucial element in the production of a memory: "Although it is often assumed that a retrieval cue merely arouses or activates a memory that is slumbering in the recesses of the brain, I have hinted at an alternative: the cue combines with the engram to yield a new, emergent entity – the recollective experience of the remembrer – that differs from either of its constituents" (70).

3 As critiques of multiculturalism have made clear, the policy reflected a political manoeuvre on the part of the federal government to manage threats to the status quo, as, for instance, Augie Fleras and Jean Leonard Elliott (1992) point out: "Political considerations ... came into play. They included the need to neutralize the impact of the Official Languages Act: to shore up Liberal electoral strength in the West, where bilingualism did not meet with widespread approval, and to capture the ethnic vote in urban Ontario. They also included the need to defuse mounting Québécois pressure on federalism, to blunt the threat of unwanted American influences on Canadian cultural space, and to replenish the void in Canadian cultural identity with the demise of anglo-conformity as a central ideological construct" (72). The policy was devised to appease the pressure from Euro-Canadian groups for recognition. Japanese Canadians, or for that matter other Asian Canadians, were not themselves considered a political presence to court. The policies, nevertheless, were appropriated in various ways to shape their own identities, often in accommodating ways as an ethnicity that accorded them the semblance, though not the actuality, of a sameness to other so-called "ethnic" groups. The translation of race into ethnicity for non-whites would cover over the racialization that continued to underwrite the lives of Japanese Canadians. For an incisive critique of the ambivalent limits of "ethnicity" in the current "era of difference" (128), see Rey Chow's (2002) *The Protestant Ethnic and the Spirit of Capitalism*, a work that came to my attention after this talk was drafted.

4 The series was called "Generations: A History of Canada's People." The financial support of the government is indicated on the Acknowledgements page: "To the Secretary of State, Canadian Citizenship Branch, Canadian Ethnic Studies, for assistance in additional funding for the National Japanese Canadian Citizens Association, History of the Japanese Canadians project." The reference to "Supply and Services Canada" is found, not in the publication, but in Multiculturalism and Citizenship Canada 1993, *Resource Guide of Publications Supported by Multiculturalism Programs, 1973–1992* (26).

5 I use the term "re-invented" specifically here. The concept of a centennial was very much a product of the times. The nation's centennial had been cel-

ebrated a decade before, and the narrative construction of the so-called settlement era was in vogue. The idea for a "Japanese Canadian Centennial" came from Toyo Takata (1983) who, in researching his book, *Nikkei Legacy: The Story of Japanese Canadians from Settlement to Today*, determined that the first settler was Manzo Nagano, who, based on historical evidence, "arrived in Canada in Spring 1877, as this country's first Japanese settler" (9). Thus the ascribed year of origin is not simply arbitrary but invented to align the history of Japanese Canadians with the history of the Canadian nation.

6 Kirsten Emiko McAllister (1999) has examined the critical implications of the processes through which Japanese Canadians narrated themselves into the nation in her essay "Narrating Japanese Canadians In and Out of the Canadian Nation: A Critique of Realist Forms of Representation." Thanks to Kirsten for sharing with me an early draft of her essay.

7 This well known and often-quoted phrase comes from Louise Pratt (1992) in her book, *Imperial Eyes: Travel Writing and Transculturation*, referring "to the space of colonial encounters, the space in which peoples geographically and historically separated come into contact with each other and establish ongoing relations, usually involving conditions of coercion, radical inequality, and intractable conflict" (6). Here, though, I'm influenced by the application of the term by Fred Wah (1996) in his biotext, *Diamond Grill*, where it functions to make visible the interstitial or in-between spaces – the spaces of the "noisy hyphen" (176) – that are the contradictory and conflicted effects of contact between the racialized bodies of "Asians" and a white-identified Canadian nation.

8 Think here of the massive efforts that went into ensuring the containment and exclusion of the "Asian": the trail of legislation that would include various Immigration Acts in which they were identified as the "undesirables"; the various levels of the "Head Tax" levied on Chinese immigrants which led finally to the euphemistically termed "Chinese Immigration Act," actually an Exclusion Act (1923); the "Continuous Journey" provisions that radically reduced the possibility for South Asians to immigrate and that instigated the Komagata-Maru incident (1914); the "Gentleman's Agreement" with Japan to restrict immigration. When the slew of legislative and administrative restrictions was supposedly lifted in the late 1940s, and after what was for Japanese Canadians the most extreme trauma in their history within the Canadian nation state, a post-war liberalism, perhaps functioning in line with the new Citizenship Act (1947), was in the making and intent on producing a more defined cultural nationalism – at least in English Canada, then still largely an Anglo-dominant identity formation.

9 From the language on the identification cards of my grandparents, Tokusaburo and Yoshi Ooto, who were registered on 7 August 1941.

10 There is an unspoken racializing syllogism that functioned to fix Japanese Canadians in the ministerial directive:
   (a) Japanese nationals are enemy aliens
   (b) Enemy aliens are "of the Japanese race"
   (c) Japanese Canadians are "of the Japanese race"
   (d) Japanese Canadians are therefore enemy aliens
11 King goes on to reassure the House of Commons: "Our aim is to resolve a difficult problem in a manner which will protect the people of British Columbia and the interests of the country as a whole, and at the same time preserve, in whatever we do, principles of fairness and justice" (quoted in Adachi 1976, 433).
12 I have placed this term in quotation marks to posit that the motivation to insert a space in the national imaginary among Japanese Canadians and other Canadian minorities was part of a larger North American politics of identity formation. Here I am thinking of the drive towards "claiming America" (16) that Sau-ling C. Wong (1995) argues constituted the cultural nationalist movement of Asian Americans in the late 1960s and 1970s.

ACKNOWLEDGMENTS

This essay is reprinted with permission from Joseph F. Kess, ed., *Changing Japanese identities in multicultural Canada*, (Victoria, B.C.: Centre for Asia-Pacific Initiatives, 2003).

REFERENCES

Adachi, K. 1976. *The Enemy that Never Was: A History of the Japanese Canadians*. Toronto: McClelland and Stewart.
Ahmed, S. 2000. *Strange Encounters: Embodied Others in Postcoloniality*. London and New York: Routledge.
Bleiker, R. 2000. *Popular Dissent, Human Agency and Global Politics*. Cambridge and New York: Cambridge University Press.
Butler, J. 1997. *Excitable Speech: A Politics of the Performative*. New York and London: Routledge.
Chow, R. 2002. *The Protestant Ethnic and the Spirit of Capitalism*. New York: Columbia University Press.
Compton, W. 1999. *49th Parallel Psalm*. Vancouver: Advance Editions.
Fleras, A., and Elliott, J.L. 1992. *The Challenge of Diversity: Multiculturalism in Canada*. Scarborough, ON: Nelson.
Japanese Canadian Centennial Project. 1978. *A Dream of Riches: Japanese Canadians, 1877–1977*. Vancouver: Japanese Canadian Centennial Project.
Kitagawa, M. 1985. *This Is My Own: Letters to Wes and Other Writings on Japanese Canadians, 1941–1948*. Ed. R. Miki. Vancouver: Talonbooks.

Kiyooka, R. "Pacific Rim Letters." Unpublished text.
Kogawa, J. 1983. *Obasan*. Toronto, ON: Penguin.
McAllister, K. E. 1999. "Narrating Japanese Canadians In and Out of the Canadian Nation: A Critique of Realist Forms of Representation." *Canadian Journal of Communication* 24: 79–103.
Miki, R., and Kobayashi, C. 1991. *Justice in Our Time: The Japanese Canadian Redress Settlement*. Vancouver and Winnipeg: Talonbooks and National Association of Japanese Canadians.
Multiculturalism and Citizenship Canada. 1993. *Resource Guide of Publications Supported by Multiculturalism Programs, 1973–1992*. Ottawa: Minister of Supplies and Services Canada.
National Association of Japanese Canadians. 1984. *Democracy Betrayed: The Case for Redress*. Winnipeg: National Association of Japanese Canadians.
Pratt, M.L. 1992. *Imperial Eyes: Travel Writing and Transculturation*. London and New York: Routledge.
Schacter, D.L. 1996. *Searching for Memory: The Brain, the Mind, and the Past*. New York: Basic Books.
Sunahara, A.G. 1981. *The Politics of Racism: The Uprooting of Japanese Canadians during the Second World War*. Toronto, ON: James Lorimer.
Takata, T. 1983. *Nikkei Legacy: The Story of Japanese Canadians from Settlement to Today*. Toronto: NC Press.
Taylor, C. 1994. "The Politics of Recognition." In *Multiculturalism: A Critical Reader*, ed. D.T. Goldberg, 75–106. Oxford and Cambridge, MA: Blackwell.
Verdery, K. 1996. "Whither 'Nation' and 'Nationalism'?" In *Mapping the Nation*, ed. G. Balakrishnan, 226–34. London: Verso.
Wah, F. 1996. *Diamond Grill*. Edmonton: NeWest Press.
Woodsworth, J.S. 1909. *Strangers Within Our Gates: Or, Coming Canadians*. Toronto: F.C. Stephenson.
Wong, S-L.C. 1995. "Denationalization Reconsidered: Asian American Cultural Criticism at a Theoretical Crossroads." *Amerasia* 21: 1–27.

ANN LAURA STOLER

Racist Visions for the Twenty-First Century: On the Banal Force of the French Radical Right

In a world in which racist perceptions and practices permeate our global space and private spheres, scholarly accountability has lain in understanding the tenacious resilience of race as a social, political, and psychological category that continues to define people and confine their options, to exclude and embrace, to grant and withhold entitlements. But scholars of racism in France have been far less attuned to asking why racist visions have such an appeal to people who in good faith hold that they are not interested in race but in defending their nation, have nothing against those of "x" origin but don't want those cultural priorities influencing "their" children in "their" schools, believe that crime and not race is the issue, and are not – and have never been – racist at all.

This essay asks why the French extreme right's policies have been "easy to think" for a broad population who neither considered themselves xenophobic, racist, nor politically "extreme" in any sense.[1] In part, it is about how we write about the abhorrent, what we treat as aberrant, and whether it is a conceit to imagine that students of racisms' histories have something to say about the quotidian face of contemporary racial politics.

Part of the task is to understand the politics of comparison in which scholars engage, what it means to argue for the similarities of racisms in different times and places, why some anti-racist scholars so adamantly claim the unchanging face of racisms on the one hand, while others argue in as principled a manner for a new cultural racism on the other. Such a discrepancy prompts a basic question: what are we willing to ask about what racisms look like on the cusp of this twenty-first century? Are racist visions taking predictable form and with familiar actors? Are racisms changing or merely the questions we're asking about them? Are scholars equipped with the epistemic tools to understand their regimes of [moral] truth? Are the forms they take what those who track racisms' archived and buried traces expect them to take? I am concerned that they are not.

For some twenty years, I have studied the making and malleability of racial categories, and the racialized regimes of imperial states.[2] Dutch and French colonialisms in the late-nineteenth and early-twentieth centuries have been my focus; public debates on immigration, multiculturalism, and declarations of the "end of racism" in Europe and the United States in the 1980s and 1990s have implicitly shaped my work. But in 1997-1998, while living in southern France, the urgency of contemporary issues pulled me away from the nearby colonial archives where I had once spent most of my time. My research took another direction: toward the racial politics in Aix-en-Provence and its surroundings, where talk of race produced a simultaneously familiar and unfamiliar social world. While far-right politics and the racial discourse that went along with it commanded enormous presence, issues of race could be strikingly effaced – irrelevant – in a space in which "nothing happened" at all. Earlier racisms resonate with these contemporary figurations, but the contours of the latter are taking shape in new sites and through new technologies unavailable in the nineteenth and through most of the twentieth century.

By one reading, 1998 was a year in which extreme-right platforms and candidates moved from the menacing margins of French politics well into the centre. It was the first time in twenty-five years (since the National Front was established in 1972) that a number of centre-right candidates in regional campaigns accepted FN (Front National) backing, acknowledged they needed them to win, and (invoking Vichy) were labeled "*collabo*" for doing so. It was the year in which France's President, Jacques Chirac, made an unprecedented address on national television to say what many already knew: that such compromises with the Front were endorsements of a "xenophobic" and "racist" France. It was a year in which media personalities who had long resisted interviewing Front leaders conceded that refusing to give them air time would not make them disappear. It was a year in which the progressive press could print headlines sounding the alarm that the "Front is everywhere" but just six months later otherwise sensible persons and public figures could applaud the World Cup victory of France's rainbow-coloured soccer team as an anti-racist victory for the real France.

But there was also this strange phenomenon of "nothing happening."[3] While well-heeled southern France with its folkloric appeal was neither obviously besieged by police nor silenced on issues of race, it was still a place where talk of "racism" was (and is) for students and the press, not for polite company, where acquaintances became palpably uncomfortable bringing up the "Front" and where "race" was a dirty word. While many university courses on issues related to immigration were offered, none listed at the universities in Aix or Marseille addressed the relationship between racism and the history of France.[4] Comments at after-dinner political discussions that turned to the FN's increasing presence in May 1998 would be met with impatience and awkward silences. When the FN began turning against itself and spiralled into decline in May 1999, there was smug satisfaction in its impending disappearance and a sense that there was no need to talk about it at all.

But this present-absence was disconcerting for Provence was also a place where the victories of the National Front – founded by Le Pen, its once charismatic leader – were daily front page news, and anti-FN demonstrations were reported as run-of-the-mill events. In Provence's towns and cities, Front-elected officials had closed down local cultural centres, censured theatre performances, banned "inappropriate" children's books (especially those illustrating parents of different hue, mixed-marriages, or toddlers of colour). Provence in 1997 is where, like in Vitrolles (a small town equidistant from Marseille and Aix), Front-elected city officials allocated municipal funds to install their own beefed-up squad of civil guard outfitted with motorcycle boots, truncheons, and black shirts, evoking memories of blackshirts of another era. The outfits were soon replaced, as one woman put it, by "more respectable" and conventional blue uniforms, but Vitrolles' city hall and central square were still well-wired with surveillance cameras aimed on its own inhabitants for their "security."

What was striking in the aftermath of the World Cup then was how sure people seemed to be that France's multicultural soccer team and the widespread support and adoration of it symbolized a defeat of the extreme right. How could the evidence of two decades of increasing support for National Front candidates (no French extreme-right party had ever survived as long) be annulled by a post-victory celebration of racial harmony? Why was one player's popularity – that of Zidane, the son of a "poor Algerian immigrant" (evinced in street chants, "Zidane for president") – interpreted as evidence of a meaningful multicultural romance rather than a one-night stand? How could the president of the French National Commission on the Rights of Man claim the World Cup "inflicted a defeat for racism" (12 August 1998). In the streets and in the press, one could hear people say, "See we've got *them* now. The FN has been silenced by this outburst of racial goodwill. The Marseillaise belongs to us again." Even left-wing weeklies wrote of a "real national communion," a French anti-racist "dream," a "plebiscite" for nationalism without exclusions – what intellectuals of diverse leanings labelled a nationalism without chauvinism that was truly

French. Similarly, what was commonly referred to as the "implosion" of the FN (as Le Pen and his former dauphin, Megret, battled for supremacy in a public standoff) was taken as further evidence that extreme right popularity was a dead issue. In both cases the confidence was myopic and misplaced. Press coverage continued in the months that followed with sanguine predictions, revelling in the Front's acceleration into a high gear of "self-destruct," its impending and much anticipated fall from grace. The sensationalism was a curious phenomenon, symptomatic of a more general trend in analyses of French racial politics: reluctance to engage what made racial thinking both commonsense and so broadly relevant.

Optimism is one thing, political delusion is another – as the April 2002 resurgence of Le Pen in the presidential primary of that year all too clearly attested.[5] The reaction to the news of Le Pen's victory over the socialist candidate Jospin in Spring 2002, four years after his "demise," was dismay and "shock" in the national and international press. Political pundits referred to the "week of surprises" and a turn that "no one expected." But one could argue that the dismay was more surprising than the victory – only understandable if one acknowledges a sustained amnesia about the place of race in France. The responses to the FN's "civil war" in 1998 and to the 2002 elections are indication of a much deeper set of misconstruals about what makes up the force of the radical right, what constitutes racism in France today, and what meaning the FN brand of racism has for its hard- and soft- line constituencies. That people *expected* the FN to be unsettled and irreparably damaged by the patriotic ecstasy surrounding the World Cup and the internecine FN battles derives in part from misidentifying what racialized discourses have looked like in the past and therefore what distinguishes them today. It disallows subtlety or complexity on the part of those who support the FN; and not least it ignores the multiple sites in which racial understandings of the social world are nurtured – and the seemingly discrepant discourses that the FN has so successfully sustained. Treatment of the celebration of multiculturalism as fundamentally subversive of racial regimes ignores basic historical evidence – that cultural hybridities can be smoothly folded back into racial social formations.

"AN-OTHER YEAR IN PROVENCE"

The research year I spent in Provence was not "fieldwork" in the sustained sense that I had been taught defines ethnography. It was instead what might be called "ethnography in the public sphere"; a tracking of the movements of people, publishing, and politics, discourses and differences that cut across local and national contexts – attention to the verbal and visual space of race in televised soundbites, websites, movies, radio, dinner parties, and graffiti. In the case of Vitrolles, the sensibilities about who was an outsider and who wasn't divided the town and was both tactile and intimate, national and European.

My movements followed those contours: from National Front demonstrations in Marseille to those against them, attendance at court hearings of provincial magistrates in Aix where the family of a "beur" girl denied access to a high school was pitted against her Front assailants. I surfed the Front's websites and newspapers overtly committed to the Front's program as avidly as those dead set against it. Women and men affiliated with the Front's parent-teacher organizations gave me their time. I followed Front candidates as they "worked" local markets in municipal elections, spoke with Front-elected city officials as well as city workers fired (because their first or family names were North African) when the Front moved in. I watched television interviews with National Front leaders, tracked the new wave of documentaries on Front-occupied towns, spoke with journalists writing on the Front in Toulon and Orange, spoke with lawyers defending those aggressed by the FN, visited the Front's national headquarters outside Paris and sought out cafés known to be friendly to FN supporters. With books on FN persons and politics something of a cottage industry, I read most and collected all I could get my hands on from the past ten years. I neither "infiltrated" the Front nor hung out with its opponents, but instead, tacked between trying to understand how race mattered in people's everyday lives and trying to figure out the space it occupied in the public sphere.

Provence's countryside is a favoured destination for those seeking out the "real" and rural souls of France. But the *département* in which Aix is located gives onto unseemly vistas and smells as well – a huge Shell refinery that takes up half of the "lake" between Marseille and Aix, an enormous shopping mall between the two cities, and row upon row of shabby subsidized housing in such towns as Vitrolles. An hour and a half's drive from Aix will bring you to one of the four towns of Toulon, Vitrolles, Marignane, and Orange – the now-infamous sites of National Front victories where as much as forty-five percent of the population have voted for platforms committed to "France for the French," "French first," expanded police forces, exclusion of welfare for "immigrants" (a misnomer in itself), and cash bonuses for couples producing "French" babies.

This area is the radical right's epicentre and the small town of Vitrolles one of its prime "laboratories," as both the Front and its opponents agree. Vitrolles-en-Provence – as its FN officials renamed it to emphasize its cultural attractions and to produce tourist appeal – is a site where the FN's national programs were rehearsed, where experiments in vigilantism, cultural censorship, barred entry to schools for those of the wrong shade, have been carried out to gauge whether such measures might produce too much publicity or not enough, whether they might scandalize too many people or prove too tepid to mobilize more support for the Front's constituencies.

The story told in this way is dramatic but the protagonists are predictable and the plot is clichéd. The politics of the Front seem excessive, unreasoned, and extreme. There is even comfort in such an account. We know its elements, we can imagine its actors – men of repressed violence, a population of uprooted ex-colonials longing for a long lost "French Algeria," people whose visions are narrow, whose employment opportunities are bleak, those desperate and too easily duped by the wrong answers to troubling questions.

But there is another side to the Front that is harder to demonize, one less dissonant with mainstream public concerns. Its proponents speak the language of democracy and liberty. They condemn violence. This side is harder to distinguish from other positions and is one those who assume they "know" the FN are less apt to hear.

For what is most striking about the platform of the Front, the persons who make up its constituency, the issues that it raises, is how unexceptional and commonplace they are. Take for instance, the FN's platform and practices on increased urban security. Virtually every effort to outline the FN's political program has described its heavy-handed crackdown on crime and juvenile delinquency. In Vitrolles in spring 1998, people talked in whispers about municipal funds siphoned off from cultural centres and reallocated to pay for more police. Vitrolles' FN city officials spoke unabashedly about the possible benefits of withholding state welfare payments to families who could not control their youth. To their minds, a critical problem in Vitrolles and elsewhere in France, has been "*laxiste*" ("permissive"), insufficiently "authoritarian" schools. They feel there are just too many families who do not know how to parent, high schools with too many left-leaning teachers catering to "problem kids" while those deserving attention and with real potential are neglected and left on their own. The "problem" students and their "negligent" families not surprisingly are those with Algerian and Moroccan family names.

On the face of it, the position is a quintessentially FN and racist one: juvenile delinquency touches poor families and many poor families in urban France are of North African origin. Withholding welfare payments is a policy, if implemented, with discriminatory effects designed to target those most dependent on state resources, those living in badly maintained state-subsidized tenements either unemployed or with low-paying jobs with dismal prospects and everything to lose. It reads as a policy invested in buttressing a disciplinary, punitive exclusionary state rather that a nurturing inclusive and liberal one.[6]

But that is both true and false. Media reports show clearly that the Front is not alone in its preoccupation with these issues. A parliamentary report on juvenile delinquency, issued by the socialist government, also recommended prison punishments for parents who could not sufficiently monitor their young (*Provence* 17 April 1998). The proposal a month later of the right-wing mayor of Aix-les-Bains – a non-FN town of 28,000 – to withhold state welfare from families with delinquent youths easily could have come from FN.[7]

At issue is the slippage between FN rhetoric and that in the wider public sphere, the chameleon-like form that FN positions assume, and the fact that it is increasingly difficult to identify a purely FN position, in part because the Front has been so effective at appropriating the rhetoric of the right, the left, the extremes, and everyone in between. As Le Pen put it so well to Mayor Michael Bloomberg in a visit to New York "I'm socially left, economically right, and more than ever and anything else, nationally for France."[8] It is not only, as the political theorist Pierre-Andre Taguieff pointed out some fifteen years ago, that the radical right has appropriated the language of the French revolution and patriotic nationalism,[9] or that it has played on anxieties over national identity prompted by a future within a borderless Europe, compounded by fears of what the substitution of the new Euro dollar for the Franc would bring (see Taguieff 1995).[10] Open discussions about immigration were disabled in part because raising the issue became synonymous with a racist position. Key words associated with the liberal state ring hollow when the language of "democracy," "individual liberty," and "the public good" appear as often in FN speeches as among those of its opponents.

Even accusations of racism – so long directed at the FN's leaders and their platforms – were no longer confined to anti-FN discourse. During 1998, the FN mounted a new discursive campaign, claiming that France's current problem was not the FN's racist tendencies but rather the anti-patriotic, "anti-French racism" of its "attackers" – a more serious threat to national heritage and the very identity of France. This could be dismissed as a clever ruse, a distorting twist of the term *racism* into its very opposite. Rather than a relationship of power in which white Frenchmen come out on top, the FN's definition of "racism" implicitly criticized the country's then-current leaders for being too swayed by a "cosmopolitan" intellectual left more committed to globalization than to local French interests. Pat Robertson's injunctions against a conspiratorial "New World Order" spearheaded by a deracinated intellectual left echo in my North American ears.[11] In the FN scenario, such "anti-French racism" produced other victims – long-standing French citizens made vulnerable to encroachments on their jobs, subject to a denigrated cultural heritage, degenerated conditions in their schools and infringements on *their* human rights.[12]

But the politics of appropriation has gone both ways: the FN may have been talking with ease about their defence of liberty, but those fiercely opposed to FN xenophobias were finding themselves working from categories not dissimilar to those of the FN. Thus public discussions unproblematically described a deluge of immigrants despite *decreased* immigration over the previous twenty years.[13] Mainstream politicians unaligned with and opposed to FN policies have been pulled in to focus on the evils or virtues of supporting the FN's platform for a "national preference." Whether or not they disagreed with its basic tenets, the *terms of the debate* were framed by the Front: demands for strict quotas on immigration, for a "return" of immigrants to their countries of origin, and for limits to medical benefits, social assistance, and rights of citizenship for immigrants.

These are more than deft language games. They are part of a broader cultural repertoire of verbal and visual images that have had broad resonance and appeal. Front tactics may be excessive and unprincipled, but their positions have offered ready answers to hard questions. What the FN conceives of as "problems" have often been more easily identifiable than those of its opponents. Front-watchers have focused on the rhetoric of Front leaders for years but there is something else more disturbing and more impressive: the discursive space the Front has provided potential non-committed sympathizers as well as its militants. Women and men I met in Vitrolles – some who avowed being supporters of the Front, most who did not – conveyed their fears and distastes in compelling terms. Almost everyone expressed distrust of mainstream politicians and politics.

Frontal attack on the Front's racist and xenophobic qualities (in a profusion of books and newspaper articles appearing in the late 1990s) has enabled some discourses and closed off others. One could argue that it created an engaged and active public sphere where racism's immorality was openly argued and multiculturalism celebrated. But one could make another case: that with such focused attention on the evils of the Front (and on its rise and fall), less heed was paid elsewhere – to the sympathies of a broader French population with visions and political principles not incompatible with those of their more overtly exclusionary FN counterparts. A frequently heard statement among those who distanced themselves from the FN (and could in no way be counted among its supporters) was one that began, "I'm not a racist, but ..." followed by a narrative about why too many immigrants was France's most pressing problem. The FN does *not* hold a monopoly on racist visions and racist practices. Assuming it does leaves little room to examine a broader space in which racial categories have been nurtured and on which FN support continues to rest.

THE FN'S COMMON SENSE: ON BEING INDEPENDENT OF POLITICS

In Vitrolles, I posed two basic questions: "What does it mean to be educated in France today?" and "What sorts of knowledge and knowhow should go into that equation?" To both questions, most people responded that they were not interested in politics (although I didn't refer to politics *per se*). They were tired of teachers' organizations, local interest groups, regional leaders and national parties that were all *"trop politisé"* (too politicized). Women in the parent-student association (APPEVE) supported by the Front, insisted that theirs was strictly an "independent" organization, unfettered by any political party. Their concern was for their children's education and safety, but unlike those associations backed by the socialist and centre conservative parties, not politics. No one with whom I spoke in APPEVE acknowledged its affiliation with the Front. They were concerned rather with an educational system too subservient to politics, teachers who brought their politics to the classroom, inadequate discipline in schools. "Laxity," "lack of discipline," "lack of limits" were the most frequent complaints.

One could say that "discipline" was their keyword. But easy answers are easy to get; for the issue of discipline is at once distinctly FN and not. "Mothers of the Front" spoke forcefully about discipline but so did those women with affiliations elsewhere. What differed was what they meant by discipline and who was deemed to lack it.

BEYOND THE EXTREMES: ARE THESE REASONING WOMEN AND MEN?

Pierre-Andre Taguieff has astutely critiqued anti-racist organizations for pathologizing those on the extreme right in ways evocative of the scapegoating so central to racist discourse itself. One could go further. FN militants and constituents have been pathologized in specific ways: as those outside reason, persons unduly swayed, deluded by crises of identity, morally weakened by disempowerment. This image of FN supporters as viscerally Other, delusional, and duped has specific effects (as though one could almost smell their politics on their breath). Deemed outside the humanist tradition, they are in *any* context and *all* instances labelled irrational and unreasonable men (sic). As such, their fear is taken as the FN's most powerful "common denominator."[14]

But let us start from a less intuitive premise: not that the radical right has been populated by insecure and fearful malcontents on the margins of French society; but rather of reasoning *women* as well as men. Not "monsters" but those who are "rather likable," or as one FN watcher put it, "faces that might occupy the ranks of any political formation."[15] What if one starts, not from the assumption that its platforms have been based on ill-will, small-mindedness, and sinister imaginings, and not just that the force of the Front derives from its trafficking in carefully crafted slogans and deft manipulations of symbols, but that the Front exercises a nuanced, even subtle cultural politics. What if racisms are not the excesses and anomalies of modern states, bureaucratic machines gone out of whack, but fundamental to their technologies of rule, as Foucault suggested some twenty-five years ago to an unreceptive College de France audience?[16] These are unpopular premises, but they may offer a better starting point to understand the FN's appeal and the popularity of its claims.

"Subtle" is not the first word that comes to mind when describing the extreme-right in the United States or Canada, much less in Germany, England, or France. The term "extreme" or "radical" indicates a set of perceptions and practices beyond the pale, exaggerated, outside the norm. In some ways this accurately describes white supremacist groups like the Canadian Western Guard or the U.S. Ku Klux Klan, as well as some members of the FN. But to stop there is to miss how far-right discourse operates. "Subtle" may not capture what typifies the FN's cultural know-how but metaphors of excess that invoke flat-footed, crass, uninspired powers of persuasion, attractive to few other than simple-minded thugs and skinheads are not either.

The National Front's commitment to the trinity of *"travail, famille, patrie"* (family, work, and fatherland) has cross-cultural relevance, cross-class and cross-national appeal. It commands a moral righteousness that touches not only those situated in the "U.S. deep south", in North America's outback west, or in France *profonde*. Such images have informed nineteenth-century racial regimes in colony and metropole, and have long appealed to women as much as men. They are common to nationalistic tracts of different political persuasions. As exclusionary invocations they are powerfully posed as defences of society against infiltrations from within. They invoke the coziness of belonging; speak in the language of protection of the majority; and promise to "weed out" the enemy within for the common good, the good of all (see figure A, a poster by the "Young People's FN," urging a "de-pollution of the city"). These images are often not unsympathetic to the plight of impoverished *cité* families of Magrehbin origin – and are not unlike the comforting politics of compassion that underwrote colonial social reforms and that underwrite programs of homeland security today.[17]

Figure A

The FN's cultural politics is well honed in other forms. The FN has its own small coterie of committed scholars that publish on the true "origins of France" and who are prominently advertised as dons of the Sorbonne.[18] Its publications are not cheap political tracts. They are printed with glossy covers on high-quality paper in paperback form. They look not unlike the 2001 publication of a member of Chirac's party, entitled *Insecurity: To Save the Republic*.[19] FN poster art is pop, catchy, and impressive. While some poster and postcard art is inspired by fascist populist imagery (bare-chested white young men with short-cropped hair, toned and taut, working tools in hand, with eyes raised to the banner of France and the Front's eternal flame) others make subtler commentaries; such as the poster I was proudly shown in the basement of the FN's national headquarters. It (figure B) showed cartoon-like figures: one wasted, dishevelled, drug-riddled student of left-wing persuasion with the year 1968 written above his head; the other a well-groomed, bright-eyed youth with 1998 over his in bold face type. Another poster (figure C) stated in bright red "REBELLE-TOI!" (REBEL!), JOIN THE FRONT." What could better invoke the fight against the status quo than an alignment with the right revolution on the side of the Front and France's future leaders? As the retired school teacher from the south who sorted posters reminded me, "see, we have our own intellectuals too."

Figure B

Figure C

It is not just their poster culture that is on the mark. The FN's cyberspace connections are informative, clear, and interactive. Its website is updated regularly with statistics on local and national elections, with new political tracts, with on-line copies of FN books and excerpts from the anti-FN popular press. In the tradition of the French communist party, whose annual festival combines family fun with cultural and political events, the FN too hosts an array of summer universities, institutes for "cultural action", scientific meetings, colloquia for journalists, and educational workshops, like the one held in Toulon's Neptune Palace concert hall that took as its theme "Liberate the Republic." In the late 1990s, FN national rallies had glitzy sound and light shows with singers of colour blasting rap and reggae music. Radio Le Pen offered non-stop news.

Until the split in 1998, the FN press provided daily and weekly analyses of national events, incisive commentaries on articles appearing in *Le Monde*, *Libération*, and the foreign press. Attacks on the FN were reported assiduously by its journalists as a badge of honour and minutely tracked, in an attempt to give credence to their claim that FN supporters are the ones who are undemocratically harassed and violently aggressed. *Canard Enchaîné* (a satirical weekly that has committed itself for years to sustained FN goading) was mocked by the FN dailies, the same dailies that scrupulously mimic its black-and-red boldface type and layout.[20] Is it significant that at a glance one cannot distinguish the FN press from that of its opponents?

Never has it been so difficult to isolate and specify what constitutes the unique discourse of the extreme right in France. This may seem contradictory but I would argue that it is not.

FIGURING THE FN: ANALYSES OF THE MAN, THE MOVEMENT, THE NATION

Problems in specifying what is specific to the FN were reflected in changes in how journalists, scholars, and activists profiled the extreme right and what sort of emphasis they placed on its founder and leader. Between 1993 and 1998 there was a virtual explosion in the literature on the "FN phenomenon" – and a distinct set of registers in which that phenomenon was cast. Typologies rarely hold fast. Still there was an identifiable shift in emphasis from a focus on the leader Le Pen, to the FN as a fascist institution, to the radical right as a reflection of French society itself.

The first register conforms to what one might call the "big man theory of history" or the "cult of the man." Here the FN's power to persuade was framed as one solely based on its extraordinary leader, his debating skills and rhetorical flourish. According to this argument, people were pulled in inadvertently, almost accidentally because of Le Pen's force as a leader (thus titles such as *In the Shadow of Le Pen*, *The Le Pen Effect*, *Le Pen: the Words*, and *The Said and the Unsaid of Le Pen*).[21] If the FN was Le Pen, then it was only a short-lived, conjunctural phenomenon that would reasonably weaken with his fall. The rise of Bruno Megret in the late 1990s did not undermine that model. With focus on Megret's more youthful, up-to-date style and panache, the "big men" were changing but not the premise of the analysis.

Journalists have a penchant for flashy newsworthy personalities, but even they could no longer argue that the Front was only Le Pen. A second wave of books took up the conflict in successionary rights from Le Pen to Megret and the growing tension between them. Those who once imagined that the FN would dissolve with Le Pen's demise were now predicting the opposite; that the FN was possibly taking on new force as the offensive brashness of Le Pen was replaced by a more stately style. Cendrine Le Chevallier, FN mayoral candidate in Toulon was hard to bill as a populist candidate with her Hermes scarves and Chanel outfits. The oppositional press lingered on her glittering jewels and the chime of her gold bracelets as she lightly brushed hands with would-be supporters in urban crowds. If being brash and outspoken were hallmarks of the FN in earlier years, future supporters were hailed as men and women of a different cloth. Megret and his cohort wore expensive-cut banker suits and preached alliances with the respectable right, not distance from it. If being outrageous and provocative was the strategy of an earlier moment, confusing the camps, blurring the distinctions, and entangling the terms of what can be discussed publicly signalled the new efforts to appeal to a different set of sensibilities.

This second register of political and historical analysis gave less emphasis to Le Pen per se than to the appeal of the Front as an organization, its recruitment strategies, its partisans, and its institutional frame. Demographic analyses of regional and national elections made effort to identify the specific populations that succumbed to the FN, with focus on their idiosyncrasies and on the susceptibilities of those that might "fall" in the future. Starting over two decades ago, with the first alarm at the FN's electoral success, the effort was to isolate those vulnerable to it. This was a reasonable effort when the FN's numbers were still small, and scattered unevenly throughout the population. In 1996, the flagship journal of Parisian intellectuals, *Nouvel Observateur*, could point to an FN constituency made up of "special" groups: for example, of "*pieds noirs*" (repatriated Frenchmen born in Algeria), of first-wave European immigrants from Italy and Portugal, or of dislocated, emasculated unemployed young men. The 2002 elections suggest a broader constituency never considered vulnerable: the rural and the elderly.

This demographics of blame has had lots of targets: some studies optimistically asserted it was really only "the aged" who were attracted, hard-line nostalgics for colonialism and/or those fearful of change. Others focused on the particular attraction of the FN for young males, ignoring the numerous women who voted for it. Many studies have addressed the regional clustering of FN support in the troubled working-class outskirts of Paris and southern France. In the latter case, the "cause" is found more specifically in a population known to have supported the Petain/Vichy government during the wartime occupation who then fled at the war's end to France's north African colonies only to be grudgingly forced back in the early 1960s with Algeria's independence.

These studies certainly have something to say about the nature of FN support, but perhaps more to say about what researchers expected to find: namely, evidence that the FN is a decidedly non-French phenomenon. Scholars shared this perspective with activists and the press. It is perhaps best captured by the favoured slogan: "F is for fascist, N is for Nazi," so often plastered across anti-FN posters, chanted in anti-FN rallies and still popular today, as though one would have to look to the history of Italian and German political extremisms for the origins of a set of sympathies that were born and bred in France.

But just as it is no longer possible to uphold that the Vichy regime was a foreign imposition on an unwilling French population, so too have analyses of the FN in its third register turned away from this search for a foreign etiology.[22] No longer seeking the anomalous nature of the FN within an otherwise republican French society, some analyses have sought other roots, those of an FN "MADE IN FRANCE."[23] Vaguely concurrent with the increasingly broad regional and class spread of the FN and its ever-widening constituencies, the third register has emphasized the FN as a product of French nationalism gone awry, as an accurate mirror of the ills of French society, or alternately as a distorted mirror of its malaise.[24] Here commentaries have turned to the making of an endemically xenophobic movement – neither foreign nor imposed – but organically French.

Not surprisingly, these shifts in exposé style and scholarship are not dissimilar to the course of Holocaust studies over the last fifty years that too have moved from studies of "the man" (Hitler/Le Pen), to those focused on the party (Front/Nazi) and those more attentive to economic depression and the anonymity of urban sprawl, to the Nazi/FN party as a product of a technocratic state machine and a swollen and alienating bureaucracy.[25] But a glaring difference remains. In the German case, the relationship between racism and the (Nazi) state is fundamental to the analysis. Studies of the FN, on the contrary, systematically beg the statist question, in part because the starting premise is that the French republican state is the FN's nemesis and by definition opposed to it.

But if Michel Foucault was right that racism is not only part of certain state formations (be they fascist, capitalist, or socialist) but fundamental to the making of the modern state itself, we need to ask other questions.[26] If state racisms take varied forms, can they be identified not only as firmly and explicitly entrenched in the state's central institutions but also in displaced sites as a shadow presence? What is the relationship between the history of the radical right and the history of the French welfare state? What does the political presence of a vocal extreme right allow or not allow states to do? One obvious question is whether a new Europe without borders is calling for a more stringently defined set of interior frontiers. Across Europe, political analysts are documenting the rise of overtly racist candidates and their electoral support in Austria, Denmark, Portugal, Switzerland, Italy, Belgium, and the Netherlands.[27]

But it may be that, as Wittgenstein once argued, these are not the wrong answers but the wrong questions. Have there been radical changes in the tactics of the Front or only in scholarly analyses of them? Assessing the force field of the FN may entail more than looking to its increased electoral successes, media presence, or organizational appeal. Perhaps we should be looking at the political habitus it has helped to create to assess how much it governs a wide range of gestures, dictates the behaviours and dispositions of those unsympathetic to it, and shapes the rules rather than the particular strategies of the game. Perhaps we should be asking another question, not only about its aim, strategies, and tactics, but also about its practical effect.

Take, for example, the "culture of fear" that was said to surround the FN. Was it produced by the FN or by those who opposed it? Was it generated out of FN practices or the result of the discourse of its opposition? During my research in Provence in 1998 and 1999 French colleagues and friends repeatedly discouraged me from continuing. I was advised to get an unlisted phone number, and to use a post office box rather than my home address. Some suggested I refrain from talking to anyone at FN rallies, not carry a camera, not attend anti-FN demonstrations. Everyone advised me to watch my back and to keep my distance from the press. At one level these were not unreasonable precautions: the FN was "known" to harass its opponents, threaten their spokespersons, and retain beefy bodyguards to protect their leaders in potentially hostile crowds. On a visit to the FN headquarters outside Paris, I deposited my Michigan driver's license at the door, and was later chided by friends for reckless bravado. How do security measures figure as intimidations? Again are these constraints produced solely by the FN or by an anti-FN caricature of it?

The answer is not obvious. In part fear of the Front permeates social relations in a wide political field. If power is defined by the capacity to impose the categories of discourse and practice, then the FN is a strong player. The FN both reproduced a culture of fear and ensured that it reproduced itself. This was strikingly evident in watching the effect of the FN victory in Vitrolles. With nearly half the population having voted for the FN in the last elections (and it did not seem to matter, as some people claimed, that many in Vitrolles had only registered a "protest vote" against the preceding spendthrift, socialist mayor), people repeatedly talked about an atmosphere in town that was tense, saying that people were uncomfortable even greeting their neighbours and that a newly heightened oppressive suspicion, distrust, and avoidance not unlike a new brand of terror had arisen.

But discourses are neither homogeneous nor shared. In returning to Vitrolles in 1999, it was clear that "security" was a prevailing trope with multiple senses. Thus the mayor's office boasted in its monthly magazine that "Security in '98 was still better than '97!" with the introduction of more police dogs, equestrian police, surveillance cameras, and a new "rapid intervention police brigade." In contrast, young women in Vitrolles' state housing (HLM) complexes saw the issue of security from another angle; they described something like a state of siege, of a police presence so intense that they and their friends were uncomfortable walking about at night – they only felt the streets were safe and "secure" in the *absence* of police in the light of day.

THE FAMILY FRONT:
ON THE GENDER POLITICS OF THE RADICAL RIGHT

The point of looking at scholarship on the FN is not to conclude that the analyses have all been wrong, but rather to question the assumptions that organize those frames. At one of the first Front demonstrations I attended in Fall 1997 on the waterfront in Marseille, two angry and vocal elderly women stood in the midst of a large crowd, chiding "France" for not upholding its democratic principles. Assuming they were anti-FN demonstrators, I was impressed with their gutsy stance in a hostile crowd, only to then realize they were staunch Front supporters and that the day's slogan "We've had enough" (of liberalism, immigrants, anti-Front attacks) was on their lips too. There was nothing out of the ordinary about the event – only my assumptions about who spoke the language of liberty, where, and in what way.

LA FAMILLE, PRIORITÉ NATIONALE !

**CERCLE NATIONAL FEMMES D'EUROPE
POUR UN REVENU PARENTAL**

11 rue Bernouli
75008 Paris
Tel : 44 70 05 72

Figure D

As one looks to the issues that have been omitted from the current research agenda on the French radical right, nothing is more striking than the singular effacement of its gender politics. Both academic and journalistic commentary and coverage have focused on the FN and men: on the male elite that formulates its policies, on the young male immigrants at which its policies are aimed, and on the insecure and unemployed male population to which it supposedly has its gratest appeal. While men have made up the majority of the Front's public, the fact remains that as much as twenty-five percent of the population who have voted for the FN are women, a percentage that has been decisive in the narrow margin by which the FN has won local elections (see figure D). Not examining the appeal of the Front for a large female constituency seems in part to be based on the unstated assumption that those women who do vote for the Front are following their fathers, brothers, sons – their men.

What is more, in the last few years women have unexpectedly emerged in key positions in the FN's leadership, as both pawns and strong players in the Front's juggling of posts and persons in local politics. As FN figures such as Le Pen, Megret, and de Chevalier have been disqualified from elections, their wives have replaced them as candidates in mayoral and regional campaigns. Following the FN's split in Fall 1998, Le Pen's daughter, Marie-Caroline, "defected" to Megret's camp, highlighting a basic tension between loyalties to political kith vs. intimate kin, especially charged because the FN's central platform has been so closely tied to "family values." The gender dynamics reflected in the fact that Megret's wife, Catherine, could legitimately "stand in" for him as Vitrolles' mayor, despite her inexperience in politics or public life, played on the relationship between family and politics yet again, snidely signalled in the non-FN press by references to her husband Bruno Megret as the "mayor consort."

Family, gender, and politics emerged again with the surprise announcement by Le Pen that his wife, Janny, would stand in for him in the European parliamentary elections rather than Megret, an event that many would argue first publicly marked the severing of the FN into two camps (*L'Evenement* 1999). The conflict (and Janny's unexpected and much publicized response to the press that she neither wanted to run nor knew anything about politics) brought the gender politics of substitutability to a new heightened level. At stake was not only the new divisions within the FN, but its very political credibility. Since the 2002 presidential victory, Le Pen's "clone" daughter Marine, "the broad-shouldered blonde" who is a 35-year-old lawyer, has taken centre stage as "the electable face of the extreme right" and his successor. It is she who London's *Financial Times* considers to be "more dangerous than her father" with her toned-down anti-immigrant language.[28]

But there is something else that makes the lack of attention to female voters surprising. And it should overshadow the coverage of the internal machinations of affinal substitutes in party politics. This is the fact that many of the major themes played out in public discourse are about areas of life thought to be controlled by, and of special importance to, women: primary school education, daycare, childrearing, family planning and sexual morality. In the Front's favoured slogan, "family, fatherland, and work," "family" comes first. Emphasis on the male contours of the Front fails to address critical arenas in which the extreme right has made its presence and power felt – all domains in which women have been actively called upon to police the boundaries between the moral and the immoral, between public and private, and between school and home.

While these are all issues that feminist scholars working on the appeal of the conservative right in the United States have addressed for some time, this is decidedly not the case for French scholarship.[29] If the issue of gender politics is examined at all, it focuses on how extreme right parties view women, rather than *how women view them*. In trying to learn something about the ways in which women of the Front process its programs and present its appeal, returning to Vitrolles in 1999, I interviewed women who worked for Vitrolles' FN-run city government, mothers with school-age children; well-educated, well-heeled, and politically learned. Unlike those women in the teacher-student organizations backed by the FN who categorically denied any association with or sympathy for its politics, these were women of the Front – young Megretistes, who characterized Le Pen as an outdated model for the FN and who bet their futures on Megret.[30]

Schools were the problem for them, but they cast their net of concern wider, using an idiom that frequently invoked the problem of figurative and literal "thresholds." Here it was the FN that policed the dangerous borders between France and its outside (with immigration quotas), the FN that understood the need to police the entries to schools, the FN that was vigilant about what belonged in school and in the home. They were disconcerted by contemporary parenting styles and blamed "some" parents for neglecting the moral rearing of their young, for not instilling a sense of "good taste," for abandoning jobs to teachers that they should be doing themselves. They blamed teachers for not leaving their politics at home. Mothers, they contended, should have the opportunity to stay at home. Asked why so many worked, one woman sighed and said it was she who suffered, that she (and France) had undergone a bit "too much feminism" when she was growing up, that work hours were not designed with women in mind. Still, both she and her co-worker adamantly opposed proposals for gender parity, which they called an "aberration of the Left." How a new feminine, domestic face of the FN in the form of a young mother, Marine, will appeal to such sensibilities is a question that FN analysts should be paying the attention it deserves.

FUTURE DIRECTIONS/OLD CONNECTIONS

What is striking about the Front's interventions in public education, welfare, immigration policy, library acquisitions, theatre openings, and scholarship is the face of racial thinking it fashions for France and a wider European community in the twenty-first century. It is neither a new racism nor a replica of the old. France today harbours a racial discourse that is flexible and porous, malleable, modernizing, and imbued with cultural currency. Those who pose this as a new racism, as a cultural racism fundamentally distinct from racisms of the past are missing how much colonial racisms spoke the language of cultural competencies, "good taste," and discrepant parenting values.[31]

The cultural ambiguities that characterized racisms in the nineteenth-century Dutch East Indies or French Indochina should serve not so much as a point of historical contrast as suggestive of the sorts of questions one might pose. Tracking what designated "race" there and then allows us to see that even those quintessential forms of racism honed in the colonies were never built on the surefooted classifications of science, but on a potent set of cultural and affective criteria whose malleability was a key to the sliding scale along which economic privilege was protected and social entitlements were assigned. In short, the porousness we assign to the contemporary concept of race is inherent in the concept itself and not a hallmark of our postmodern critique – much less of our postcolonial moment.

Still, what the face of racism looks like on the cusp of this twenty-first century cannot be derived from its eighteenth- and nineteenth-century templates alone. Nor can it be derived from the years of the FN's rapid ascension, followed by a succession of splits, failures, and weakenings in mainstream politics. That two-thirds of France in a summer 1998 poll avowed that it was sympathetic to at least some of the National Front's platform was largely ignored then but cannot be now. It should remind us that racisms never have existed (and do not today exist) in distilled form. They are as easily embraced by those eager for change as by those who are not. Racial discourses can serve central state concerns as much as it serves those opposed to them. They can herald utopian visions as much as nostalgic ones. Predicating an understanding of today's racism on a flattened, reductive history of what racism once looked like may be consoling but it is neither helpful nor redemptive. Genealogies of racisms must reckon with racism's power to rupture with the past and selectively and strategically recuperate it at the same time. We should take seriously the ways in which exclusionary politics have created and continue to produce a repertoire of responsive solutions that its adherents see neither as racist nor exclusionary, but as reasonable, measured, even compassionate and commonsensical.

NOTES

1 This paper is based on a presentation delivered as a keynote address for the conference "Making History, Constructing Race," University of Victoria, and for the workshop "Europe and Algeria," held at the Johns Hopkins Center in Bologna in May 1999. Funding for the project was provided by the LSA faculty fund, the Office of the Vice President, and the Institute for Research on Gender at the University of Michigan. Initial research was conducted in 1997 with the help of Chantal Février, Annie Roquier, and Frédéric Cotton. Research in 1999 was carried out with Delphine Mauger of the University of Michigan.

2 See my *Race and the Education of Desire: Foucault's History of Sexuality and the Colonial Order of Things*. Durham: Duke UP 1995, and "Racial

Histories and their Regimes of Truth." *Political Power and Social Theory* 13, (Fall 1997).
3. On this phenomena "in which nothing ... appears to happen," see John Pemberton's *On the Subject of Java*. Ithaca: Cornell University Press 1994, 7, where he describes the normalized, quotidian terror of Suharto's long-ensconced regime in Indonesia, finally ousted in 1998.
4. Colonial history, on the other hand, has suddenly become, a new favourite subject in the popular and academic press but somehow still removed from the deep genealogies of racisms in France today.
5. See "Chirac-Le Pen: la semaine de toutes les surprises." *Le Figaro*, 28 April 2002, and "Far Right Eclipses Socialist in France." *The New York Times*, 22 April 2002: 1,6.
6. In April 2002, when Le Pen resumed his campaign, he did not bother to speak against immigration. As Le Figaro noted, "This time, it was enough to just speak of insecurity" *Le Figaro*, 25 April 2002.
7. *Le Monde*, 25 May 1998.
8. Quoted in Erwan Lecoeur, *Un Neo-Populisme à la Française: Trente ans de Front National*. Paris: La Découverte 2003, 11.
9. See Pierre-André Taguieff's rich and subtle analysis of the multilayered mobilizing tactics of the Front in "The Doctrine of the National Front in France (1972-1989)." *New Political Science* 16–17 (fall/winter 1989): 29–70.
10. Taguief, Pierre-André. *Les Fins de l'antiracisme*. Paris: Michalon 1995.
11. The comparison between far right political discourse in the U.S. on the perils of immigrants and of globalization, as embodied in Pat Robertson's *The New World Order*. Dallas: Word Publishing 1991, and that of the French National Front is yet to be made.
12. In a public colloquium on "Anti-French Racism" organized by the municipal library of the FN-run city of Marignane in June 1998, at least one prevailing definition targeted those who "spoke of" and "encouraged *metissage* (mixing)." Compte Rendue d'un colloque publique à Marignane sur le theme: "Le racisme anti-français." 12 Juin 1998.
13. The confused use of "immigrant" to include "jeunes Françaises d'origine immigrée" and "jeunes immigrés non-français" is not fortuitous but part of the racial politics of this discourse. See Yannick LeFranc, "Comment le parti de l'exclusion traité un mouvement pour l'intégration." *Mots* 58 (Mars 1999): 60.
14. Michalina Vaughn. "The Extreme Right in France: 'Lepenisme' or the Politics of Fear." In *The Far Right in Western and Eastern Europe*, ed. Luciana Cheles, Ronnie Ferguson, and Michalina Vaughn. London: Longman 1995, 215–33.
15. As Mark Hunter put it, "There are, in reality, monsters in the Front; I have met several of them. But one equally finds people rather likable, attractive (*"sympathetique"*) which raises another question: what are they doing here

among these monsters?" (See Mark Hunter. *Un Américain au Front: Enquête au sein du FN*, Paris: Stock 1997, 11; Jonathan Marcus. *The National Front and French Politics*. New York: NYU Press 1995, 2.)

16 Stoler. *Race and the Education of Desire*. 1995, 55–94.

17 On the distancing and differentiating politics that underwrite "empathy" see Julie Ellison's "A Short History of Liberal Guilt." *Critical Inquiry*, (Winter 1996).

18 Among some of these are *Les Origines de la France*, published "under the direction of Professor Jacques Robichez" among others with the names of Bruno Megret and Jean-Marie Le Pen included as co-authors. This volume, published by the FN press, Editions Nationales, was a product of its "12th Colloque du Conseil Scientifique du Front National"; Pierre Milloz. *L'Immigration sans haine ni mépris: les chiffres que l'on vous cache* ("Immigration without hate or misapprehension: the numbers that are hidden from you") 1997.

19 Christian Estrosi. *Insécurité: Sauver le République*. Paris: Editions du Rocher 2001.

20 After the split between Megret and Le Pen, the FN articles became noticeably innocuous, aiming at safe and familiar targets, like immigrants, but with no comment on the divisions that sundered the party.

21 Examples of this genre of analysis include: Pascal Perrineau's *Le Symptome Le Pen: Radiographie des électeurs du Front National*. Paris: Fayard 1997; Maryse Souchard, Stephanie Wahnich, Isabelle Cuminal, Virginie Wathier. *Le Pen Les Mots: Analyse d'un discours d'extrême-droite*. Paris: Le Monde éditions 1997; Lorrain de Saint Affrique and Jean-Gabriel Fredet. *Dans l'ombre de Le Pen*. Paris: Hachette 1998, the latter a former press officer for Le Pen.

22 Among the first in this genre of Vichy exposé, see Henry Russo. *Le Syndrome de Vichy: De 1944 à nos jours*. Paris: Seuil 1987.

23 Hubert Huertas. *FN: Made in France*. Paris: Autres Temps 1997

24 Alain Bihr. *Le Spectre de l'extrême droite: les Français dans le miroir du Front National*. Paris: Les Éditions de L'atelier 1998.

25 On the Holocaust as "deeply rooted in the nature of modern society and in the central categories of modern social thought," see Zygmunt Bauman. *Modernity and the Holocaust*. Ithaca, NY: Cornell University Press 1989.

26 See Foucault's final set of lectures in 1976 on "the birth of modern racism," discussed in *Race and the Education of Desire* (1995) and now available in English as Michel Foucault. *Society Must be Defended. Lectures at the Collège de France, 1975–1976*. New York: Picador 1997.

27 See Julio Godoy. "Politics: The Right Is on the Rise across Europe." *Global Information Network*, New York, (17 December 2003): 1.

28 Jo Johnson. "Marine le Pen in a Dawn Raid on French Voters." *The Financial Times*, 28 February 2004.

29 See, for example, Caludie Lesselier and Faimmetta Venner. *L'extreme droite et les femmes*. Paris: Golias 1997.
30 This was just a month before the court decision that the logo, name, and funds designated as those of the FN rightfully belonged to Le Pen and that Megret could not use them without severe penalty.
31 On the importance of a proper moral and culturally attuned education for European colonials, see my *Carnal Knowledge and Imperial Power: Race and the Intimate in Colonial Rule*. Berkeley: University of California Press 2003, especially chapters four and five.

PAUL MAYLAM

Unravelling South Africa's Racial Order: The Historiography of Racism, Segregation, and Apartheid

When South Africa entered the post-apartheid era in the mid-1990s it basked in international acclaim for its negotiated transition and new democratic order, and in the universal reverence accorded its new president, Nelson Mandela. At the same time the country had to deal with the awful legacy of apartheid. This challenge gave rise to many questions, two of which require consideration here. First, what was to be done with the country's ignominious history of racial oppression? Should it be swept under the carpet so that old divisions and hatreds could be buried and a new, united South Africa could blossom? Second, should this new South Africa be built firmly on the principle of non-racialism, thereby breaking entirely free from its racialized past? If this was to be the path, how could the victims of past racial oppression obtain redress, given that such redress would inevitably involve the continued existence of racial categories? Herein lay a fundamental dilemma – one which has shaped much of the discourse and analysis surrounding "race" and racism in post-apartheid South Africa.

In response to the first question the ANC-led government of national unity established a Truth and Reconciliation Commission (TRC) as a compromise measure. Its task was to uncover some of the more brutal episodes of the apartheid era, while stopping short of punitive retribution. It would strive to reveal "truths" about the ugly past, and to achieve reconciliation through disclosure. There is already a massive body of literature on the TRC, and it is not the intention of this essay to add to that – except to say that one of the many criticisms directed against the TRC is that it concentrated too much on specific acts of brutality carried out in defence of apartheid, and not enough on the broader destructive impact of the whole system. This is a harsh criticism, given that the TRC lacked the resources and the time to investigate and report upon the wider impact of apartheid. However, such was the specific focus of the TRC that it had the effect of shifting public attention away from those broader aspects that made apartheid "the crime against humanity" that it was – aspects such as forced removals, the pass laws, labour exploitation, and other multifarious forms of racial discrimination. Some see a danger that future generations will lose sight of South Africa's long history of racism, segregation, and apartheid. The focus of this essay is historical and historiographical – as it tries to show how, through much of the twentieth century, different writers, scholars, observers tried to explain – or explain away – the country's deeply racialized past.

Trends in South Africa in recent years suggest, in answer to the second question, that non-racialism still remains a distant ideal. Paul Gilroy's utopian project of transcending and abandoning racial categories looks to be a remote possibility.[1] "Race" still matters in South Africa in the early twenty-first century.[2] Racial categories are still built into census-taking and into job application forms. National and provincial sports teams are subject to racial quotas. "Paradoxically," as Deborah Posel observes, "one of the principal legal instruments for redressing the racial imbalances of the apartheid past – the Employment Equity Act (Act 55 of 1998) – reproduces the racial categories enacted in the Population Registration Act [of 1950] as the basis on which affirmative action is to be instituted and measured."[3]

This is the dilemma already mentioned – redress requires racial categorization. But this is not just a matter of "race" serving the needs of affirmative action. Racial assumptions continue to pervade public discourse in South Africa. Again there is a paradox. Racism is rigorously proscribed – instances of racism draw wide media attention. At the same time popular understandings of South African society remain heavily racialized, even if more implicitly than explicitly. Moreover, although proscribed, there is no doubt that racism persists in South Africa. The effect of the proscription has been to push it below the surface, or to confine it to the private domain. No whites want the ignominious charge of racism hanging over them, but racialized assumptions still permeate the consciousness of South Africans, black and white.

All this has given rise to a further paradox – that social scientists and other commentators have come to concentrate their attention on the persistence of racism and racialization in the post-apartheid era. Thus in recent years much less attention has been paid to the history of racism over the centuries when racial differentiation, discrimination, and oppression were so deeply embedded in the South African social, political, and economic order. One of the aims of this essay is to re-focus on the historical – or, rather, historiographical – dimensions of racism in South Africa. The essay explores how the development and dynamics of South Africa's racial order have been explained in different ways and at different times. Attention will be paid to approaches and paradigms that became dominant at particular moments as well as to paradigm shifts and the contexts in which they occurred.[4]

The first of these approaches, "pluralist analysis," enjoyed a considerable following among social scientists, especially during the 1950s and 1960s. The pluralist approach contains different strands, and it can give rise to diverse, even opposing, political programs, as we shall see. But the approach docs rest on one basic assumption – that in many societies the fundamental divisions are racial, ethnic, and cultural. Such heterogeneous societies are deemed to be potentially unstable, with the likelihood of one racial or ethnic group assuming dominance and the consequent danger of interracial or interethnic conflict. In the South African case the pluralist approach gave rise to two lines of analysis – one ultra-conservative, the other liberal. According to the former, social and political stability in South Africa could only be achieved by recognizing the reality of racial differentiation and by securing power firmly in white hands. According to the latter, racial and ethnic cleavages posed a challenge best met by striving for interracial and interethnic cooperation. While both lines of analysis contained particular political agendas, they also both offered historical interpretations of how South Africa's racial order had evolved. It is these interpretations which now require consideration.

White supremacist ideology has not, of course, been the exclusive preserve of Afrikaner nationalism in South Africa. But for the purpose of this essay the focus will be on Afrikaner nationalist writing as an example of an ultra-conservative, essentialist, primordialist approach. We shall also see that this approach went through shifts during a period of about forty years in the 1930s. As Saul Dubow has observed, "Afrikaner nationalism was markedly slow to address directly the relationship between black and white South Africans."[5] It was only in the 1930s that leading Afrikaner thinkers began to examine that relationship. And when they did so they operated within a rigid racial pluralist framework. The existence and salience of racial categories went unquestioned. Racial groups were perceived as biological entities, and the distinctive character of each group was taken for granted. This basic assumption was propounded in the 1930s and 1940s by Afrikaner nationalist writers such as Badenhorst, Preller, Eloff, and Cronjé – with Eloff even going so far as to define Afrikaners themselves as a separate biological race group.[6] As late as 1959 Du Preez was still able to claim "it is an undeniable fact that racial differences actually exist, whether we can explain them or not. The Bantu and White man in South Africa belong to two different racial groups with distinctive and immutable racial characteristics."[7] The proponents of this view drew upon both science and theology to back their claim. Preller, for instance, writing in the late 1930s, referred to scientific analysis which was "gradually discovering the remarkable physiological differences between the brain of the white man ... and that of the Bantu, – differences which are innate and constitute the measure of their respective intellectual capacities."[8] And Cronjé and Du Preez, among others, saw racial differences as divinely ordained, as part of God's plan.[9]

This assumption had various implications. One was that there was no real need to explain, sociologically or historically, South Africa's racial order. Racial groups were considered to be natural components of human society – as natural a component as the family. Therefore race consciousness and a sense of identity with one's own race group was equally a natural part of the human make-up. The race instinct was normal, and a consciousness that was not race-oriented was deemed to be false consciousness.[10] This meant that the historical foundations of South Africa's racial order were taken for granted – racial separation was a natural process and in keeping with God's will.[11]

In time there came to be something of a departure from this assumption among Afrikaner nationalist writers. Indeed, by the late 1950s, Rhoodie and Venter were bemoaning the fact that, apart from Cronjé's writings, there was not "a single work which gives a reasonably detailed socio-historical or fundamental exposition of apartheid."[12] And so from this time some of these old assumptions about racial difference came to be taken less for granted among Afrikaner nationalists, and attempts were made to explain the country's racial order in historical terms.

While there may have been a shift away from the crude primordialist assumptions of this earlier generation of Afrikaner nationalist writers, those who attempted to explain the racial order in historical terms still remained firmly tied to an idealist line of analysis. Central to this historical explanation were a number of key ideas. Perhaps foremost among these was the notion that the history of the boers/Dutch/Afrikaners should be read as a long struggle to protect their racial/national identity. Rhoodie and Venter, for instance, wrote of the Afrikaners' particular "moral characteristics" which were based on Afrikaners' "determination to preserve their racial identity and an inherent realization of the 'difference' between themselves and the non-whites."[13] But there was more to it than simply protecting their identity. Other Afrikaner nationalist historians came to represent the history of the "volk" as a history of sheer survival. It is suggested that historical experience and the force of circumstance did much to shape boer racial attitudes from the nineteenth century. The voortrekkers who migrated into the South African interior after 1836, so the argument goes, did not develop a race policy but rather engaged in a straightforward struggle for survival. This was a quest for security which could only be achieved through the military subjugation of blacks, as well as their political exclusion and territorial separation. Thus security and survival became linked to the "race question." As one historian, Moolman, put it, for the Boers in the nineteenth century the daily fight for survival became a racial fight.[14]

In later Afrikaner nationalist historical writing attention was also paid to the development of racial attitudes. It was argued that virtually from the beginning of white colonization at the Cape in the mid-seventeenth century, the early Dutch colonists saw indigenous people as uncivilized and inferior. Three days after landing at the Cape, Van Riebeeck referred to the indigenous Khoi people as "wild" and "brutal."[15] According to this interpretation such attitudes soon became widely held among the white community. Because people of colour were deemed to be uncivilized and inferior it was therefore appropriate for them to be enslaved. A circular argument developed: people of colour were inferior and therefore naturally servile – and their enslavement and servitude confirmed this inferiority. When the trekboers came into contact with African communities on the eastern frontier in the late eighteenth century, white racial attitudes strengthened. Contact with Xhosa chiefdoms, so the argument continues, reinforced the developing image of Africans as treacherous and savage. Thus in the minds of the early Dutch/boer colonists, Christianity and civilization came to be associated with whiteness, while heathenism and barbarism were equated with blackness.[16]

Racial segregation could therefore be represented by Afrikaner nationalist historians as the logical consequence of these different levels of civilization. According to Van Jaarsveld, because whites regarded themselves as civilized and Christian, and saw blacks as uncivilized and heathen, the idea and practice of race differentiation came into being.[17] Moolman argues that the difference in the levels of civilization made political equality and social contact between white and black impossible.[18] And so it was easy for Afrikaner nationalist historians to claim that racial segregation developed naturally out of the historical relations between Dutch/boers/Afrikaners and indigenous communities.[19] Moreover, racial segregation was represented not only as logical and natural, but also as divinely ordained. In the nationalist version of South African history the boers were driven by devout Calvinist beliefs – by the idea that they were a chosen people with a special calling. Any idea of black-white equality would have contravened the word of God – they believed blacks were pre-ordained to serve whites.[20]

This brief survey of Afrikaner nationalist historical interpretations of South Africa's racial order reveals a few fundamental features. First, the writing falls within a racial pluralist paradigm. Racial difference was deemed to be a basic element of South African society and history. In its crudest form, as expressed in the 1930s and 1940s, this pluralist approach rested on the premise that races were distinct biological categories, and on the primordialist assumption that a strong sense of racial identity was an ingrained human instinct. Thus South Africa's racial order could be taken for granted, assumed to be part of the natural order of things. It needs to be said that such thinking was not at the time some bizarre South African aberration. It was a paradigm that enjoyed some degree of acceptance and legitimacy elsewhere. As Saxton has remarked, "Until about the third decade of the present century, most people in the so-called western world, including most social scientists and historians, took for granted the hereditary inferiority of non-white peoples. Differential treatment required no special explanation so long as it could be understood as a rational response to objective reality."[21] Indeed, some of the early Afrikaner proponents of racial theory studied during the 1930s in Germany where Nazi ideas about race were gaining adherence.[22]

A later generation of Afrikaner nationalist writers departed somewhat from these crude racial theories, but still remained solidly within a pluralist, idealist paradigm. Attempts were now made to explain racial differentiation and segregation through recourse, not to racial science, but to history. However, within this historical approach the existence of distinct racial categories still went unquestioned; and it continued to be assumed that a sense of identification with one's race and nation was a key force motivating human behaviour – and, therefore, also a crucial factor explaining the course of South African history.

There was, of course, a strong ideological dimension to Afrikaner nationalist historical writing. Many of these historians claimed that they were producing "objective-scientific" work in the Rankean tradition,[23] but in reality they were writing history to promote Afrikaner nationalism and to justify apartheid. Whereas the earlier generation of writers in the 1930s had had it somewhat easier in terms of the international acceptability of their ideas, however crude those ideas now seem, the later generation was engaged in an uphill battle. Amidst the post-war reaction against Nazism, racial theory came to be widely discredited. From the 1950s African decolonization proceeded apace. South Africa's apartheid policies flew in the face of the changing international order. Apartheid's apologists thus drew upon South African history to make their case. It was important that apartheid be represented, not as a crazy piece of National Party social engineering, but rather as a product of the country's past, as the culmination of a long evolutionary process of racial differentiation going back to the first days of white settlement, and therefore as a phenomenon that was "traditional" to South Africa, a special feature of the country's unique history and character.[24]

Some have questioned whether one can talk of a "liberal" school of South Africanist historians. However, there is little doubt that during a period of four or more decades from the late 1920s there appeared a body of writing, produced by historians and social scientists, that investigated and analysed South Africa's racial order on the basis of certain underlying ideas and premises. There were variations in these ideas from writer to writer, but there was a common overall framework that enables one to view these works as a body of writing. This framework was essentially pluralist, and it was one that enjoyed a considerable degree of hegemony in South African historical discourse during these decades.

When liberal pluralist writers set about trying to explain the origins and evolution of the South African racial order they did so, of course, with a different political agenda from that of the Afrikaner nationalists. While the latter were trying to justify a system of racial differentiation, the former were striving for interracial cooperation and harmony. However, what is striking is the degree to which the two shared similar assumptions about South African society and the course of history. Although each drew different conclusions and lessons from their study of the country's past, both proceeded from similar premises.

The most important shared assumptions were that racial categories were fundamental realities of South African society, that relations between different racial and ethnic groups were the central theme in South African history, and that those relations were characterized by a high level of antagonism and conflict. By the 1950s and 1960s this assumption had come to pervade much of the literature on South African society and history. Marquard, for instance, in his brief survey of South African history, wrote that by 1700 "the three main elements of South Africa's population were present, European, African, and Coloured."[25] These were crucial categories used in attempting to explain South Africa's past. For Van der Horst the census classification of South Africa's population into four major groups was "not simply a statistical abstraction or a legal classification but a social reality."[26] Perhaps the chief exponent of liberal pluralist analysis in the South African case was Van den Berghe, who described South Africa as "one of the world's most pluralistic societies."[27] For him the deepest cleavage in South African society was the racial one, accompanied by significant cultural divisions and a general absence of value consensus among different groups.[28] His view of South Africa was asserted unequivocally: "The only principle which pervades the whole society is that of 'race'."[29]

From this premise, that South Africa has long been a racially polarized society, there followed logically a further assumption – that racial division had, throughout South African history, given rise to racial conflict. Marquard stated this assumption explicitly: "The history of South Africa is the story of strife between the various groups composing the political union ... Until 1910, when Union was established, the story is one of war between tribe and tribe, between black and white, and between English and Afrikaner."[30] For Van den Berghe relations between South Africa's four main "racial castes" were "based mostly on conflict."[31] Conflict was thus deemed to be the natural outcome of racial division. It was further assumed that one of the sources of conflict was white race prejudice. From the early days of white settlement, so the story goes, whites developed a strong racial identity and sense of superiority over racial "others." From white racism flowed many evils – labour exploitation, land-grabbing, and a host of discriminatory measures against people of colour. In Van den Berghe's view white race prejudice was, and had long been, South Africa's fundamental problem: "At the very root of the 'South African Dilemma'," he claimed, "lies White racialism."[32] Take away this and the course of South African history would have been very different: "Had it not been for the development of a strong form of racial ... prejudice, South Africa could have developed into the same type of harmonious society, racially mixed and culturally Western, as is found in Latin America."[33]

Not all writers belonging to this "liberal" school saw race prejudice as being endemic from the very beginning of the white settlement. Indeed, there has been debate among historians as to whether racism originated in Europe or developed in the particular conditions of South Africa. Some argue that racism was brought to the Cape from Europe by the Dutch.[34] Others stress the local rather than metropolitan sources of white racism. Among the latter historians there are further differences. Some trace the origins of racism to Van Riebeeck, arguing that attitudes of white superiority developed from the 1650s. Others argue that the main cleavage in the early years of white settlement at the Cape was not racial, but religious – between Christian and non-Christian. They claim that white racism developed mainly during the frontier era of South African history, from the eighteenth century. Walker and Mac-Crone, writing in the 1930s, were the two chief proponents of this view. They argued that the remote frontier zones of the Cape and beyond were isolated from centres of "civilisation." So the white frontier pioneers, removed from colonial authority and competing with indigenous communities for resources, developed a lawless, individualist lifestyle, as well as a strong race consciousness – a sense of in-group solidarity and hostility towards racial "others" with whom they were competing. This era of white frontier expansion, argued Walker and MacCrone, was the crucial phase in the emergence of South Africa's racial order. It was crucial because the racist attitudes that were formed in the frontier environment were later carried over into the twentieth century – and so formed the basis of segregation and apartheid.[35]

Liberal pluralist writing on South Africa stressed not only the racial cleavage and conflict between white and black, but also ethnic divisions. One of these divisions deemed to be important historically was that between the English and the Afrikaners. And in the view of many liberal writers this division reflected, at least in part, different degrees of racism, with the boers/Afrikaners deemed to be generally more racist than English-speaking colonists – and therefore more blameworthy for segregation and apartheid. It has been common, for instance, to refer to two traditions of race relations in South Africa: the northern tradition of the nineteenth-century Boer republics, characterized by harsh race prejudice and rigid discrimination against people of colour, and the Cape liberal tradition, supposedly less discriminatory and more open to assimilationism and interracial cooperation.[36]

This dichotomization is seriously flawed. It is now well-established that the contribution of white English-speaking colonists and British imperial officialdom to the making of South Africa's racial order was no less significant than that of the Dutch/boers/Afrikaners. It is also ironic that this idea of a distinction between two traditions should have been propounded by historians and social scientists who shared many of the premises and assumptions of Afrikaner nationalists when it came to explaining South African history and society. As we have seen so far from this brief historiographical survey, both Afrikaner nationalist and liberal writers operated within the paradigm of racial pluralism, assuming race groups to be real categories and discrete entities, and deeming racial cleavages to be the primary divisions in South African society. Both, too, developed their analyses in the idealist tradition, stressing the significance of racial and ethnic consciousness as a major factor in South African history, and presuming political objectives to have been primary, while generally neglecting economic interests. Furthermore, according to both schools, South Africa's racial order had deep roots in the country's past and evolved over a long period of time from the early colonial era.

Although both these schools proceeded within a similar framework they were driven by very different political agendas. Whereas Afrikaner nationalists were trying to present a view of South Africa's history that would legitimize both apartheid and Afrikaner nationalism, liberals were striving to promote interracial cooperation and individualist values. The liberal view of South African history, as outlined above, gained ground from the 1930s. Before the 1930s a number of liberal thinkers in South Africa had supported segregationist policies as the best means to ensure social and political stability in South Africa.[37] However, from the early 1930s, liberals steadily moved away from segregationism. This was largely because they saw that greater economic and social integration was becoming a reality of South African life, and that a policy of racial segregation flew in the face of that reality. So they came to argue that the country's socio-political system should be amended along more liberal lines so as to adapt to this reality. They believed that its failure to adapt was largely the result of the ingrained, archaic, racist attitudes of most whites. As Van der Horst put it, "Yet while economic forces have been drawing black and white together, social and political adaptation on the part of the dominant white group has not kept pace. There has been a constant attempt by the whites to retain the benefits of economic integration and yet to insist upon a large measure of social and geographic segregation; to retain a monopoly of political power."[38] As part of their effort to promote interracial cooperation and harmony, some liberal writers argued that South Africa's past had not only been marked by racial division and conflict. These writers drew attention to past interracial cooperation, trying to downplay the emphasis on conflict.[39]

In trying to contextualize this liberal analysis of South African history and society it is also necessary to see how liberal writers came to pin the responsibility for segregation and apartheid on the boers/Afrikaners. This tendency became more pronounced in the 1950s and 1960s – for the obvious reason that during these decades the Afrikaner-dominated National Party government was tightening its system of racial discrimination and oppression at the very time that racism was becoming reviled in international circles. In this context it became much easier to represent Boers/Afrikaners as the chief proponents of racist thought and practice throughout South African history – a representation that is thoroughly misleading.

It was not just a political agenda that shaped the liberal idealist approach to South African history. Idealists were working within a paradigm that enjoyed a certain degree of hegemony in Western social science circles at that time, especially in the United States. A social psychologist has recalled how his "work of the 1950s was still largely conducted within the theoretical frame that dominated race relations research during the decade. That frame involved an emphasis on attitudes and stereotypes while paying scant attention to the macroinstitutional level of analysis."[40] This paradigm was certainly dominant, at least until the 1970s, among South Africanist historians and social scientists attempting to explain the evolution and dynamic of South Africa's racial order. However, from the early 1970s this dominant approach came to be seriously questioned and challenged.

It was fifty years ago that Oliver Cox suggested that "The interest behind racial antagonism is an exploitative interest – the peculiar type of economic exploitation characteristic of capitalist society."[41] It was more than twenty years before this idea gained significant or widespread application to the South African case. But when the analysis of racial oppression in South Africa did come to be based on this premise, the idea gained considerable adherence. Some might even say that the growth of Marxist analysis in the 1970s marked a significant paradigm shift in South African studies. The emergence of a "school" of radical, revisionist South Africanist scholars at that time is a story that has been told many times. All that is required here is a brief recapitulation of some of the salient points – or, more particularly, those aspects of the revisionist analysis which related to the history of South Africa's racial order.

The first thrust of this radical challenge was a forthright rejection of those pluralist and idealist assumptions which had been predominant for some decades. Pluralist analysis was deemed to be fundamentally flawed because it treated racial and ethnic categories as given realities, and because it saw relations between racial and ethnic groups as the crucial dynamic in divided societies. As Wolpe put it, such an approach wrongly conceived of race "as the irreducible constituent and determinant of social relations."[42] Johnstone rejected out of hand the very concept of "race relations" in his study of the South African gold mining industry.[43] Hand-in-hand with this critique of pluralism went an assault on idealist explanations of South Africa's racial order. Such explanations were deemed to focus too heavily on race attitudes and prejudice, and to rest on the false presupposition that the racial order was essentially a political/ideological phenomenon.[44] For Legassick, such an emphasis on white race attitudes failed to explain "the unfolding dynamics of South African society."[45] Segregation and apartheid were not primarily about separating races.

Two further commonly held liberal assumptions about the history of South Africa's racial order were also challenged by the revisionists. First, they rejected the notion that the racial order had evolved over a long period of time, from the early years of white colonization. Rather they viewed racial oppression as an essentially modern phenomenon, integrally bound up with the development of industrial capitalism in South Africa. Second, they questioned the view that the Boers/Afrikaners had been the most virulent racists in South African history and the main culprits responsible for segregation and apartheid. The racial order was seen not as an outgrowth of Afrikaner ethnicity, but rather a product of material forces.

So how did revisionist writers explain the making of the racial order in South Africa? There was no single explanation – different writers had different emphases – but there clearly was a dominant theme, within which there were variations. An unequivocal, perhaps extreme, statement of the revisionist interpretation was put forward by Davies, O'Meara, and Dlamini: "The national oppression of black people in South Africa is a product of, and was indeed the necessary historical condition for, the development of capitalism in that country."[46] They are quite explicit in stating that racial discrimination was "a product of" capitalism. Similarly, Johnstone set out to explain "the racial system not as some dysfunctional intrusion on the economic system from such outside, non-material factors as prejudice, racism, and 'social and cultural pluralism', but as a system generated and determined by the economic system of which it formed a part."[47] In short the racial order was essentially a system of class domination, designed to further the interests of capital.

The close connection between racial oppression and capitalism was central to this revisionist line of analysis. To establish this connection it became necessary to argue that the racial order was born of capitalism – hence the rejection of the older view that apartheid had deep roots in the past. If racial oppression grew out of capitalism such oppression could not have occurred on any significant scale in the precapitalist era. Rather, the growth of the racial order could only be explained if it was viewed in the context of South Africa's mining revolution in the last third of the nineteenth century. The revisionist argument started from a structural analysis of the gold-mining industry in its early phase when it came up against serious constraints on its profitability. These constraints placed an absolute imperative on the minimization of production costs. From this imperative there developed a system of racial oppression which made possible the ultra-exploitation of cheap black labour. A number of revisionist writers propounded the "cheap labour thesis" in the 1970s and 1980s. It is stated succinctly, for instance, by Lacey, for whom the policy of racial segregation "was designed as a coercive labour system geared to ensure capitalist profitability."[48]

An examination of one specific issue – the racial division of labour – serves to illustrate the difference between the pluralist, idealist interpretation and the materialist approach. According to the former, there was a racial division of labour in the mining industry because white workers had since the seventeenth century developed an aversion to performing unskilled manual labour which they deemed to be degrading and therefore the preserve of black people. The racial division of labour was thus explained as a manifestation of this long-held, irrational prejudice.[49] In contrast, some revisionists argued that the racial division of labour was a deliberate strategy of the mining industry and the state to divide the working class along racial lines so as to eliminate any threat that a united, organized working class might have posed to capitalist profitability. This position has been clearly stated by Ticktin: "the rigidities in the system, the common superiority of the whites, do not derive from previous history or from a shared 'whiteness' or common culture but rather from the need of the capitalist class, in order to survive, to find a means of dividing the working class."[50]

This shift away from pluralist, idealist explanations of the history of South Africa's racial order was not simply a change of intellectual direction in South African studies. It was rather part of a wider tendency. As one American sociologist recently recalled, "During the sixties and seventies there was this strong tendency to privilege structural explanations of all types and to downplay – almost with scorn – the relevance of cultural values or the importance of racial prejudice."[51] This was certainly the case among revisionist South Africanist social scientists and historians who became dismissive of cultural, ideological, and psychological factors, claiming that they had little significance in explaining the history of racial oppression in South Africa. At best it was conceded that racial ideologies could take on a life of their own once formulated.[52] But the generally held view was that the main function of racial ideology was to justify the extreme exploitation of black labour, and that the apparatus of racial discrimination was designed primarily to facilitate such exploitation.

While being influenced by international theoretical tendencies, the work of revisionist South Africanist writers was also fashioned in a particular political context. The new wave of Marxist writing appeared in the early 1970s, after the heavy political repression of the 1960s, when the apartheid system was being tightened and when extra-parliamentary opposition movements had been quelled. The prospects for a white change of heart and reform of the racial order – the hope of liberals – had all but vanished. Equally bleak was the likelihood of any popular uprising to overthrow the apartheid regime, at least in the near future. So the situation demanded new lines of analysis and innovative ways of conceptualizing South African society and history. Marxist theory and class analysis seemed to point to a new way forward.

The revisionist analysis of South African history and society was highly influential and had a considerable impact in the 1970s. However, the shortcomings of the approach were soon to become apparent.

A number of historians and social scientists who were broadly sympathetic to the overall materialist approach were, by the 1980s, critically re-evaluating some of the earlier revisionist assumptions about the history and nature of South Africa's racial order. The thrust of the critique was that the earlier writing had been too determinist, reductionist, functionalist, and mechanistic. The connection between capitalism and racism had been represented in a too stark and oversimplified way. Racism could not, argued the critics, be explained simply as the invention of capitalism.[53] The racial order could not just be viewed as a modern phenomenon with minimal roots in the distant past. Moreover, the materialists' overriding emphasis on political economy in their explanation of apartheid precluded any thorough investigation of "race" and racism. As Posel has observed, the research generated by the race-class debate "tended to say little, if anything, about racist institutions and practices which seemed more remote from the capitalist nexus."[54]

Those revisionist writers of the 1970s who were drawing conclusions about the history of the South African racial order were for the most part concentrating their focus on the era of industrial capitalism.[55] Apart from Legassick and Freund, few revisionist historians at that time were concerned with exploring the history of racial division and discrimination in the pre-industrial era.[56] So the view that racism was not rooted in the distant South African past tended to be asserted rather than substantiated with reference to historical evidence.

It may well have been this revisionist assumption, with its rather thin foundations, that prompted a rush of research into the history of South Africa's racial order in the pre-industrial era. Within a period of four years, between 1979 and 1983, there were published a number of important historical works which aimed to throw light on the subject of white racism during the first two hundred years or so of white settlement.[57] One significant feature of these works is that none of them can be fitted into the paradigms that have been considered thus far in this essay. They avoided the assumptions of pluralist analysis; and, although open to the materialist perspective, they were wary of its reductionist conclusions. Ross, for instance, was struck by "the general lack of a cogent Marxist theory on the origins of racist stratification in South Africa."[58] And Fredrickson set out "to comprehend the interaction and inter-relationship of 'race' and 'class' – of ethnic consciousness and economic advantage – without assigning a necessary priority to either."[59]

Accordingly their conclusions represented a departure from orthodox pluralist and materialist views. They rejected, for instance, the idea that rigid white racist attitudes had been ever-present since the early days of white settlement. Fredrickson saw a pattern of free fraternization between racial groups in Cape Town well into the twentieth century –

what he refers to as the city's "special tradition of multi-racialism."[60] Ross, Elphick, and Giliomee agree that in the pre-industrial Cape there was no systematic expression of race attitudes, no racist ideology or racial theory, no system of racial classification.[61] As Ross observes, "The eighteenth-century Cape was in no way a plural society in the sense that Furnivall, M.G. Smith, or Leo Kuper would define it, with specific ethnic blocks maintaining identities of their own and meeting only under specific, defined conditions."[62]

In this particular debate around the question of whether a racial order developed in the pre-industrial Cape, much attention has been given to the issue of miscegenation. For primordialist pluralists and the apologists of apartheid, the incidence of miscegenation in the early Cape was an awkward topic. Their response was usually one of denial – claiming that the only white men to consort with women of colour were transient sailors and soldiers. By contrast, some revisionist writers highlighted the occurrence of miscegenation to substantiate their point that racism was not a significant feature of the pre-industrial order. Both views were too simplified. The work of Elphick, Shell, and Fredrickson, based on more careful historical research, provides a necessary corrective. They show that in the seventeenth and eighteenth centuries, especially in Cape Town, it was common for white men to take women of colour as concubines and that there was a regular occurrence of intermarriage. White masters might cohabit with slave women, and by the late eighteenth century white trekboers in the eastern frontier districts were consorting with Khoi women. There was at the time no commonly held view that white racial purity should be preserved, that miscegenation was a form of contamination. However, these writers do qualify their view. Elphick and Shell suggest that miscegenation was more common in Cape Town than in the rural districts of the western Cape; and they insist that miscegenation and intermarriage did not threaten white dominance at the Cape.[63]

It is on this last point that this group of writers part company with the revisionist view that the racial order was barely developed before the nineteenth century. Indeed, Elphick and Giliomee see "the racial order as largely in place by the end of the eighteenth century."[64] They argue that there was a high coincidence of race and class in early Cape society: whites exercised power and made up the landholding class, while Khoisan and slaves formed the labouring class.[65] Fredrickson reinforces this point, arguing that the long experience of black servitude and enslavement "established a presumption that whites were naturally masters and members of a privileged group while nonwhites were meant to be their servants and social inferiors."[66] Ultimately Fredrickson adopts a compromise position in the race-class debate: "One way to comprehend the social structure of the late eighteenth- and early nineteenth-century Cape is to see it as a class society in which race mattered in the determination of status but was not all-important."[67]

These historians adopting an intermediate position also addressed the teleological question – was the eighteenth-century racial order an antecedent of twentieth-century segregation and apartheid? Ross is somewhat ambivalent on this issue. He states that apartheid institutions "must have had their roots in pre-industrial South Africa," but also argues that "the racial order of modern South Africa was in no way inherent in colonial society from its foundation."[68] These two statements can be reconciled with each other, but they do reflect the author's attempt to steer a course between the older liberal position with its emphasis on continuity and the revisionist stress on discontinuity. Elphick and Giliomee are less equivocal in their conclusion. They have no doubt that whites in eighteenth-century Cape Colony had a conviction of their own distinctiveness and enjoyed "virtually exclusive access to power and wealth." The long-term implications of this are made clear in the final sentence of the book: "These convictions and social realities formed the fateful legacy of the pre-industrial Cape to the modern people of South Africa."[69]

In this survey, admittedly a sketchy one, I have identified four main approaches to explaining the history of South Africa's racial order – they can be loosely labelled as primordialist pluralist, liberal pluralist, materialist, and "intermediate." Not all writing can necessarily be placed squarely in one or other of these categories. But most historians who have ventured interpretations of the history of racial division in South Africa can probably be identified more or less with one of those four schools – although there are exceptions. What is striking about the first three of these approaches in particular is that each fitted into a paradigm that enjoyed a level of international credibility at the time. For instance, the idea of racial groups being real, discrete entities displaying distinctive cultural traits was standard fare in the early decades of the twentieth century.[70] From the 1930s this idea gained extreme expression in some Afrikaner nationalist writing, and was reinforced by Nazi ideology. The idea also informed liberal pluralist analysis which was a widely supported approach in Western social science in the 1950s and 1960s. What separated the primordialist pluralists from the liberal pluralists was their different political agendas. The primordialists saw racial difference as an essential feature of human society and therefore argued that political systems should accommodate this deep-seated difference – an argument presented as an obvious apologia for apartheid. Liberal pluralists on the other hand, while recognizing that racial division and conflict had been a major factor shaping the course of South African history, still believed in an individualist ethos and a sense of common humanity, both of which could transcend or erode racial and ethnic divisions. Hence the agenda of the primordialists was conservative, and that of the liberals was reformist, even though both shared pluralist and idealist assumptions.

The materialist approach tended, at least in its most determinist form, to reduce racial ideology and racial discrimination to material forces. Again, this was a fashionable approach in the 1960s and 1970s, and it was adopted by a number of South Africanist social scientists and historians. In disavowing liberal reformism it seemed to offer a fresh, more radical approach to challenging the apartheid regime of the time. Only the last of the four lines of analysis, the so-called "intermediate" approach, cannot be linked to any dominant paradigm or to any particular political agenda at the time. This approach is labelled "intermediate" because its practitioners tried to steer a middle course in the race-class debate, avoiding the pitfalls both of pluralism and of economic determinism. Each of the scholars pursuing this line was a historian working in an empirical tradition according to which interpretations of the past had to be based on a careful examination of available evidence. (This, of course, does represent a paradigm in itself – a long-standing one within the discipline of history.) Moreover, each of the scholars would have been, in their private lives, firmly opposed to apartheid, but there is little in their historical writing to suggest a particular strategy for opposing or ending apartheid. It appears that their project was more purely historical – to explain the origins and evolution of South Africa's racial order.

Research into the history of South Africa's racial order probably peaked in the early 1980s. The work of Fredrickson, Ross, Elphick, and Giliomee placed questions about the origins and nature of that order at the forefront of South African historiography. However, the main focus of these scholars was on the pre-industrial era. So how would the industrial era – the era of segregation and apartheid – be revisited and reconceptualized? Or would the materialist have the last word in the race-class debate?

Since the mid-1980s there have been two main developments in the historiography of the South African racial order. The first has been a growing interest in the history of racial ideology. Here the work of Dubow, Rich, and Bank has been particularly important.[71] The critique of the economism and reductionism of the Marxists demanded that ideology no longer be treated as a mere epiphenomenon, that it be accorded both investigatory and explanatory weight. So from Dubow's work in particular comes a fuller understanding of racial theory and scientific racism, as propounded by eugenicists, social Darwinists,

South African scientists and Afrikaner nationalist intellectuals from the late nineteenth century and through much of the twentieth.

However this work on racial ideology did leave a key question unanswered: what was the significance of racial theory and scientific racism in the making of South Africa's racial order? Dubow himself was well aware of the difficulty, noting that "one of the most intractable problems in intellectual history" is to gauge the impact of ideas on society.[72] Did the ideas emanating from racial theorists in any way determine and shape the discriminatory policies and institutions of twentieth-century South Africa? Or was it more a case of the power-players and policymakers seizing upon these ideas in an attempt to render some legitimacy to their racial projects? These are difficult questions, but it is evident that some elements of racial theory did become deeply embedded in popular consciousness and discourse. Foremost among these was the notion that race groups constituted real, distinct entities. This was a notion endorsed not only by "science," but also by the common-sense view that physiological differences between people basically corresponded with cultural differences.[73]

While Dubow and others have brought a sharper focus on racial ideology, Adam Ashforth has used discourse analysis to bring a fresh perspective to the study of South Africa's racial order. He has analyzed the reports of a series of twentieth-century official commissions of inquiry set up to investigate the "native question" in South Africa. He has studied these reports as texts that deployed metaphorical techniques to convey an authoritative sense of South African realities, based on "expert," "scientific" knowledge.[74] Ashforth was one of the first scholars to adopt a postmodernist approach to understanding South Africa's racial order. His work is an exploration of the relationship between knowledge and power, with a strong emphasis on the importance of language. He makes no attempt to uncover any kind of underlying dynamic determining patterns of differentiation and discrimination in South Africa.

The most overtly postmodernist text on apartheid is Aletta Norval's book, *Deconstructing Apartheid Discourse*. The focus of her work is "the discourse of apartheid: the multifarious practices and rituals, verbal and non-verbal, through which a certain sense of reality and understanding of the nature of society were constituted and maintained." She concentrates on the surface of apartheid, rejecting as problematic any attempt to search for some hidden, underlying essence, "for such attempts tend to be bewitched by a metaphysical illusion of depth."[75] She disavows class reductionism, preferring to examine those elements of apartheid discourse which enabled whites, particularly Afrikaners, to make sense of their everyday life.

Norval's work is in line with other postmodernist work on "race" and racism that rejects both essentialist and reductionist approaches.[76] Foremost among the essentialist approaches is one that rests on a biological definition of "race" – a view that had wide adherence in the earlier decades of the twentieth century (and has already been considered in this essay). It is a view that is rightly and readily dismissed – but its rejection cannot be specially attributed to postmodernist analysis. For the past few decades such biological essentialism has been anathema to any credible social scientist, whether postmodernist or not.

While the dismissal of essentialist notions of "race" is now commonplace, the postmodernist critique of Marxist analysis as reductionist is more problematic. Here the danger is that the baby gets thrown out with the bathwater. It is one thing to reject crude reductionism and economic determinism, but quite another to throw out materialist analysis altogether. Indeed, a striking feature of Norval's work is the degree to which she draws upon the writing of Marxist scholars in her analysis. It can be argued that Marxists may have too easily dismissed racism as false consciousness and therefore paid too little attention to the phenomenon. At the same time, though, they made a crucial contribution in linking racial differentiation and discrimination to broader social and economic forces. It is simplistic to dismiss that linkage as reductionism. And it is important to build upon the insights of materialist scholars who have analyzed South Africa's racial order. The findings and conclusions of these scholars were never definitive – no findings ever are – but they did represent a significant analytical and interpretative breakthrough which has not been matched by subsequent generations of scholars who have tried to explain the history of racism in South Africa.

NOTES

1 See Deborah Posel, Jonathan Hyslop, Noor Nieftagodien. "Debating 'Race' in South African Scholarship." *Transformation* 47 (2001): xiii.
2 See Gerhard Maré. "Race Counts in Contemporary South Africa: 'An Illusion of Ordinariness'." *Transformation* 47 (2001).
3 Deborah Posel. "Race as Common Sense: Racial Classification in Twentieth-century South Africa." *African Studies Review* 44, no. 2 (2001).
4 See also Paul Maylam. *South Africa's Racial Past: The History and Historiography of Racism, Segregation and Apartheid*. Aldershot 2001.
5 Saul Dubow. *Illicit Union: Scientific Racism in Modern South Africa*. Johannesburg 1995, 248–49.
6 Ibid., 273; F.G. Badenhorst. *Die Rassevraagstuk*. Amsterdam 1939, 14, 20; Gustav Preller. *Day-Dawn in South Africa*. Pretoria 1938, 149–51; G. Cronjé. *Voogdyskap en Apartheid*. Pretoria 1948, 31.

7 A.B. Du Preez. *Inside the South African Crucible*. Pretoria 1959, 41.
8 Preller. *Day-Dawn*. 149–50.
9 J.M. Coetzee. "The Mind of Apartheid: Geoffrey Cronjé (1907-)." *Social Dynamics* 17, no. 1 (1991): 9; Du Preez. *South African Crucible*. 56, 85.
10 Coetzee. "Geoffrey Cronjé." 12.
11 Johannes du Bruyn. "Swartes in die Afrikanergeskiedskrywing." In *Afrikaanse Geskiedskrywing en Letterkunde: Verlede, Hede, en Toekoms*, ed. H.C. Bredekamp. Bellville 1992, 72–73.
12 N.J. Rhoodie and H.J. Venter. *Apartheid*. Pretoria 1960, 6.
13 Ibid., 49.
14 J.P.F. Moolman. "Die Boer se Siening van en Houding Teenoor die Bantoe in Transvaal tot 1860." MA thesis, University of Pretoria, 1975, 14. See also G.D. Scholtz. *Die Ontwikkeling van die Politieke Denke van die Afrikaner: Deel II 1806–1854*. Johannesburg 1970, 398, 401, and *Deel III 1854–1881*. Johannesburg 1974, 223, 228.
15 Moolman. "Die Boer se Siening," 7.
16 Ibid., 2, 7, 13, 16–17, 33, 35, 101; Scholtz. *Deel I 1652–1806*, 206, 216–19, and *Deel II 1806–1854*, 213–14; F.A. Van Jaarsveld *Die Evolusie van Apartheid*. Cape Town 1979, 3.
17 Van Jaarsveld. *Die Evolusie van Apartheid*, 5.
18 Moolman. "Die Boer se Siening," 80–1.
19 Du Bruyn. "Afrikanergeskiedskrywing," 72.
20 Moolman. "Die Boer se Siening," 15, 23, 79, 83; F.A. Van Jaarsveld. *The Afrikaner's Interpretation of South African History*. Cape Town 1964, 5–6. For a refutation of this view, see A. Du Toit, "No Chosen People: The Myth of the Calvinist Origin of Afrikaner Nationalism and Racial Ideology." *American Historical Review* 88 (1983).
21 Alexander Saxton. *The Rise and Fall of the White Republic*. London 1990, 2.
22 Dubow. *Illicit Union*, 255, 270; Albert Grundlingh. "Politics, Principles and Problems of a Profession: Afrikaner Historians and Their Discipline, c.1920-c.1965." *Perspectives in Education* 12, no. 1 (1990): 9.
23 Grundlingh. "Afrikaner Historians," 1.
24 It is worth noting that some Afrikaner nationalist writers found it necessary, particularly from the late 1950s when South Africa faced mounting international criticism, to produce work in English – in an attempt partly to appease international opinion and partly to win support from white English-speaking voters in South Africa. See, for instance, Du Preez. *South African Crucible*, and Rhoodie and Venter. *Apartheid*.
25 Leo Marquard. *The Peoples and Policies of South Africa*. London 1962, 2.
26 Sheila Van der Horst. "The Effects of Industrialisation on Race Relations in South Africa." In *Industrialisation and Race Relations*, ed. Guy Hunter. London 1965, 99–100.
27 Pierre Van den Berghe. *Race and Ethnicity*. New York 1970, 81.

28 Ibid., 83; Pierre Van den Berghe. *South Africa: A Study in Conflict*. Middletown 1965, 38.
29 Van den Berghe. *South Africa*, 72.
30 Marquard. *Peoples and Policies*, 32.
31 Van den Berghe. *South Africa*, 267. See also K.L. Roskam. *Apartheid and Discrimination*. Leyden 1960, 9. It should, though, be recognized that not all liberal scholars stressed the conflictual nature of South African history – some focused on instances of interracial cooperation during the country's past. See below.
32 Van den Berghe. *South Africa*, 245.
33 Ibid., 41.
34 See, for instance, L. Guelke. "The Origins of White Supremacy in South Africa: An Interpretation." *Social Dynamics* 15, no. 2 (1989).
35 Eric A. Walker. *The Frontier Tradition in South Africa*. London 1930, 7, 12, 22–4; I.D. MacCrone. *Race Attitudes in South Africa*. London 1937, 98–101, 109, 135–6. A number of other historians and social scientists adopted this "frontier thesis" which was still being propounded in the 1950s and 1960s. See, for instance, Van den Berghe. *South Africa*, 23–4, and Sheila Patterson. *The Last Trek*. London 1957, 9–11, 17–19.
36 Walker. *Frontier Tradition*, 8; Marquard. *Peoples and Policies*, 14–16; Van der Horst. "Effects of Industrialisation," 105–6; Ralph Horwitz. *The Political Economy of South Africa*. New York 1967, 10–11.
37 See Saul Dubow. *Racial Segregation and the Origins of Apartheid in South Africa 1919–36*. Basingstoke 1989, 21–45.
38 Van der Horst. "Effects of Industrialisation," 101.
39 C.C. Saunders. *The Making of the South African Past*. Cape Town 1988, 95–96.
40 Thomas F. Pettigrew. "How Events Shape Theoretical Frames: A Personal Statement." In *A History of Race Relations Research*, ed. John H. Stanfield II. California 1993, 164.
41 Oliver C. Cox. *Caste, Class and Race*. New York 1970, xxxi.
42 Harold Wolpe. *Race, Class and the Apartheid State*. London 1988, 12. For another trenchant critique of pluralism, see Frederick A. Johnstone. *Class, Race and Gold*. London 1976, 5–6, 208–10.
43 Johnstone. *Class, Race and Gold*, 5.
44 Ibid., 8, 206; Wolpe. *Race, Class*, 25.
45 Martin Legassick. "South Africa: Forced Labour, Industrialization and Racial Differentiation." In *The Political Economy of Africa*, ed. Richard Harris. Cambridge MA 1975, 232.
46 Rob Davies, Dan O'Meara and Sipho Dlamini. *The Struggle for South Africa*. London 1984, i, 2.
47 Johnstone. *Class, Race and Gold*, 215.

48 Marian Lacey. *Working for Boroko*. Johannesburg 1981, xi. See also, Johnstone. *Class, Race and Gold*, 22–5; Harold Wolpe. "Industrialism and Race in South Africa." In *Race and Racialism*, ed. Sami Zubaida. London 1970, 168–70; Bernard Magubane. *The Political Economy of Race and Class in South Africa*. New York 1979, 14; Martin Legassick. "Gold, Agriculture, and Secondary Industry in South Africa, 1885–1970: From Periphery to Sub-Metropole as a Forced Labour System." In *The Roots of Rural Poverty in Central and Southern Africa*, eds. Robin Palmer and Neil Parsons. London 1977, 193.

49 See G.V. Doxey. *The Industrial Colour Bar in South Africa* (London, 1961).

50 Hillel Ticktin, *The Politics of Race Discrimination in South Africa*. London 1991, 12. See also Robert H. Davies. *Capital, State and White Labour in South Africa 1900–1960*. Brighton 1979, 100; Magubane. *Political Economy*, 16.

51 Bob Blauner. "'But Things Are Much Worse for the Negro People': Race and Radicalism in My Life and Work." In *Race Relations Research*, ed. Stanfield, 30.

52 Magubane. *Political Economy*, 225.

53 Shula Marks and Richard Rathbone. "Introduction." In Shula Marks and Richard Rathbone. *Industrialisation and Social Change in South Africa*. London 1982, 5. See also Belinda Bozzoli. "Class, Community and Ideology in the Evolution of South African Society." In *Class, Community and Conflict*, ed. Belinda Bozzoli. Johannesburg 1987, 1–2; and D.B. Posel. "Rethinking the 'Race-Class Debate' in South African Historiography." *Social Dynamics* 9, no. 1 (1983).

54 Deborah Posel. "Apartheid and Race." In *A Companion to Racial and Ethnic Studies*, eds. D. Goldberg and J. Solomos. Oxford 2001, 77.

55 I am here excluding those historians (such as Guy, Bonner, Wright, Peires, and Delius) who worked in the field of pre-colonial African history – they were generally not trying to explain the history of South Africa's racial order.

56 See Martin Legassick. "The Frontier Tradition in South African Historiography." In *Economy and Society in Pre-industrial South Africa*, eds. Shula Marks and Anthony Atmore. London 1980, and W.M. Freund. "Race in the Social Structure of South Africa, 1652–1836." *Race and Class* 18, no. 1 (1976).

57 Richard Elphick and Hermann Giliomee, eds. *The Shaping of South African Society 1652–1820*. Cape Town 1979; George M. Fredrickson. *White Supremacy*. Oxford 1981; Robert Ross. "Pre industrial and Industrial Racial Stratification in South Africa." In *Racism and Colonialism*, ed. Robert Ross. The Hague 1982; Robert Ross (with D. Van Arkel and G.C. Quispel). "Going Beyond the Pale: On the Roots of White Supremacy in South Africa." In Robert Ross. *Beyond the Pale*. Hanover 1993 – this essay was originally published (in Dutch) in 1983.

58 Ross. "Racial Stratification in South Africa," 83.
59 Fredrickson. *White Supremacy*, xx.
60 Ibid., 258–60. This assumption has recently been challenged – see Vivian Bickford-Smith. "South African Urban History, Racial Segregation and the 'Unique' Case of Cape Town." *Journal of Southern African Studies* 21, no. 1 (1995).
61 Ross. "Going Beyond the Pale," 85–6, 90; Richard Elphick and Hermann Giliomee. "The Origins and Entrenchment of European Dominance at the Cape, 1652-c.1840." In *The Shaping of South African Society, 1652–1840*, eds. Richard Elphick and Hermann Giliomee. Cape Town 1989, 532. For the purpose of this discussion, I will be referring to the revised, expanded edition of this work.
62 Ross. "Going Beyond the Pale," 72.
63 Richard Elphick and Robert Shell. "Intergroup Relations: Khoikhoi, Settlers, Slaves and Free Blacks, 1652–1795." In *Shaping of South African Society* (1989 edition), eds. Elphick and Giliomee, 194–204; Fredrickson. *White Supremacy*, 110–17, 122–3.
64 Elphick and Giliomee. "European Dominance," 522.
65 Ibid., 559–60.
66 Fredrickson. *White Supremacy*, 92–3.
67 Ibid., 88.
68 Ross. "Going Beyond the Pale," 71, 90.
69 Elphick and Giliomee. "European Dominance," 561.
70 Dubow. *Illicit Union*, 20, 74.
71 See, for instance, Dubow. *Illicit Union*; P. Rich. "Race, Science, and the Legitimization of White Supremacy in South Africa, 1902–1940." *International Journal of African Historical Studies* 23, no. 4 (1990); Andrew Bank. "Liberals and Their Enemies: Racial Ideology at the Cape of Good Hope, 1820 to 1850." Ph.D thesis, Cambridge University, 1995.
72 Dubow. *Illicit Union*, 286.
73 Posel. "Race as Common Sense," 94.
74 Adam Ashforth. *The Politics of Official Discourse in Twentieth Century South Africa*. Oxford 1990.
75 Aletta Norval. *Deconstructing Apartheid Discourse*. London 1996, 2.
76 See, for instance, Ali Rattansi, "Just Framing: Ethnicities and Racisms in a 'Postmodern' Framework." In *Social Postmodernism: Beyond Identity Politics*, eds. Linda Nicholson and Steven Seidman. Cambridge 1995, 251–5.

FRANCES HENRY AND CAROL TATOR

A Critical Discourse Analysis of the *Globe and Mail* Editorials on Employment Equity

Media representations are discursive formations that are part of our everyday culture. Their discourses have enormous power not only to represent social groups but also to identify, regulate, and even construct social groups – to establish who is "we" and who is the "other" in the "imagined community" of the nation state. At the level of public discourse, this creates an ideological climate that seems invisible and natural to those immersed in it, but that contains unchallenged assumptions about marginalized groups circulated and disseminated by the mass media and other systems of cultural production and representation. These cultural instruments play a critical role in controlling the access of those marginalized groups to cultural, social, economic, and political power.[1]

The images circulated by Canada's media (newspapers, television, and radio, film, music, videos, literary works, theatre, and other vehicles of cultural production) are not images that African Canadians, Asian Canadians, or First Nations people would present of themselves. Members of the dominant culture can feel secure in the wide spectrum of representations they see of themselves in the media. However, minority communities do not have that luxury, and instead are sensitive to the biased and frequently negative images with which they are portrayed in the media. Such images contribute to the sense of "otherness," which they experience in the cultural and representation systems of society.

In this paper the *Globe and Mail*'s discourse on the subject of employment equity as contained in a series of editorials is examined to demonstrate how this newspaper sustains an anti-equity ideological position. The authors use two different forms of critical discourse analysis (CDA). The first form of CDA we apply (influenced by Wetherell and Potter 1992) utilizes a macro-level framework to explore the erroneous assumptions, myths, and misrepresentations that underpin the *Globe*'s editorials. This approach focuses on the broad rhetorical strategies, central themes and topics, and argumentative statements used to "other" minorities, and to critique the policy of employment equity. This macro-analysis will help illuminate how "text" and "talk" (van Dijk 1988) are used to promote, support, and communicate a particular ideology – in effect, to maintain the power held by white, able-bodied males. The *Globe* uses a form of argumentation that draws on democratic liberal values and principles.

The second method of CDA focuses on the linguistic structures the *Globe*'s editors use in constructing their editorials. Following both van Dijkian categories (1991) and Fairclough's classifications (1992), we examine the organization of the text, and show how through the choice of specific words, images, and sentence structures, a discourse is constructed. Fairclough (1992) notes that there are three dimensions to CDA: description of text; interpretation of the interaction processes and their relationship to text; and an explanation of how the interaction process relates to social action. The editorials we have selected come from time periods when the issue rose to the top of the public agenda.

Van Dijkian critical linguistic analysis (1998) strongly emphasizes the significance of editorial writing. It is important to analyze editorials because they are not merely idle statements of senior writers' opinions; often they express the broader ideological stance of the newspaper's owners and managers. They are evidence of the interlocking power structures of any given society; in fact, they are often addressed not only to the reading public but more narrowly to society's economic and power elites. Van Dijk (1991) categorizes editorials according to the following elements:

- Definition. The editorial defines a situation or event.
- Explanation. The editorial explains the situation.
- Evaluation or moral commentary. The editorial discusses "what will happen, what should happen, or what should be done" about an event or situation.

At the time these editorials were written, the *Globe* was the only national newspaper in the country. It was also the main media vehicle for Canada's conservative elements and political right wing. Its criticisms of employment equity legislation did much to undermine that legislation, and may well have helped ensure that it was rescinded in the province of Ontario. It is worth noting here that in the debate on Bill 8, the job Quotas Repeal Act 1995, that took place in the Ontario Legislature, a Conservative MPP stated: "Let me also quote very briefly from a *Globe and Mail* article 'Designed by well-meaning people to encourage integration, employment equity in fact works against it, encouraging Canadians to huddle together in groups and feed the unhealthy obsession with race and gender that has seized Canadian society in the 1990s'." Later, the same MPP quoted the *Globe* again: "Every Canadian should give it hearty good riddance" (Hansard, 30 October 1995, session 36.1).

BACKGROUND TO THE ENACTMENT OF EMPLOYMENT EQUITY LEGISLATION

Concern over employment discrimination against people of colour (visible minorities), women, people with disabilities, and Aboriginal peoples led the federal government to establish a royal commission on equality in employment (Abella 1984). Its task was to inquire into the employment practices of eleven designated Crown and government-owned corporations and to explore the most effective means of promoting equality for the four groups cited above. Its findings echoed earlier studies and public inquiries: bias and discrimination were endemic in the employment system. The commissioner, Judge Rosalie Abella, argued in the commission's report that strong measures were needed to remedy the impact of discriminatory attitudes and behaviours.

She recommended employment equity legislation. The Employment Equity Act became law in 1986, and applies to Crown corporations and federally regulated employers with 100 or more employees. The act was intended to establish equality in the workplace and to correct the conditions of disadvantage in employment experienced by four designated groups: women, Aboriginal peoples, people with disabilities, and members of visible minorities (Agocs et al. 1992). Employment equity legislation provided a framework to support a diverse workforce. Employment equity was supposed to identify workplace policies and practices that, though neutral in their intentions, were discriminatory in their effects or results. The goal of employment equity was fair treatment and equitable representation throughout the workplace (Agocs and Jain 2001; Jain et al. 2003).[2]

Equality in employment means that no one can be denied opportunities for reasons that have nothing to do with inherent ability (Abella 1984). The act required all federally regulated employers to file an annual report with the Canadian Employment and Immigration Commission. This report was to provide information for a full year on the representation of members of designated groups by occupational group and salary range, and on members of those groups who had been hired, promoted, or terminated. Employers were also required to prepare an annual employment equity plan with goals and timetables, and to retain this plan for at least three years. The Employment Equity Act was revised by Parliament in 1995; the legislation was strengthened, and the public service, the RCMP, and the military were brought under the purview of the act.

The language of the federal act was not itself racialized; however, responses to the legislation within and outside government were racialized in a number of ways. Efforts to make the Canadian public service more representative of the Canadian public had failed. The 1996 Annual Report of the Canadian Human Rights Commission documented in stark numbers the huge gap between the government's commitment to a fully diversified public service and its dismal record in promoting minorities.[3] Census data from 1996 and 2001 demonstrate that racial discrimination in employment continues to be pervasive in Canadian workplaces. Research studies (Mensah 2002; Samuel 1997) show that the federal government is "among the worst violators" of national employment equity policies. In examining some of the reasons for the failure to eradicate discrimination, Senator Noel Kinsella – a one-time senior bureaucrat with Heritage Canada – noted that "Institutions act as collective memory carrying forward values, principles, and traditions" (quoted in Samuel and Karam 1996).

Faced with the finding that discrimination against designated groups was widespread, persistent, and systemic, in 1993 Ontario became the first province in Canada to introduce employment equity legislation. As one of their first acts of governance, on 13 December 1995, the newly elected conservative government led by Premier Mike Harris rescinded the legislation. In retracting employment equity legislation the government incorporated the rhetorical strategies that the *Globe* had utilized in the campaign against employment equity. The title of the act, Bill to Repeal Job Quotas and the name given to the new legislation, Equal Opportunity Plan, reflected a discursive shift away from the discourse of the former NDP government. The Conservative government was rejecting the concept of systemic discrimination, in effect declaring that the Ontario Human Rights Code and Commission could deal with any individual cases of discrimination (Goldberg 1996).

RHETORICAL ARGUMENTS USED BY THE *GLOBE AND MAIL*

We analyze the first set of editorials by focusing on the central arguments the editors used to challenge the concept of employment equity and the legislation pertaining to it. Our analysis shows that the editors utilized a discourse that was based on the idea of liberalism. These editorials also utilized discursive elements that were based on a number of misrepresentations, unsubstantiated assertions, anecdotes, and erroneous assumptions. They disguised their attacks on employment equity as defences of traditional Canadian values. The central discourses, which were closely interlinked, were as follows:

"Employment equity is reverse discrimination."

In their editorial "The Discrimination Clause" (8 March 1995, A18), the editors argued that the law "effectively discriminates against some individuals on the basis of colour and gender." Farther down it became clear that the editor's target was "overt discrimination in hiring against white, able-bodied males." In "Why Merit Matters" (13 October 1995), the editors contended: "The bill is clearly discriminatory. By requiring employers to favour members of designated groups, it effectively requires them to discriminate against members of the undesignated group: that is, able-bodied white men."

"Employment equity is hiring by quotas and ignores the merit principle."

In "Why Merit Matters" (13 October 1995), the editors argued that the legislation "was unquestionably a quota law ... The main evil of the law is its implicit attack on the principle of merit." The editors went on to argue that the merit principle has

always been cherished most dearly by the disadvantaged who regard it as a ladder to better things. For generations, even centuries, disadvantaged people have pleaded to be released from the pigeonholes in which others place them and evaluated on their ability as individuals ...

The supporters of employment equity would throw all this out the window ... Instead of disregarding the group identity of people in hiring and promotion, we will fixate on it. Instead of encouraging employers to hire the best person for the job, we will require them to tote up their workers like so many jelly beans.

On the editorial page, on 18 March 1995, in an opinion piece titled "This Is No Way to Run a Railroad. Or a Newspaper. Or a Province," the *Globe*'s editor-in-chief, William Thorsell, argued that "ambitious social engineers in Ontario have taken us beyond the negative option of human rights law ... and into the affirmative option of hiring quotas." He went on to contend that affirmative action requires discrimination in hiring based on sex, race, and ability.

The *Globe* editorial "Real Employment Equity" (13 June 1995) supported the election promise of the Conservative government to rescind employment equity. It stated that the legislation "set up a quota system for hiring in Ontario. It would have prevented some companies from hiring the most talented people. It would have required employers to discriminate against some individuals (especially able-bodied white males) to benefit others." This editorial went on to argue that employment equity encourages "Ontarians to think of each other – and resent each other – as racial and gender units."

The theme of identity politics was revisited in the editorial "Please Identify Yourself" (18 June 1996, A14), in which the editors contended: "The decomposition of true liberalism into identity politics afflicts more than interest groups such as the National Action Committee on the Status of Women." This same piece said of the rescinding of employment equity in Ontario: "Ontario came within a hair's breadth of state employment quotas based on race and disability."

This same editorial concluded by sharply criticizing the University of British Columbia's advertisement for a president for including a statement of concern about the under-representation of women, Aboriginal people, visible minorities, and people with disabilities. The *Globe* understood the statement "the university welcomes all qualified applicants, especially members of these designated employment equity groups" to mean that "UBC is prepared to discriminate in hiring on the basis of race, gender, and disability in hiring its president."

"Employment equity challenges the fundamental tenets of liberalism such as individual rights and equal opportunity"

On 18 March 1995, in a piece titled "There Are Not Two Kinds of Equality in the World," Thorsell wrote that there are not two kinds of equality: equality of opportunity as enshrined in Section 15(1) of the Charter of Rights and Freedoms, and equality of outcomes as sanctioned by Section 15(2) of the Charter. The Charter sanctions affirmative action laws, programs, and activities as means of ameliorating the conditions of disadvantaged groups. He maintained that "the individual's right to equal protection and benefit of the law" in Subsection (2) is a right that "defines our democracy." He rejected the notion of substantive equality – that is, that the state must ensure that all social groups reap equal benefits from the law, even if different or special treatment is required to ensure such equality. He argued that equal opportunity allows all individuals to participate in all aspects of Canadian life. In his article of 18 March, he declared that we are in "a moral and philosophical mess. The nullification of individual rights in favour of group preferences mocks the very foundation of our democracy." The ideological schemata underpinning Thorsell's perspective are based on the following implicit and erroneous assumptions:

1 The only "qualified," meritorious individuals for jobs or promotions are white, able-bodied males.
2 Discrimination may exist in isolated instances, but women and minorities do not suffer from systemic discrimination. Most employers are "colour-blind," and neutral in their attitudes toward hiring and promoting women, people with disabilities, and Aboriginal peoples.
3 In a liberal democracy, individual rights must take primacy over group rights. Any recognition of group rights leads directly to the unravelling of the democratic state.
4 Equal opportunity is presumed to exist, so employment equity is an unnecessary intrusion and intervention by the state. Fairness is best achieved by treating everyone the same.
5 Employment equity requires that white, able-bodied males be excluded from workplaces and results in an epidemic of reverse discrimination.
6 Any legislation or public policy that targets a particular group for "preferential treatment" leads to victim-focused identities, conflict, and division.
7 Employment equity and other proactive, affirmative-based programs are a serious threat to a liberal democratic society.

A MICRO-LEVEL LINGUISTIC ANALYSIS OF THE DISCOURSE OF EMPLOYMENT EQUITY

In the following section, we carry out a more detailed linguistic (micro-level) analysis of the *Globe*'s discourse on employment equity, examining the actual structure of news-making through editorial writing.

Editorial 1: "Time for Debate on Employment Equity" (17 February 1995)

This editorial's headline calls for a debate, but the editorial itself does not. The use of the term "debate" makes it sound as if the editorial writers want a true dialogue or debate to take place, rather than unilateral actions. The article does not really call for debate except in the last paragraph, where it asks political parties to take a stand on the issue of employment equity. In sum, it is not asking Canadians to debate employment equity but to fight it. "Canadians like to think of themselves as more liberal and progressive than Americans, but in at least one area, the United States has been 'ahead' for years ... Pollsters say Californians would approve [employment equity legislation] by a big majority. No doubt Canadians would too, if asked a similar question."

The source, or evidence, for this assertion is "pollsters." No other source for this or the following statements is offered. That Canadians would also follow this lead shows presupposition without evidence; there is no indication that Canadians would also approve the proposal. "Though most would support removing barriers to equal employment in the workplace, the idea that governments ... is as repugnant to most Canadians as it is to Americans. Some opinion polls here have shown a three to one majority against affirmative action." The phrase "though most would support" is not backed by any evidence that most Canadians would support removing barriers. It is based on an assumption which refers back to the "liberal and progressive" ethos of this society which implies that Canadians really are progressive people and that this legislation is not in keeping with such progressiveness. Moreover, by citing the three-to-one majority against affirmative action, the editorial is playing a numbers game the intent of which is to impress readers with how many are against the policy.

This quotation is also vague in that nowhere does it state the actual numbers in the three-to-one judgment. "Last year, it brought in the country's most heavy-handed employment equity law ... How are Canadians going to fight these laws?" The use of language such as "heavy-handed" is an example of hyperbole, or exaggerated language. So is the idea that such laws need to be "fought." "Not obviously through human rights commissions ... not through direct democracy either ... not even through the charter." By calling into play other government agencies created through legislation, the editorial is impugning the human rights laws that already exist in Canada and dismissing them as incapable of "fighting" against employment equity legislation. Furthermore, it is planting by autosuggestion the idea that the people have lost their voice because "direct democracy" and its procedures will not work. It is suggesting that employment equity legislation is so terrible that ordinary democratic procedures cannot stop it. In saying "Not through the Charter of Rights and Freedoms" the *Globe and Mail* rejects constitutional remedies.

How are Canadians going to fight these laws? The editorial argues that the fight must use "ordinary political processes" and calls on political parties to show how this legislation "accords with Canadian values of fairness and equal opportunity." By again referring to these Canadian values, the article is once more framing the employment equity legislation as negating or being against these basic and positive Canadian values.

The moral of this editorial is that employment equity needs to be placed again on the "political agenda" and that every party should be "forced" to take a stand. The implication is that not every party wants to take up this issue. The editorial is castigating the present government for introducing this legislation in the first place; it follows that the party that needs to be "forced" is the NDP. So this editorial is not only criticizing the legislation but the government as well.

Editorial 2: "Employment Inequity," 1 September 1994

The headline begins with negativization in that the word "inequity" is used rather than equity; the headline thus sets the tone for a negative appraisal of the issue. It immediately alerts the reader to how the editorial views the legislation, and without any delay offers its opinion about it. One of the most common strategies used in presenting an editorial argument is frontage – that is, placing a key point, idea, or item at the very beginning of an article. This point is the most important one to be made in the piece and the one the writer wants to impress on the reader immediately. In this editorial, the point placed at the front or first position is that employment equity is responsible for the unemployment of Ontarians who are not Native or people of colour – more specifically, people of African origins. "Unemployed Ontarians would be well advised to ferret out that ancestor who claimed native roots or a history on an African slave ship. Or they might even consider inventing such a relative." The words "ferret out" are suggestive of furious digging. The suggestion is that as a result of employment equity legislation, unemployed Ontarians need to dig furiously to make claims to an ancestor of colour in order to ensure they will be eligible for employment.

The reference here to Native roots and African slave ships trivializes the history of both groups. But the most striking form of argumentation being resorted to here relates to the word "inventing." The implication is that unemployed Ontarians have been made so desperate by this iniquitous legislation that they must falsify or "invent" relatives of colour. These are the depths to which such people must sink in order to find employment in present-day Ontario.

In the very next paragraph the editorial hedges its bets: "That, it seems, is the doorway to a job." Through the use of the words "it seems," the writers are retreating somewhat from the strong position they took in the opening paragraph. This linguistic technique, known as hedging or vagueness, allows writers to distance themselves from responsibility for their statements. Having caught the reader's attention to the point being made, the editorial retreats slightly. In this way it can claim a degree of objectivity.

The editorial then turns its sights on the minister. It states that the legislation, "which comes into effect today and promises, at least as far as Citizenship Minister Elaine Ziemba is concerned, a new tomorrow." Here the minister's words are being subjected to a degree of mockery and ridicule. The implication of this statement is that the promise of a new tomorrow holds for the minister but not for anyone else. It continues: "Ms. Ziemba says in a recitation of high principle that is so much a part of her government." "High principle" is yet another example of arguing by opposites. In fact, the editorial believes there is no high principle involved here, and is using those words sarcastically to make the point that there is not.

The editorial continues: "Employers have been given the word, explicitly or otherwise." The words "explicitly or otherwise" send a vague, but also threatening, message to the reader. This is because the term "otherwise" is not further explained or defined. What are we to read into the term "otherwise"? What will happen to an employer who ignores "the word"?

"Rather than deal with the hiring process, the government has chosen to monitor the results and has created a 63-member bureaucracy to deal with the masses of reports that businesses will have to feed into the system to make sure the universe is unfolding as it should." This sentence is based on an unproven assumption that the government is not interested in dealing with the hiring process. It could be argued that the whole point of employment equity legislation is to deal with exactly that! The editorial then notes that a bureaucracy has been created. In specifying the exact number of members, the editorial is using the numbers game to frame its argument. The reader is supposed to be aghast at the vast number of bureaucrats who will deal with the issue. It could be argued, however, that governments are in the business of creating and maintaining bureaucracies – so why make an issue of this? At heart, the argument is framed in terms of contrast: instead of dealing with the hiring process – which they rightly should – the government is creating more bureaucracies. Yet the argument is based on the faulty premise that employment equity does not deal with the hiring process.

"Masses of reports" is another example of playing the numbers game; furthermore, these words are an example of exaggeration and hyperbole, in that they imply there will be large numbers of reports. This is based on an unproven premise.

The trite expression "the universe is unfolding as it should" is used to trivialize the issue. It ridicules the government for believing that its legislation is important enough to influence the universe; at the same time, it trivializes the legislation itself.

Later, "there is still the occasional woman who chooses to describe herself as an unpaid homemaker. Such options will wreak havoc for the bureaucrats who crunch numbers at Queen's Park." Use of the term "occasional woman," when the editorial writer knows there are far larger numbers of women who are homemakers, is an example of minimalization. This strategy is used here to question the *methods* that bureaucrats will use to measure the results of the equity act, and suggests that the legislation is flawed because the results cannot be measured properly. Moreover, this one supposed flaw is used to besmirch the entire process. The next sentence goes even further by resorting to strong hyperbolic language, such as "wreck [sic] havoc," to describe the work of the "number crunchers".

"The NDP government is nothing if not reasonable, and it does not expect all this to fall into place overnight." This is argumentation by reverse or sarcasm, in that the meaning is exactly the opposite of what has been written. The editorial writers really believe that the NDP government is unreasonable, and they frame this point not only by sarcastically reversing it but also by using the double-negative. A double-negative often requires the reader to read slowly or several times to fully comprehend its meaning. It is used here to imply that the government is not reasonable, but that the writers are too charitable, objective, or fair to say so.

Finally, "Of course, this utopian ideal carries a price tag, and the Ontario taxpayer will be billed $9.3 million in 1994–95 for the exercise. The cost of compliance for businesses is anyone's guess." Here the legislation is ridiculed by being described as "utopian." The assumption is that it cannot be effective; after all, utopias are unattainable by definition. The real moral or conclusion of this editorial is that a great deal of money is going to be spent in an attempt to attain an unrealizable objective. By citing the amount of $9.3 million, the writers are again employing a numbers game: readers are to be shocked by the size of the amount. Furthermore, the cost is to be born by Ontario taxpayers. The language here resorts to personalization techniques to bring the issue home. It is made to sound as if each and every Ontario taxpayer will be billed in order to reach the budgeted figure. It is hoped that such an appeal to each individual Ontarian's pocket will make the reader more readily agree with the editorial's criticism of the legislation. It is also superfluous to point out to the sophisticated readers of the *Globe and Mail* that the costs of implementing the employment equity legislation are to be borne by the taxpayer, considering that all government programming is paid for by the public purse. The only reason to include such an obvious point – especially at the very end of the editorial – is to further convince the reader by personalizing the issue.

Editorial 3: "Employment Equity's True Colours," 12 November 1993

By using the word "true" in the headline, the writers are establishing the assumption that there has been something hidden in the past. "In politics, a gaffe is when you tell the truth." This lead sentence places in the forefront the claim that the government is not telling the truth. This is an example of topoi, a special form of argumentation that involves resorting to commonplace or common-sense notions to explain events. The idea that politicians are dissemblers is widely held. What makes this fronted argument especially noteworthy is that the government being impugned has been formed by the NDP, a party that the generally conservative *Globe and Mail* is highly critical of.

"On Tuesday ... made a whale of a gaffe ... slicing the great beast open, allowing its putrescent vapours to fill the air." In this extract, several techniques are used. The size of the gaffe is being compared to that of the world's largest animal – an example of metaphor. The language throughout this line – "great beast," "putrescent vapours" – is highly exaggerated and hyperbolic. The reader is meant to be repulsed by the magnitude of the government's actions.

"There is an opening ... a position paying $74,000–$111,000 a year." By including the salary, the editorial again uses the numbers game. The hidden message is that this government is paying out substantial sums of money. Yet in all likelihood, the sum is drawn from the civil service schedule of salaries and is in line with what senior managers are generally paid.

"Nice work if you can get it." This short expression coming immediately after the job description is rather snide in tone. The bulk of the criticism in this editorial focuses on the job posting being restricted to members of the employment equity groups, so it is really irrelevant to the main argument. It is used, it seems, mainly to take another pot shot at the NDP government and its legislation.

"English-speaking white males, thank you for not applying." By describing those who need not apply, the editorial is playing to the sentiments of the readers. The article has already assumed that "many of those reading this newspaper" could not apply for the position. With this line, the editorial is identifying many of its readers as being in the mainstream majority group. In this way it is reinforcing and legitimizing any biases these readers already have. The final phrase thanking them is an example of sarcasm being used to hammer home a point.

"Honesty is one thing that has been missing from the debate on employment equity, with the truth obscured by layer upon layer of carefully scripted pseudo-science, bafflegab and out and out lies." The descriptive words used in this passage – "pseudo-science," "bafflegab," "out and out lies" – are examples of the technique of parallelism, in that it unites three different word/phrase combinations and culminates in the hyperbolic "out and out" to strengthen the claim of dishonesty.

"Behind the rhetorical Potemkin Village that Queen's Park has built around employment equity." Here the techniques of metaphor and strong negative imagery are being used. "Potemkin village" is a historical allusion associated with secrecy, hiding, spying, and hypocrisy. It reflects the writer's attempt to get the *Globe*'s elite and educated readers to compare the government's secrecy about employment equity with a particular period of Russian history characterized by negative features such as extreme secrecy.

"Such 'positive measures' are now government policy." By putting quotation marks around the words "positive measures," the editorial is suggesting just the reverse. Actually, it believes these measures are negative. "Goes on to explain that blatant discrimination – whoops, 'positive measures'." Here, the writers are clearly expressing their opinion that the measures constitute blatant discrimination. However, by injecting the childlike word "whoops" into the argument, they are trivializing the meaning of "positive measures." A similar form of argumentation is involved in the following sentence, which begins, "Funny, that's not what the government has been telling the public." Usually a sentence in an editorial in such a newspaper would not begin with the word "funny," but this one does, for the sake of trivializing the issue.

"The truth about Bill 79, ... can hardly be seen for all the saccharine coating." Continuing with the theme of disguise that the term "saccharine coating" suggests, the editorial now states with a degree of assertiveness that it knows the real truth behind this legislation. It then goes on to provide some carefully chosen excerpts from the bill. This is an example of the strategy of incompleteness. Not all aspects of the legislation are cited, but only those which the editorial writer can disagree most convincingly.

"The goings-on in the Ontario Public Service make it clear that employment equity is about quotas, pure and simple. Yet the government insists that the great virtue of its legislation is that it contains no quotas, only 'goals' and 'timetables.' There's no difference, of course, but the government assumes its citizens will never figure that out." The expression "pure and simple" reflects the strategy of simplifying or even oversimplifying ideas that are rather more complex. It continues in this assertive manner, stating "there's no difference" without providing any evidence or proof that there is no difference. It then underlines the point by adding the words "of course." In so doing it is also resorting to topoi – that is, it is suggesting that the fact that there is "no difference" is patently clear and obvious to all except the government, which has stated that there *is* a difference. Finally, it argues that the government is deliberately misleading the public, who are too stupid to realize it. In this way the editorial is insulting not only the government but the people who support it as well.

"As the OPS shenanigans show ... in the interest of getting the 'right numbers' ... this is what ... calls 'equal treatment and fairness.' This is what the NDP calls 'social justice'." This paragraph begins by using the pejorative word "shenanigans" to describe the government's actions. It continues by placing quotation marks around all the words drawn from either the legislation or the words of the minister. This is again an example of calling into question the veracity of the claims, in order to suggest reverse or opposite meanings: the editorial does not believe that the legislation will create "right" numbers, or that it is an example of "equal treatment," or that it will bring about "social justice."

"And so his lunacy on stilts marches on, mindless of the warped society it is dedicated to creating." The phrase "lunacy on stilts" is a clear example of hyperbole. So is the term "warped society." In both instances, an extreme form of language is being employed to degrade the government's objectives.

"The only way to stop it is [sic] for the NDP government to make a few more gaffes. The only way to stop it is for a few more people to speak the truth." In this final paragraph, the editorial reaches its concluding moral. It reverts back to the theme of the NDP government's alleged dishonesty, saying it should make more gaffes because only through its inadvertent mistakes will the real truth – which it wants to keep hidden – come out. The technique of substitution is used so that the word "gaffe" really means inadvertently telling the truth.

CONCLUSIONS

In this case study we have a clear example of how editorials are used to communicate with particular constituencies in their reading audience, and in this case to express support for a particular position in the course of a parliamentary debate. Through these editorials, the *Globe and Mail* is addressing the social, economic, and political elite which constitute its main readership. The central narrative, and the myths, assumptions, and images that the editors draw on to construct this discourse resonate with those who do not need proactive programs and measures to preserve their power and privilege. The editorials reassure white, able-bodied males that they are not unqualified recipients of unfair advantage; they are not demanding special interest groups; and they are not the recipients of costly government assistance programs. The *Globe* presents the privileges of maleness, whiteness, and able-bodiedness as natural and normal. It also presents any attempt to change the status quo as a threat to the nation's most cherished liberal values.

Many scholars (Fiske 1994; Hall 1997; van Dijk 1998) have noted that the discourses and representations that permeate much of the press are not haphazard and isolated, but rather are part of a deep and complex ideological foundation. In a racially divided society, the assumptions and beliefs that underpin the dominant discourse of much of the media and other members of the power elite serve an important function: they explain, rationalize, and resolve contradictions and tensions in society. For example, employment equity profoundly upsets the understood balance of relationships in society at the psychological, social, and economic levels. It threatens the infrastructure of white organizational space, as well as the sense of entitlement of those who have unrestricted access to employment and who have benefited from systemic discrimination.

The *Globe*'s editors frame almost all their arguments with the notion of liberal equality or equal opportunity, which is premised on the claim that all people begin from the same starting point. From the liberal, meritocratic point of view, society merely provides the conditions by which individuals who are differently endowed can make their way. The individual is seen as autonomous, as essentially unconnected to others, and as dedicated to pursuing his or her own interests. If all begin with the same opportunity and have the same rights, then the outcome must be fair. Thus, according to the "liberal" arguments employed by the *Globe and Mail* editors, neither collective (group) rights nor state intervention are required to ensure justice and equality (see Goldberg 1993; Wetherell and Potter 1992).

The *Globe*'s unconditional support for equal opportunity and opposition to employment equity reflects an ideology that rejects the need to dismantle white institutional spaces and power. The central argument against employment equity is that there is no need for white social capital to be redistributed.

This case study also illustrates how dominant or backlash discourse draws clear connections between marginalized groups in order to marginalize them even more. To make its case against employment equity, the *Globe*'s editors had to trivialize the multiple social disadvantages experienced by the disabled, racial minorities, women, lesbians, and so on. It had to draw on the discourse of liberalism and the reassuring ideals of individualism, equal opportunity, fairness, and merit to reinforce the message that what is at stake in this debate is not only the well-being of white, able-bodied males, but also the future of the democratic state. It resorted to the rhetorical strategies of hyperbole, exaggeration, mitigation, oversimplification, trivialization, and ridicule to tell its master narrative.

The analysis of the *Globe and Mail*'s editorials on employment equity (like the case studies presented by the authors in the *Discourses of Domination: Racial Bias in the Canadian English Language Press*, 2002) reveals a profound tension in Canadian society. A conflict between the belief that the media are the cornerstone of a democratic liberal society and the key instrument by which its ideals are produced and disseminated, and the actual role of the media as purveyors of racialized discourse, and a vehicle for reinforcing racism in Canadian society. A truly democratic liberal society requires a less biased and more inclusive, responsible, and accountable media.

NOTES

1 This paper is a revised version of a case study appearing in Henry and Tator. *Discourses of Domination: Racial Bias in the Canadian English Language Press*. Toronto: University of Toronto Press 2002, 93–107. Since it was written, new materials, including the 2001 census and reports relevant to this chapter have been published.
2 Equitable representation depends on the following factors: the number of designated group members in the working age population in a certain geographic area, the number of trained or skilled members who are employable or can be readily available, and the existence of equal opportunities in each workplace.
3 In March 1987, visible minorities made up 2.7 percent of the public service and 6.3 percent of the Canadian population. By March 1996, their share of government employment had risen to 4.5 percent, but their representation in the population had jumped to 13 percent. In management, minorities held only 2.3 percent of the executive positions in the public service (Samuel and Karam 1996).

REFERENCES

Abella, R. 1984. *Report of the Commission on Equality in Employment*. Ottawa: Supply and Services Canada.
Agocs, C., Burr, C., et al. 1992. *Employment Equity: Cooperative Strategies for Change*. New York: Prentice Hall.
Agocs, C., and Jain, H. 2001. *Systemic Racism in Employment Practices in Canada: Diagnosing Systemic Racism in Organizational Culture*. Toronto: Canadian Race Relations Foundation.
Fairclough, N. 1992. *Discourse and Social Change*. Cambridge: Polity Press.
Fiske, J. 1994. *Media Matters: Everyday Culture and Political Change*. Minneapolis: University of Minnesota Press.
Globe and Mail. 1993. Editorial. "Employment Equity's True Colours." November 12.
– 1994. Editorial. "Employment Inequity." September 1.
– 1995. Editorial. "Time for Debate on Employment Equity." February 17.
– 1995. Editorial. "The Discrimination Clause." March 8.

- 1995. William Thorsell (editor-in-chief). "This is No Way to Run a Railroad. Or a Newspaper. Or a Province." March 18.
- 1995. Editorial. "Real Employment Equity." June 13.
- 1995. Editorial. "Why Merit Matters." October 13.
- 1996. Editorial. "Please Identify Yourself." June 18.

Goldberg, D. 1993. *Racist Culture: Philosophy and Politics of Meaning.* Oxford: Blackwell.

Goldberg, M. 1996. *Can the Government's Discursive Shift Legitimize its Shift in Equity Definitions?* MA thesis, Graduate Dept of Education, University of Toronto.

Hall, S. 1997. *Representation: Cultural Representations and Signifying Practices.* Thousand Oaks CA: Sage.

Henry, F., and Tator, C. 2002. *Discourses of Domination: Racial Bias in the Canadian English Language Press.* Toronto: University of Toronto Press.

Jain, H., Sloane, P., and Horwitz, F. 2003. *Employment Equity and Affirmative Action: An International Comparison.* Armonk, NY: M.E Sharpe.

Mensah, J. 2002. *Black Canadians: History, Experience, Social Conditions.* Halifax: Fernwood Publishing.

Samuel, J. 1997. *Racism in the Public Service.* Ottawa: Canadian Human Rights Commission.

Samuel, J., and Karam, A. 1996. "Employment Equity and Visible Minorities in the Federal Workforce." Paper presented to Symposium on Immigration and Integration. Winnipeg, October 25–27.

van Dijk, T. 1988. *News as Discourse.* Hillsdale: Lawrence and Erlbaum.

- 1991.*Racism and the Press.* Newbury Park, CA: Sage.
- 1998. *Ideology: A Multidisciplinary Approach.* London: Sage.

Wetherell, M., and Potter, J. 1992. *Mapping the Language of Racism.* New York: Columbia University Press.

YASMIN JIWANI

Orientalizing "War Talk": Representations of the Gendered Muslim Body post-9/11 in The Montreal *Gazette*

Imperial logic genders and separates subject peoples so that the men are the Other and the women are civilizable. To defend our universal civilization we must rescue the women. To rescue these women we must attack these men. These women will be rescued not because they are more "our" than "theirs" but rather because they will have become more "ours" through the rescue mission ... In the Islamic context, the negative stereotyping of the religion as inherently misogynist provides ammunition for the attack on the uncivilized brown men."

(Cooke 2002, 468)

The ideological function of the news media as the bearer of "news," as a sentinel, and as a purveyor of hegemonic views of the nation vis-à-vis the world, lends it a certain kind of influence and legitimacy (Gitlin 1979; Hall 1984, 1990; Hartley 1982; van Dijk 1991). The portrayal of the orientalized, gendered body in the news media thus demands interrogation on at least two levels – in its strategic use to define the boundaries of nation or imagined community (Anderson 1983), and in its role as the contemporary signifier of an "Other" who is considered to be the repository of all that is the antithesis or projection of the "self." The current and shifting nature of the news enables one to examine representations of an "Other" from different historical vantage points, in other words, to explore how these representations are being constructed at a given point in time in order to facilitate their consumption, and hence legitimization, as part of common sense.[1] Furthermore, to what political ends are these representations being used?

In this chapter, I analyze the Montreal *Gazette's* coverage of the events following the destruction of the Twin Towers in New York on 11 September 2001. I contextualize this analysis within the framework of orientalism as defined by Edward Said. In so doing, I explicate the links between colonial and post-colonial representations of the orientalized body. I pay particular attention to the ways in which the news media both construct a gendered interpretation of this orientalized body and draw upon a cumulative stock of authoritative knowledge (Said 1978) to build upon and stabilize its materiality. Drawing on Yegenoglu (1998), my aim is to highlight the connections between the textually situated discourses that are present in *The Gazette*'s representations and the sedimented or historically constituted materiality of the discourse of orientalism. However, by drawing upon the discursive features used in the stories covered in *The Gazette*, I also highlight the nuances of contemporary representations, underscoring their fluidity, yet reflecting also on their deep-seated resonance with the collective stock of knowledge that informs orientalist thought.

In the sections that follow, I present an analysis of fifty-six stories that included some mention of women in *The Gazette*. I describe the ways in which Muslim women and men are represented, and how these representations differ according to their location in the East or West. Further, I outline the ways in which stories concerning the threat of backlash as experienced by Muslims living in the West serve to reinforce the containment of Muslim women, as well as underscore the presumed superiority of the West. Finally, I draw on excerpts from these stories to demonstrate the ways in which the discourse of backlash seeps into and is reinforced by the prevailing anti-immigrant sentiments of news media, and in particular of *The Gazette*.

THE GENDERED AND ORIENTALIZED BODY

Much has been written about the ways in which the binaries inherent in colonial discourses have feminized representations of subject nations as well as their inhabitants (see for example, Fanon 1965; Hammond and Jablow 1977; Huttenback 1976; Lazreg 1988; Stott 1989; Wyn Davies, Nandy, and Sardar 1993). The seepages of such representations into common-sense thought through popular culture have also been documented in numerous instances (Greenberger 1969; Grewal 1996; Hall 1990; Isaacs 1958; Lalvani 1995; McBratney 1988, McClintock 1995; Schneider 1977; Shohat and Stam 1994; Stam and Spence 1985; Stott 1989). The continuity between past representations and contemporary portrayals have also been researched (van Dijk 1993).

Said (1978) has argued that the Orient has been conceptualized as feminized terrain, weak yet dangerous and ready to be subjugated/domesticated through the civilizing forces of the "progressive" West. Within this context, women are seen in terms of their role as signifiers of culture: the boundary markers between the "us" and "them" which underlie and structure the relationship of the dominant colonizers to the subordinated colonized (Fanon 1965; Lévi-Strauss 1966; Yegenoglu 1998). Thus, women's bodies have been used to solidify national boundaries, and/or to differentiate out-groups (Anthias & Yuval-Davis 1992). The portrayal of women as gendered beings then carries particular connotations and is located at multiple sites of discursive manipulation (Lalvani 1995). On the one hand, women are represented as the keepers of culture and the maintainers of tradition. On the other hand, they are represented as exchange commodities to be used to cement alliances, or to be used as sexual objects by occupying forces and indigenous patriarchal institutions.

The gendered discourse of power as underpinning colonialism and subsequently neo/post-colonial relations is also evident in the ways in which the news media cover stories about "other" nations and "other" peoples. Existing studies point to the multiple ways in which "developing" nations are portrayed as backward, barbaric, traditional, and "primitive" (Dahlgren with Chakrapani 1982; Hackett 1989). On the other hand, and in keeping with the Manichean allegories of colonial thought (JanMohamed 1985), the "natives" of these countries are also seen to be innocent, childlike, and pure relics of a distant past (Wyn Davies et al. 1993). In the case of women, dominant representations tend to exoticize them, highlighting their perceived excessive sexuality, and representing them as dangerous and engulfing (Jiwani 1992; Lalvani 1995; Mohanty 1991a). A critical feature of many of these representations is their inherent ambivalence (Bhabha 1990). As Stuart Hall (1990) has pointed out, if the representation of black women, for example, has centred on the magnetism of their perceived sexuality, this very sexuality is also seen as threatening because of its "otherness" and its perceived potentiality to overcome and invade the male psyche. Similarly, and in keeping with the ambivalence inherent in these stereotypes, the figure of the black woman is also contained through her depiction as the "mama" figure or the tragic mulatto. Here, her transgressive potential is defused and evacuated through discursive and representational strategies of containment, trivialization, erasure, and symbolic annihilation (in which she is completely denied any representation (Gross 1991)). The containment of these representations is also evident in Hollywood's depictions of the gendered and orientalized body which range from the geisha girl or dragon lady, to the victimized and oppressed woman of colour.

ORIENTALISM

Edward Said's (1978) significant contribution in defining the organizational features of orientalism and examining it as a discursive regime has been critiqued by feminists on the grounds that it does not adequately address the issue of sexuality, and that it tends to be a totalizing discourse devoid of any spaces of resistance or counter discourses (Karim 2000; Lalvani 1995; Yegenoglu 1998). Nevertheless, Said's definition of orientalism offers a useful point of departure for the present inquiry primarily because it highlights the existence of a repository of images from which the collective stock of knowledge – everyday common-sense knowledge – continually draws upon to make sense of the world. The articulation of these images reveals a degree of fluidity based on the changing circumstances to which these images are called upon to respond. As instantiations fashioned and wrought by contemporary events, as well as by the inherent constraints and enabling influences of various institutions and technologies, they tend to echo elements of that collective and cumulative reservoir of knowledge (Hall 1990). To use Foucault's terminology, orientalism constitutes a regime of truth based on an authoritative corpus of knowledge.

The discursive regime of orientalism overlaps with, and is derived from, discourses of colonialism and imperialism. Hence, commonalities shared by these discursive traditions lie in the binary oppositions that form and inform the power coordinates of these "regimes of truth." These include a perception of cultural practices as indicative of inherent and innate traits, a collapsing of differences among subject peoples so that they appear as monoliths, and taxonomies of knowledge which situate subject peoples in particular relations of inferiority which are then naturalized. According to the tradition of orientalism, then, the Orient is a place of mystery and danger; the orientalized body discursively situated within this landscape serves to legitimize and naturalize unequal power relations. The orientalized body becomes a projection of all that the West finds strange, alien, and abhorrent, but simultaneously exotic, inviting, and alluring. In short, the orientalized body essentializes otherness (Lazreg 1988; Said 1981).

Methodology

Montreal has been described as "more like Europe" than other parts of Canada. Carrying a legacy of both French and English colonialism, the city is a remarkable site of uneasy co-existence between these two dominant cultures, with a medley of exoticized "other" cultures thrown into the mélange. The city has a significant Jewish population, as well as a growing number of diverse Middle Eastern communities.² As the only major English daily in Montreal, *The Gazette* is rather peculiarly situated. Owned by CanWest Global Communications Corporation (a corporation that also owns many other of Canada's largest daily newspapers), it is obviously influenced by the mainstream conservative political values of the dominant groups. However, in addition to serving the minority anglophone community in Quebec, it is equally seen to represent the voice and interests of a significant number of English-speaking minority/immigrant communities. Hence, *The Gazette* is caught in the difficult position of trying to cater to both the traditional anglophone and the more recently arrived English-speaking immigrant communities, while still adhering to the conservative bias of its owners.³

For the purposes of this analysis, daily editions of *The Gazette* over the two-week period following 11 September 2001 were scanned and input into the FileMaker Pro database program.⁴ A search using the keywords "women," "veil," and "burqa" was conducted. Out of a total of 362 articles dealing with the destruction of the Twin Towers and its immediate aftermath, only fifty-six articles either centred on women or made some mention of women. Of these, twenty-nine primarily addressed Muslim women living in the West, eighteen primarily addressed non-Muslim women living in the West, and nine primarily addressed Muslim women in the East. The other 393 articles either explicitly mentioned men, or assumed an androcentric perspective.

The fifty-six articles containing references to women were examined using a combination of textual analysis and certain aspects of informal discourse analysis (van Dijk 1985, 1993). Central to discourse analysis are issues revolving around accessed voices (who gets to speak), types of description, semantic moves, and discursive strategies. Representations were scrutinized in terms of their denotative and connotative meanings (Barthes 1973a), as well as their resonance with orientalism as defined by Said (1978). The combination of an informal discourse analysis with Said's epistemological perspective serves to delineate the various ways in which orientalism is transformed at the level of *parole* – in terms of its instantiation within a particular news story – while at the same time reproducing the larger discursive formation of orientalism as *langue* (as defined in de Saussurean linguistics and explicated by Barthes 1973b).⁵

In the analysis that follows, the major themes and signifiers to be found in these stories are detailed. No differentiation is made between stories filed by regular columnists, on-site reporters, the paper's editors, or informed citizens. While recognizing that there are important differences between these categories, the principal aim here was to examine all of the various representations that referenced the category "women."

It should also be stressed that even though the articles selected were chosen because of their mention or inclusion of the keyword woman/women, the resulting analysis includes an examination of male representations in so far as these were portrayed in relation to women. This point is predicated on the notion that gender is a relational category that derives its meanings from its contextual and social location vis-à-vis other categories.

Analysis and Discussion

In examining the coverage printed by *The Gazette*, it was apparent that descriptions of Muslim men far outweighed those pertaining to Muslim women. Of the total number of stories examined, thirty-two explicitly contained descriptions of Muslim men while only twenty-three referenced women or dealt specifically with Muslim women. The majority of these stories, especially those dealing with events related to Afghanistan, tended to utilize binary oppositions – pitting the oppressive, harsh, dictatorial and barbaric characteristics of Afghanistan to the liberal, democratic, and superior character of the United States. I will discuss this further in the section pertaining to the representations of Muslim men.

There were also significant differences in the ways in which Muslim women residing in Afghanistan, Pakistan, and other parts of the Muslim world were represented, as compared to their counterparts living in Canada or the United States. A significant corpus of stories pertaining to Muslims living in the United States or Canada focused on the threat of backlash. Further, and in contrast to Muslim women living in Afghanistan, Pakistan, or other parts of the Middle East, Muslim women living in the West tended to have a modicum of active representation in that they were interviewed, and their words were often quoted in print. However, whether the stories dealt with the threat of violence experienced by them here in the West or the conditions of patriarchal oppression confronting them in the East, Muslim women tended to be portrayed as victims.

Overall, however, it was difficult to separate out the representations of Muslim men from those of Muslim women given that the two were intertwined in the coverage, with the framing of one giving meaning to the framing of the other. Nonetheless, for analytical reasons I have separated out the main discursive themes used to represent women and men in the sections below. Additionally, I outline the various ways in which the discursive constructions of Muslim women in the West, under the auspices of expressing concern for the backlash they might face as a result of their presence, in fact served to contain women in ways that converged with their containment in the East.

MUSLIM WOMEN IN THE EAST

Of all the stories referencing Muslim women, orientalist themes were especially apparent in those that focused on Muslims living directly under Islamic rule. For example, several stories used the image of women veiled in burqas – appearing mute and fleetingly in the streets – as a backdrop against which the horrors and barbarism of the Taliban were more fully described. In a sense, there is nothing new here. In contemporary Western media, the veil remains a symbol of Muslim women and their oppression by tribal, primitive, and conservative upholders of Islam (Ahmed 1992; Hoodfar 1993; Jafri 1998). As Anouar Majid (1998) remarks, "For the Western media, the picture of the veiled woman visually defines both the mystery of Islamic culture and its backwardness."[6] Yet, as Yeğenoğlu (1998) suggests, the veil also serves another function:

The veil attracts the eye, and forces one to think, to speculate about what is behind it. It is often represented as some kind of a mask, hiding the woman. With the help of this opaque veil, the Oriental woman is considered as not yielding herself to the Western gaze and therefore imagined as hiding something behind the veil. It is through the inscription of the veil as a mask that the Oriental woman is turned into an enigma. Such a discursive construction incites the presumption that the real nature of these women is concealed, their truth is disguised and they appear in a false deceptive manner. They are therefore other than what they appear to be. (44)

Notwithstanding the possibility that the veil might serve as a shield, in the corpus of the coverage examined, women's alleged victimized and subordinate status was generally linked to the excessive patriarchal nature of Islam and of Afghan men by association. The following story underscores this kind of reporting:

It's midday in Pakistan's deeply conservative northwest. Bearded men sit in small groups sipping sweet black tea. The rare woman hidden in an enveloping head-to-toe cloak called a burqa scurries through the dusty market. The call to prayer sounds. The voice is soothing, almost mournful. Then the cleric begins to preach. His voice changes, suddenly shrill and angry and his message violent. Bellowing from a loudspeaker atop the mosque, the voice rails against internationally financed aid organizations and their promotion of women's rights, girls' education and small home-based businesses. It hurls curses at the women who work for these groups, calling them evil handmaidens of a decadent West that wants to destroy traditions, culture and the Islamic religion. They should be punished, the voice says.

Islamic clerics urge the faithful to shun women involved with such groups as prostitutes – or, alternatively, to kidnap them, force them into marriage and keep them locked away at home. "Don't allow these sinful women to enter our villages," roars Maulana Zia-ul Haq, a cleric in Banda, a village in the Dir district. "If you see any one of them, just take her home and forcibly marry her. If she is a foreigner, kill her." (Gannon 2001, C7)

Entitled "Where equality is 'obscene': Conservative Pakistani clerics vow to crush women's rights" and appearing just two days after the destruction in New York City, this article strategically brings together several orientalist tropes. For instance, orientalist imagery is evoked in the language used to describe the setting. The alleged laziness of the "natives" comes through in the representation of men sitting around sipping tea while the women hurry about their business. Women are not to be seen or heard under Taliban rule (Franks 2003). Men, on the other hand, are charged with maintaining the patriarchal order as exemplified in the role of the clerics. The clerics then become the point men for the media, symbolizing fanaticism, ruthlessness, barbarity, and excessive patriarchal violence. Lazreg (1988) notes that "[t]he fetishism of the concept, Islam, in particular, obscures the living reality of women and men subsumed under it" (95). Thus, Islam becomes the paradigm by which women's and men's lives are understood as opposed to a force for identification and mobilization as a response to external circumstances and conditions. Interestingly, news stories *such as the one above* conflate or collapse the differences between Palestinians and Afghanis, or Palestinians and Pakistanis, and reflect the tendency of dominant Western media to resort to homogeneous and totalizing representations (see also the Canadian Islamic Congress's evaluation of Western media bias 2002).

However, ambivalences still abound. The voice of one of the clerics vowing to crush women's rights, for example, is described as "shrill and angry and his message [as] violent." This loaded description offers a view of the clerics as irrational and insane in their ultra-patriarchal insistence that women remain subjugated, but also as weak and feminized given that emotion is stereotypically considered to be the province of women. Similarly, the women who are interviewed are presented simultaneously as victims and as active agents who, although somewhat deceptive by necessity, are resisting the patriarchal onslaught by organizing a shelter for women and setting up educational programs to make other women aware of their rights.

One of these "active" women, for instance, is described elsewhere in the story as "cover[ing] her head in a large sweeping shawl." Her victimization is made evident from the inclusion of her experience of being in an abusive marriage with her first cousin whom she has not yet divorced. She is further described as being engaged in educational efforts to make other women aware of their rights. Commenting on other women, she says, "Their self-esteem is not there. *They think of themselves as something akin to animals*" (my emphasis). The victimization of Afghani women is thus rendered complete – as animals, they need to be saved.

Another young female worker at the shelter, Ruhi Tabassum, is also interviewed. "[S]miling beneath the shawl," as the reporter puts it, she is quoted as saying, "they [the men] know that if their women know their rights, they won't be able to control them." The reporter's insertion of the smile is suggestive of Tabassum's duplicity. In other words, the overall portrayal of Afghani women in this article resonates with the colonial representation of women of colour as secretive, deceptive, and as appearing to be meek and submissive while plotting against their benevolent colonizers – or, for that matter, against their own men (Jiwani 1992).

This profile is carried over into a story about the necessity for increased security measures at airports (Smith & Philps 2001, A4). Here, the traditional notion of Arab or Middle Eastern women as quintessential victims is shattered by the Israelis' contention that they have successfully identified Arab women travelling alone as constituting a high risk. In contrast, Israeli or Jewish women are considered to be low risks. Others who constitute a high risk include Arab males, priests, and individuals who purchase "their tickets at the last minute." By framing such travellers as hiding behind deceptive appearances, the article manages to justify racial profiling and to legitimize extensive state surveillance methods.

Again, this confusing and sometimes contradictory conflation of woman as helpless victim and manipulative activist is found in another article that contrasts the innocence of those female victims who turned up to work in the Twin Towers on that fateful day with the callous and uncanny behaviour of the Palestinian women in Ramallah who were shown celebrating in response to the tragic news (Schnurmacher 2001, A19). Here, active agency in the form of Palestinian women's militancy is presented in an extreme fashion by the writer who then goes on to make nebulous links between Palestinian women, their celebration, and their commitment to a cause beyond reason.

Such unquestioning and irrational commitment to a cause "beyond reason" is then harnessed to the female biological body by presenting Palestinian women as reproducers of terror – as mothers of suicide bombers. As this writer described it:

[A] Canadian broadcast reporter whose coverage had always leaned strongly toward the Palestinian position recently became more even-handed after an encounter with the mother of a suicide bomber who told him she was happy with what her son had accomplished. Her only regret was she did not have other sons who could do the same thing. (Schnurmacher 2001, A19)

The same ambivalent framing of the victim/activist Muslim female is captured in a photograph and caption that accompanies a story on the U.S. movement of arms to areas around Afghanistan. The photo shows women in burqa with guns protesting at a rally in Lahore. The caption reads: "Veiled women activists of a Pakistani religious-political party hold toy guns and the Koran as they chant anti-U.S. slogans at Lahore protest rally" (Blanchfield & MacKenzie 2001a, A1). That women are depicted as actively engaged in protest as opposed to their usual stereotypical depiction as passive victims should, according to the gender liberation rhetoric of the West, suggest a disruption that is progressive. However, here, the very act of holding "toy guns" and the "Koran" makes their action suspect and indicative of an emergent threat. In contrast, women educating other women and setting up shelters for their sisters – in short, women who behave like "us" – are acceptable. However, women who are militant "activists" are not (Thobani 2003).

In all these articles, Afghanistan and surrounding nations are also gendered with negative "feminized" qualities. They are portrayed as "allies of convenience" that cannot be entirely trusted, given that they are also deceptive and motivated by their own agendas (Goldstein 2001, B1; Wallace 2001, A13). "Dependency" is a gendered term used to describe many of the countries surrounding Afghanistan, as well as the country itself.

Images of failed states, primitive technologies, and peoples come through in these stories. Afghanistan was described by American observers as having been bombed "up to the Stone Age" (Dowd 2001, B3). What is implicitly understood, and what is even sometimes explicitly stated, is that these countries have failed because of their own inherent shortcomings rather than because of any involvement by the Western or Soviet imperial powers (Friedman 2001, B3). There is a complete erasure of history in the kinds of representations that are used to justify American intervention in Afghanistan. Thus, it is the "failure" of these countries that is deemed to be the motivating factor sparking resentment towards, and retaliation against, the West.

Primitivism, then, becomes one of the discursive means by which to explain women's subordinate position (Bagnall 2001, B3), the rejection of leisure through consumption (i.e., the banning of television sets, music, and even kites), (Dowd 2001, B3), and the brutality of Afghani men (Gannon 2001, C7). In contrast, America and Americans are represented as emblems of freedom, liberation, and democracy. While they might have a few failings, these are not equivalent to the crimes committed by the Taliban. As one writer concludes:

Before September 11, it might have been possible to feel pity for the men who joined the Taliban, with their feelings of dislocation after 20 years of Soviet invasion and civil war, their poverty, their desire to make sense of their world. But not now. By now we know how they intend to order their world: women under house arrest; the rest of the world their enemy. (Bagnall 2001, B3)

The very notion of "pity" is suggestive of Western benevolence which, as Sherene Razack (1998a) reasons, is the underside of Western racism.

MUSLIM MEN IN THE EAST

The "lowness" of the Afghani men and the Taliban in particular (who are also Afghanis) comes through not only in the imagery of primitiveness, but also in descriptions of their brutality and zeal. Several stories underline this brutality by linking it to the treatment of women, and more importantly, to fanaticism. One mullah is described as "reputed to be so crazed that when shrapnel hit his eye in the battle with the Russians, he simply cut it out with a knife and kept going" (Dowd 2001, B3). Another story discusses the attack on the World Trade Centre in 1993, concluding that "The mastermind, Ramzi Yousef, later boasted that he had hoped to kill 250,000" (Spector 2001, B3). Overall, the message is that primitivism leads to brutality and fanaticism, and to a violent opposition to the West. Add poverty to this potent mix – a poverty which would seem, according to these stories, to be self-inflicted by inherent laziness – and what we are left with is a confluence of factors that lends itself perfectly to the development of human weapons of mass destruction. These themes are exemplified in a story by a reporter who visits a Madrasa in Pakistan where orphan boys and refugee men are schooled in the practice and theological foundations of one particular interpretation of Islam. He calls it a "jihad factory" populated by "poor and impressionable boys who are kept entirely ignorant of the world and largely ignorant of all but one interpretation of Islam. They are the perfect jihad machines" (Goldberg 2001, B1).

Nowhere in this article is mention made of the fact that the type of Islam taught in this particular Madrasa is akin to the Islam practised by the ruling elite in Saudi Arabia, a significant ally of the United States, nor is there any mention of the diversity that exists within the Islamic world, or of the history of U.S. involvement in the region. Nor why these young boys and men are orphans and refugees in the first place.

Another common trope in the coverage of Muslim men concerned their perceived envy of, and anger against, the West. As this writer argues:

And this Third World War does not pit the U.S. against another superpower. It pits it – the world's only superpower and quintessential symbol of liberal, free-market, Western values – against all the super-empowered angry men and women out there. Many of these super-empowered angry people come from failing states in the Muslim and Third World. They do not share American values, they resent America's influence over their lives, politics and children, not to mention its support for Israel, and they often blame America for the failure of their societies to master modernity.

What makes them super-empowered, though, is their genius at using the networked world, the Internet and the very high technology they hate to attack the United States. Think about it: they turned its most advanced civilian planes into human-directed, precision-guided cruise missiles – a diabolical melding of their fanaticism and American technology. Jihad Online. And think of what they hit: the World Trade Centre – the beacon of American-led capitalism that both tempts and repels them, and the Pentagon, the embodiment of American military superiority. (Friedman 2001, B3)

The above excerpt from this article illustrates both the ambivalence inherent in these representations – the juxtapositioning of primitiveness (failure to master Western modernity) with expertise in computer technology – and the strategic moves which underscore the differences between "us" versus "them." The latter includes those moves which minimize the grounds of "their" grievances. In other words, those grievances – regardless of how founded they might be – are simply translated into the emotions of anger, resentment, and envy. "They" are thus rendered as undeserving "children" who have no legitimate basis for their anger. However, "their" anger, perceived as illegitimate, is dangerous enough to signal the advent of a third world war. Additionally, the excerpt illustrates the binary of the benevolent West which shares its technologies with the primitive East only to have the latter use it against their benefactors. The theme of betrayal is underscored in the above quote constructing the inhabitants of the "failed states" as beyond redemption and thus deserving of extreme retaliatory action.

The inferiorizing of Muslim men, then, is achieved through representing them as emotional, irrational, deceptive, resentful, untrustworthy, and above all, as child-like in their irrationality. This latter rendering serves to emasculate these men – reducing them to entities who are weak, vulnerable, and conquerable. Another part of this strategy of emasculation is to render these men more feminine. The use of emotional descriptors to describe their motivations serves this function as do other more explicit discursive devices. Witness for example, the following description of Osama bin Laden offered by one of the reporters:

The image has flickered across North American television screens so many times in the last five days it will probably take years to fade – the liquid-eyed Osama bin Laden, almost girlishly pretty despite the breast-long beard, sits in the dust in flowing robes, firing an automatic weapon and smiling at the strength of its recoil. The film was shot years ago, but in the pictures, the charismatic gunman seems almost to be mocking the West and its grief. (Waters 2001, B1)

The feminized portrayal of Osama bin Laden cited above coalesces a number of different signifiers and connotations, producing an overall picture of bin Laden as the beguiling yet ultimately menacing arch-villain who is cold, calculating, ruthless, and sinister – all characteristics, incidentally, that are commonly associated with women of colour in colonial literature and popular culture (Jiwani 1992). A cartoon in the paper a week later also feminizes bin Laden, portraying him as a woman in a burqa. What is interesting about the cartoon and the above portrayal is its use of feminized terms such as "liquid-eyed," "girlishly pretty," "breast-long beard" combined with his representation in a burqa complaining about the heat generated by wearing such a garment.

At this point, it should be mentioned that, in the course of The *Gazette*'s post-11 September 2001 coverage, several reporters *do* attempt to explain Islam and its variegated nature to the Western audience, but all too often, dichotomous interpretations of Islam – as a religion of peace on the one hand and a religion advocating war on the other – are juxtaposed. These stories tend to draw heavily on the accessed voices of various elite Islamic scholars in the West and the East (Watanabe 2001, B1). They also privilege a sense that the message of peace in Islam is particularly vulnerable to being hijacked, and that this very vulnerability is itself a function of the inherent flaws of Islam's religious structure. Thus, a structure which is perceived to be without a central authority, without policing mechanisms, and with a kind of communal orientation is seen to lend itself to a collective ethos that then becomes the antithesis of Western capitalism with its hierarchal structures and its centralization of power. Within such a framing, even the intellectual tradition within Islam is seen to be at fault for encouraging this kind of hijacking. As one reporter puts it, "All of this flexibility and questioning mean that a clever leader or scholar with a bitter and often not very well-informed audience can twist Koranic ideas to his own ends. The jihad for example" (Waters 2001, B1). This statement follows that of a Muslim advocate in the West who counters the stereotypical view of Islam by emphasizing its intellectual tradition and its encouragement of questioning and internal search. That Christianity, as Karim Karim (2000) has suggested, has been similarly hijacked is an observation significantly missing from these articles.

"BACKLASH STORIES"

A significant number of stories printed by *The Gazette* during this period cohered around the theme of "backlash," or the threat of backlash as experienced by Muslim communities in the United States and Canada. What is interesting about these backlash stories is that they served a dual ideological function. On the one hand, they communicated to minority groups that their interests were considered important enough to garner press coverage – in other words, they counted. On the other hand, and from a somewhat cynical perspective, the inclusion of backlash stories served the strategic function of "balance." As Stuart Hall (1974) has argued, the codes of objectivity, balance, and impartiality are critical to the ideological functioning of the news media with respect to their position as the "fourth estate" and their role in maintaining the hegemonic order. For the news media to appear to be partisan would not only detract from their credibility as the fourth estate and the voice of the "nation," but also make them vulnerable to boycotts, advertiser reprisals, charges of biased reporting, and a disaffected audience.

Several interesting themes emerge in the stories concerning Muslim fears of a backlash. Of the fifty-six articles, thirteen dealt specifically with the actual or potential threat of a backlash against the Muslim population living in the West. Of ten such stories to appear in the first week following the event, two dealt with the Muslims in the United States. Another concerned a personal account of a Pakistani woman and her experience of racism upon moving to a particular part of the province of Quebec many years ago. Two are editorials decrying the incidence of racist assaults and the targeting of Muslims in Montreal. One other story revolves around the reporter's overhearing of racist comments by non-Muslim women in the aftermath of the collapse of the Twin Towers. In many of these stories, incidents of assault – whether they are projected or fully realized – are noted. Most of these focus on women wearing the veil and their fears of doing so in the immediate aftermath of September 11.

In the single article that focuses on an actual assault of a young Saudi female resident at a local hospital, the reporter makes no mention of a veil or hijab, though the assault itself is graphically described. Further, there is no mention of how the attacker actually identified the woman as being Saudi or a Muslim (Macfarlane 2001, B6). According to the report, the woman is "a fourth year resident in obstetrics and gynecology, described by her supervisors as a brilliant resident." Her dedication to her work is further emphasized by the mention that she stayed for most of her shift despite having being attacked and traumatized. While she is not interviewed, the Dean of McGill's Faculty of Medicine is quoted as saying that "female Muslim residents will not be on call during nights, effective immediately." What is striking about the Dean's response is that measures were not invoked to increase the protection of those who are rendered vulnerable to such assaults. Equally striking is that while the story appears to be sympathetic to the young woman and laudatory of her status, her own voice is erased.

In this story, as in the majority of the other backlash stories, the themes of fear and the possibility of retaliation emerge clearly. However, in most of them, it is the male authoritative figures (in general, key spokesmen or presidents of various organizations) who are interviewed or quoted extensively. Muslim women are directly interviewed in only three stories. An example of this trend is evident in the following story which appeared on 13 September 2001:

In Canada, the backlash began Tuesday, said Shafiq Hudda, chairman of the Islamic Humanitarian Service, a national charitable organization based in Kitchener, ON. "One of our lady volunteers was actually verbally assaulted on the highway," Hudda said.

"Somebody called her an effing terrorist." Hudda said the woman, who is in her 50s and was wearing a head scarf, was shaken by the incident, which occurred near the downtown area of Kitchener.

The Islamic Assembly of North America, which is based in the United States but also has an office in Quebec, is advising Muslims in both countries to stay home. "All Muslims in the U.S. and Canada must take precautions and care from the possibility of retaliatory attacks," said the group's Web site. "Do not leave home unless absolutely necessary, especially women, who wear Muslim dress." (Richards 2001)

While the backlash stories serve the important function of highlighting the vulnerabilities of the Muslim population living in North America, their resulting message ends up reinforcing notions of the weakness and victim status of this particular group. This is especially evident in the references to women. The majority of the articles underline the view that women wearing the veil or the hijab are most vulnerable to attacks because they are easily identifiable (see, for instance, Fitterman 2001a, 2001b). Male spokespeople for the various organizations that are interviewed all caution women who wear the hijab or veil to stay at home. One Muslim woman specifically mentions how her daughter was afraid of wearing her hijab to school and had to be accompanied by her brother to ensure her safety (Davenport 2001, A3).

These words of caution, though well-intentioned, end up legitimizing Muslim women's containment in the private sphere of the home. That home might well be located in America or Canada, but the end result is a strategy of containment, ironically reminiscent of that which the Taliban in Afghanistan had been enforcing upon women. Gendering terror, then, becomes in part about the various ways in which the *threat* of violence and retaliation forces women to refrain from being seen, or from occupying space as legitimate citizens.

In yet another article, reference is made to a woman who now refrains from wearing the veil *precisely* because of this threat of backlash. In the same article, two female students recount their experiences of terror. One is told to "go home. You're just a terrorist." The other student states, "I do have a feeling of insecurity because of the looks I am getting of anger and suspicion" (Block 2001, A17). In other words, fear, heightened security, and potential threats are all ways in which Muslim families and individuals are terrorized into "going home" or staying at home.

In these latter stories, then, Muslim women are framed as victims who are acted upon by others rather than as active agents who are capable of determining their own course of safety or resistance to the perceived threat from the outside (see Franks (2003) for a more detailed discussion of this phenomenon). Such a framing accords with one of the main features of news reporting, namely, the tendency to create binaries between the victims and the perpetrators (Connell 1980). But interestingly, it also converges with the dominant ideology which, as evident from the controversial case of Émilie Ouimet, (a twelve-year-old girl who, despite having been sent home from school in Montreal for having worn the hijab, chose to wear the veil) suggests that symbols such as the veil communicate a reluctance to assimilate on the part of a minority group member and hence justify their further marginalization. Thus, the victim of discrimination is seen as being responsible for her own victimization, and blamed for "inciting" discriminatory attitudes by refusing to adhere to the dominant norms (Lenk 2000). In other words, by insisting on wearing the hijab, Émilie Ouimet marginalized herself.

As for Muslim men living in the West, these backlash stories tend to depict them as authoritative, reasonable, compassionate and desperate to distance themselves from the acts of not only those who attacked the Twin Towers, but also from the more fundamentalist clerics who advocate a literal and conservative interpretation of Islam. Such a social distancing is symbolic of a retreat. By distancing themselves from those who attacked the Twin Towers and those who represent the Taliban and the Afghanis, Muslim men who were interviewed in many of *The Gazette* articles are, by their very geographic location, rendered more like "us." Such a sentiment is clearly articulated by one Muslim spokesperson – a professor at the University of Waterloo and president of the Canadian Islamic Congress – who is quoted as saying: "We are part of you and you are part of us" (Waters 2001, B1).

The Gazette's representations also serve to reinforce the binary of East versus West, and tradition versus liberation. By locating these Muslim males in the West, the connotation is that these men are more "Westernized," and hence liberated. At the same time, the backlash experienced and articulated by these men serves to underline their subject position as members of weak and victimized minorities left to suffer the consequences of events far beyond their control. The terrorizing nature of the backlash becomes even more apparent with the subsequent forced incarceration of Muslim men in the United States, and with the racial profiling of men who appear to be Muslim or of Arabic heritage.

However, despite the widespread publicity about unfair stereotyping, not to mention the stigmatizing of, and threats of physical and psychological violence against, Muslim communities, there was virtually no mention in this coverage of an active or assertive involvement of state authorities, such as the police, in working with these communities to safeguard them from acts of violence. On the contrary, the coverage seemed at times to oscillate between the backlash and racial profiling discourses, with the latter seeping into the ever-present anti-immigration discourses extant in Canadian news coverage (Henry & Tator 2002; Jiwani 1993; Mahtani 2001).

HARNESSING THE FEAR TO SUPPORT ANTI-IMMIGRANT SENTIMENTS

This seepage between the two dominant discourses – the anti-immigrant discourse on the one hand, and the backlash discourse on the other – is evident in several cases. For example, in one of the few cases where a Muslim woman is interviewed, her interview is used to support the view that Canada's refugee system should be tightened to exclude "extremists and nationalists." She herself is described as a refugee from Kyrgystan, and as an Uzbek woman (Sevunts 2001, A19). In the same story, the reporter interviews two other men, one of whose name sounds Muslim. In recounting these men's experiences, their observations regarding the vulnerabilities of the immigration system are emphasized:

Bakhtiar said the Immigration and Refugee Board needs not to tighten the screws but train real professionals. "The sad truth that I learned while interacting with other refugees," Bakhtiar said, "is that a convincing liar can become a refugee because the tribunal members have no way of checking his story. But a real refugee who is so nervous that he makes one mistake might be denied his claim."

Another man who didn't want his name used said instead of tightening the refugee determination system Canada might want to invest more in its immigration screening process. "I know a thing or two about interrogation," the man said. "And I was appalled by the security screening interview I had." "The first thing the RCMP officer asked me was whether I had ever killed anybody. The second question was whether I belong to any terrorist organizations. As if I had been a terrorist and a killer I would have admitted to it." The whole interview lasted no more than 15 minutes, the man said. "No wonder they missed that Algerian terrorist and others like him. I'm sure they asked him the same questions and he said no. Now we all have to pay for it."

These men's accounts are then used to underscore the weakness of the current system which supposedly allows terrorists to enter the country undetected. A forum intended for the open discussion of backlash stories is itself hijacked in order to reinforce the hegemonic interests of another dominant discourse.

ACCESSED VOICES:
WHO GETS TO SPEAK AND WHO IS SILENCED

Throughout the two weeks of coverage that were analyzed, the voices of authority accessed to make judgments and articulate a position on the issues at hand tended to be male. Furthermore, virtually all of these accessed voices belonged to men living in the West, and in only a minority of instances were these voices those of clerics in Pakistan. Where white male authoritative voices were accessed, they subordinated those of the Muslim spokespeople. The predominant pattern that emerged was that men spoke for women, and this was particularly true of Muslim men speaking on behalf of Muslim women living in the West.

Muslim or Middle-Eastern women who were directly quoted tended to be highly educated or enrolled as students in recognized institutions (e.g., at McGill University or Concordia University, or in one case, with a doctorate from the University of Western Ontario) (Block 2001, A17; Fitterman 2001b, A13; Moore 2001, A4). In only one instance was a Muslim woman living in the West quoted without these kinds of identifiers (Davenport 2001, A3). The subtext seems to suggest that if these women are educated, then they are credible and their stories can be believed. They are, in other words, more like "us." On the other hand, no female activists in Afghanistan – for instance women representing organizations such as RAWA (the Revolutionary Association of Women in Afghanistan) – were cited or quoted despite the fact that they have long been advocating an end to the oppressive conditions imposed by both the Northern Alliance and the Taliban (Kolhatkar 2002b; Moghadam 1999, 2001).

Interestingly, this emphasis on citing Muslim women educated and sometimes born in the West seems to strategically underscore the West's representation of itself as the land of progress, gender equality, and liberation for women. This sets the West ("us") apart from the Taliban ("them") which is, according to one reporter and several scholarly sources, specifically aiming their policies of containment at educated, middle- and upper-class urbanized Afghani women who they see as having been "contaminated" by Western notions of progress and liberation (Bagnall 2001, B3; Hirschkind & Mahmood 2002; Moghadam 2001). That Afghani women are silenced in Afghanistan but allowed to speak in the West works ideologically to seal the dominant interpretation of the Western ethos of egalitarianism and its sense of superiority.

"Overcomplete" descriptions which are replete with unnecessary but identificatory details were also prevalent in the coverage of Muslim men and women living in the West. In one instance, a Muslim in Brooklyn was interviewed "as he stood behind a counter filled with incense sticks, surrounded by shelves of essential oils, trays of olives and jars of pistachios" (Richards 2001, B4). In another instance, a reporter talking to a Muslim man living in Montreal notes his gray hair and beard, as well as the fact that he is reclining on "deep red velvet cushions atop an ornate Afghan carpet in his sparsely furnished Longueuil apartment" (Montgomery 2001, B1). These descriptors are replete with signification about the Orient: its exotic lush colours and almost hedonistic lifestyle. In the same article, the reporter notes how this man's wife, Sabera, "laid out a plastic sheet on the floor, then proceeded to cover it with large pots full of rice, chicken stew, salad and plates of home-made flatbread." Here, the exoticization of the food and the simple manner of the serving style all work to underscore the otherness of this family, as well as its incongruous appearance in a Western milieu.

CONCLUSION

Within the context of post-11 September 2001 news coverage, representations of the gendered orientalized body did not depart from the existing pool of stereotypical images. The militant martyr or suicide bomber was a constant figure (perpetuated in part by the coverage of the situation in Palestine), as were hostage takings and violent upheavals. Likewise, the veiled woman received much media attention, depicted as being both oppressed by and subjugated under Islam, as well as unable to liberate herself without the help of Western powers (Hoodfar 1993; Jafri 1998; Lenk 2000; Todd 1998). As far as these stereotypical representations are concerned, *The Gazette* shared much in common with the dominant Western media, albeit with an interesting twist given the demographic it serves and Quebec's unique political and linguistic climate.

Nonetheless, the particular cluster of "backlash" stories examined also demonstrates that the meta-narrative of orientalism is not simply static but reproduced in a way that is responsive to contemporary circumstances. In the latter situation, the ethos motivating the coverage on backlash was likely mediated by the structural and institutional constraints of the print medium – the necessity to constantly provide fresh stories, continuity with previous stories, and the requirement for "balance" and impartiality. The latter factor is undoubtedly influenced by *The Gazette's* readership and the concentration of Muslims in the Montreal area, as well as the Western tradition of liberalism. However, and despite the mitigating force potentially available to audiences, the fact that Muslim women and men in the East were represented in orientalized ways underscores how the media constantly shift our attention to the problems "out there" which are then presented as requiring our intervention "from here."[8]

These stories illustrate the imbricated nature of the gendered and orientalized discourse of the news media in their coverage the events following September 11. Further, they demonstrate the ways in which such imagery becomes commonplace and commonsensical in the kinds of explanations being proffered. Woven throughout this gendered discourse are descriptive tropes that identify one side as being evil, manipulative, and deceptive, while the other, notably the United States, is presented as moral, open, and explicit about its intentions. The ultimate rescue is then presented as the liberation of the oppressed by the "free world," and as the annihilation of evil by the powers of good: a belief reflected in the media's acceptance and replication of the U.S. christening of their intervention as "Operation Enduring Freedom," and grounded in the framework of orientalism. In the final analysis, these news stories reinforce a sense of "nation-ness" – of "us" versus "them" – and analytically, offer insights into the ways in which contemporary forms of racism draw upon orientalism but, in the process, reproduce it in ways that "make sense" of the contemporary political and social climate.

ACKNOWLEDGMENT

I would like to acknowledge the support and assistance of Ross Perigoe in providing me with access to his database of coverage, as well as Jo-Anne Lee, Christine Khalifah, Linnet Fawcett, Holly Wagg, and Amin Alhassan for their insightful comments and feedback. The title of this chapter is inspired by Arundhati Roy's work aptly entitled *War Talk* (2003). A version of this paper was originally printed in *Critique: Critical Middle Eastern Studies* 13(3), Fall 2004. This research was made possible by a grant from the Social Sciences and Humanities Research Council (410-2004-1496).

NOTES

1 I am using the term "common sense" in the Gramscian sense of denoting the common stock of knowledge that is taken for granted, but that in itself contains contradictory bits of information that are then selectively used to make sense of the world (see Hall 1979).
2 According to Statistics Canada (2001), 100,200 Muslims live in the Montreal area.
3 *The Gazette's* readership has been expanding after a decline over the last decade. Today, the paper has a readership of over half a million on the weekends, and between 360,000 and 380,000 during the week.
4 This database was created by Ross Perigoe, Department of Journalism, Concordia University.
5 Barthes (1973b) defines the difference between *langue* and *parole* as follows: "the systematized set of conventions necessary to communication, indifferent to the material of the signals which compose it, and which is a language (*langue*); as opposed to which speech (*parole*) covers the purely individual parts of language (phonation, application of the rules and contingent combinations of signs)" (13).
6 However, as she goes on to explain: Despite its close association with Islam, the veil is in fact an old eastern Mediterranean practice that was assimilated to Islam in its early stages of expansion. In the two suras in the Qur'an that refer to the veil, not only is there no specific mention of veiling the face but certain parts of the body in fact are assumed to be visible (Majid 1998, 334).
7 In this regard, see Razack (1998b) in terms of her analysis of the use of "degenerate spaces" in Thailand in particular, as a way to reinforce the legitimacy of the moral spaces of the West.

REFERENCES

Ahmed, L. 1992. *Women and Gender in Islam: Historical Roots of a Modern Debate*. New Haven: Yale University Press.

Anderson, B. 1983. *Imagined Communities: Reflections on the Origin and Spread of Nationalism*. London: Verso.

Anthias, F., and Yuval-Davis, N., in association with Cain, H. 1992. *Racialised Boundaries: Race, Nation, Gender, Colour and Class and the Anti-racist Struggle*. London and New York: Routledge.

Bagnall, J. 2001. "Tale of the Taliban: Once, you could feel sorry for the dispossessed men, but no longer." *The Gazette*, 27 September: B3.

Barthes, R. 1973a. *Mythologies*, trans. A. Lavers. London: Paladin (Original work published 1957).

— 1973b. *Elements of Semiology*, trans. A. Lavers and C. Smith. New York: Hill and Wang (Original work published 1964).

Bhabha, H. 1990. "The Other Question: Difference, Discrimination and the Discourse of Colonialism." In *Out There: Marginalization and Contemporary Cultures*, eds. R. Ferguson, M. Gever, T.T. Minh-ha, and C. West, 71–87. New York and Massachusetts: The New Museum of Contemporary Art and MIT Press.

Blanchfield, M., and Mackenzie, H. 2001a. "U.S. Flexes Muscle: Warplanes ordered to Gulf bases; Bush to address his nation tonight; Pakistan tries to defuse unrest." *The Gazette*, 20 September: A1.

— 2001b. "Saudis in a Squeeze: U.S. bid for air base runs contrary to policy, Sentiment." *The Gazette*, 23 September: A1.

Block, I. 2001. "City Muslims Appeal for Calm: 'We Thank God until now there is no acceleration (of Violence) in the Montreal Area'." *The Gazette*, 14 September: A17.

Bromstein, E. 2001. "Feeling Racism's Imperceptible Grip." *The Gazette*, 19 September: A4.

Canadian Islamic Congress. 2002. *Anti-Islam in the Media: Summary of the Fifth Annual Report*. Waterloo, ON, Canada. http://www.canadianislamiccongress.com/rr/rr_2002_1.php.

Connell, I. 1980. "Television News and the Social Contract." In *Culture, Media, Language*, eds. S. Hall, D. Hobson, A. Lowe, and P. Willis, 139–156. Britain: Hutchinson in association with the Centre for Contemporary Cultural Studies, Birmingham.

Cooke, M. 2002. "Saving Brown Women." *Signs* 28, no. 1: 468–70.

Dahlgren, P., with Chakrapani, S. 1982. "The Third World on TV News: Western Ways of Seeing the 'Other'." In *Television Coverage of International Affairs*, ed. W.C. Adams, 45–65. Norwood, NJ: Ablex.

Davenport, J. 2001. "Muslims Wary of Reprisals: 140 at mosque denounce terror attacks." *The Gazette*, 16 September: A3.

Dowd, M. 2001. "History Throws Knuckleball to Bush." *The Gazette*, 25 September: B3.

Editorial. 2001. "Good vs. Evil." *The Gazette*, 15 September: B6.

Fanon, F. 1965. *Studies of a Dying Colonialism*, trans. H. Chevalier. New York: Grove Press.

Fitterman, L. 2001a. "Hate Hits Canada: Muslims, even Sikhs, targets of backlash." *The Gazette*, 15 September: A24.
– 2001b. "Montreal's Pakistani Muslims Feel the Heat: 'We are here; we are not the terrorists'." *The Gazette*, 21 September: A13.
Franks, M.A. 2003. "Obscene Undersides: Women and Evil between the Taliban and the United States." *Hypatia: A Journal of Feminist Philosophy* 18, no. 1: 135–56.
Friedman, T.L. 2001. "It's World War III: America will have to fight on several fronts, and need all its will to win." *The Gazette*, 14 September: B3.
Gannon, K. 2001. "Where Equality Is 'Obscene': Conservative Pakistani clerics vow to crush women's rights." *The Gazette*, 13 September: C7.
Gitlin, T. 1979. "News as Ideology and Contested Area: Toward a Theory of Hegemony, Crisis and Opposition." *Socialist Review* 9, no. 6: 11–54.
Goldberg, J. 2001. "Taking Courses at Jihad School: All-Islamic Classes." *The Gazette*, 15 September: B1.
Goldstein, S. 2001. "Ex-Soviet States Will Be Key for U.S.: Most of the 'stans' have Muslim majorities." *The Gazette*, 29 September: B1.
Greenberger, A. J. 1969. *The British Image of India: A Study in the Literature of Imperialism, 1880–1960*. London: Oxford University Press.
Grewal, I. 1996. *Home and Harem: Nation, Gender, Empire, and the Cultures of Travel*. Durham and London: Duke University Press.
Gross, L. 1991. "Out of the Mainstream: Sexual Minorities and the Mass Media." In *Gay People, Sex and the Media*, eds. M.A. Wolf and A.P. Kielwasser, 19–46. New York and London: Harrington Park Press.
Hackett, R. 1989. "Coups, Earthquakes and Hostages? Foreign News on Canadian Television." *Canadian Journal of Political Science* 22, no. 4: 809–25.
Halbfinger, D.M. 2002. "Make-over Rush after the Burqa." *The Gazette*, 3 September: A1.
Hall, S. 1974. "Media Power: The Double Bind." *Journal of Communications* 24, no. 4: 19–26.
– 1979. "Culture, the Media and the 'Ideological Effect'." In *Mass Communication and Society*, eds. J. Curran, M. Gurevitch, and J. Woollacott, 315–48. London: Sage Publications.
– 1984. The Narrative Construction of Reality. *Southern Review* 17: 1–17.
– 1990. "The Whites of Their Eyes." In *The Media Reader*, eds. M. Alvarado and J.O. Thompson, 9–23. London: British Film Institute.
Hammond, D., and Jablow, A. 1977. *The Myth of Africa*. New York: Library of Social Sciences.
Hartley, J. 1982. *Understanding News*. London and New York: Methuen.
Henry, F., and Tator, C. 2002. *Discourses of Domination: Racial Bias in the Canadian English Language Press*. Toronto: University of Toronto Press.
Hirschkind, C., and Mahmood, S. 2002. "Feminism, the Taliban, and Politics of Counter-insurgency." *Anthropological Quarterly* 75, no. 2: 339–54.

Hoodfar, H. 1993. "The Veil in Their Minds and on Our Heads: The Persistence of Colonial Images of Muslim Women." *Resources for Feminist Research* 22, no. 3/4: 5–18.

Huttenback, R. A. 1976. *Racism and Empire: White Settler and Coloured Immigrants in the British Self-governing Colonies, 1830–1910*. Ithaca and London: Cornell University Press.

Isaacs, H. 1958. *Scratches on Our Minds*. Connecticut: Greenwood Press.

Jafri, G.Y. 1998. *The Portrayal of Muslim Women in Canadian Mainstream Media: A Community-based Analysis*. Afghan Women's Organization, ON, Canada. http://www.fmw.org/Articles%20and%20Presentations/muslim%20women%20&%20media%20-report.PDF.

JanMohamed, A.R. 1985. "The Economy of Manichean Allegory: The Function of Racial Difference in Colonialist Literature." *Critical Inquiry* 12, no. 1: 59–87.

Jiwani, Y. 1992. "The Exotic, the Erotic and the Dangerous: South Asian Women in Popular Film." *Canadian Woman Studies* 13, no. 1: 42–6

– 1993. By Omission and Commission: "Race" and Representation in Canadian Television News. Doctoral Dissertation, Department of Communication Studies, Simon Fraser University.

Karim, H.K. 2000. *Islamic Peril*. Montreal, QC: Black Rose Books.

Kolhatkar, S. 2002a. "'Saving' Afghan Women: (How Media Creates Enemies)." *Women in Action* 1: 34–6.

– 2002b. "The Impact of US Intervention on Afghan Women's Rights." *Berkeley Women's Law Journal* 17: 12–30.

Lalvani, S. 1995. "Consuming the Exotic Other." *Critical Studies in Mass Communication* 12, no. 3: 263–86.

Lazreg, M. 1988. "Feminism and Difference: The Perils of Writing as a Woman on Women in Algeria." *Feminist Studies* 14, no. 1: 81–107.

Lenk, H-M. 2000. "The Case of Emilie Ouimet, News Discourse on Hijab and the Construction of Quebecois National Identity." In *Anti-Racist Feminism*, eds. A. Calliste and G.J. Sefa Dei, 73–88. Halifax, NS: Fernwood.

Lévi-Strauss, C. 1966. *The Savage Mind*. Chicago: University of Chicago Press.

Lindgren, A. 2001. "Arabs Don't Face Tougher Flight Checks: Officials." *The Gazette*, 19 September: A9.

Macfarlane, J. 2001. "Medical Resident Tells of Assault." *The Gazette*, 18 September: B6.

Mackenzie, H. 2001. "Taliban to bin Laden: Get Out: Afghanistan's hard-line regime is forcibly blocking its own People from leaving the country, even as its leader, Mullah Mohammed Omar, asks its most notorious guest to move on." *The Gazette*, 28 September: A1.

Mahtani, M. 2001. "Representing Minorities: Canadian Media and Minority Identities." *Canadian Ethnic Studies* 33, no. 3: 99–133.

– 2002. "Interrogating the Hyphen-Nation: Canadian Multicultural Policy and 'Mixed Race' Identities." *Social Identities* 8, no. 1: 67–90.

Majid, A. 1998. "The Politics of Feminism in Islam." *Signs* 23, no. 2: 321–61.
McBratney, J. 1988. "Images of Indian Women in Rudyard Kipling: A Case of Doubling Discourse." *Inscriptions* 3, no. 4: 47–57.
McClintock, A. 1995. *Imperial Leather.* New York: Routledge.
Moghadam, V.M. 1999. "Revolution, Religion, and Gender Politics: Iran and Afghanistan Compared." *Journal of Women's History* 10, no. 4: 172–95.
– 2001. "Afghan Women and Transnational Feminism." *Middle East Women's Studies Review* 16, no. 3/4: 1–9.
Mohanty, C.T. 1991a. "Cartographies of Struggle: Third World Women and the Politics of Feminism." In *Third World Women and the Politics of Feminism*, eds. C.T. Mohanty, A. Russo, and L. Torres, 1–47). Bloomingdale, IN: Indiana University Press.
– 1991b. "Under Western Eyes: Feminist Scholarship and Colonial Discourses." In Mohanty, Russo, and Torres, eds. *Third World Women and the Politics of Feminism*, 51–80.
Montgomery, S. 2001. "Loss Felt among Local Afghans: Rights Activist Hopes Level Heads Will Prevail as U.S. Mulls Retaliation." *The Gazette*, 18 September: B1.
Moore, L. 2001. "Learning the Nature of True Islam: Mosques Educating Non-Muslims." *The Gazette*, 24 September: A4.
Razack, S.H. 1998a. *Looking White People in the Eye, Gender, Race, and Culture in Courtrooms and Classrooms.* Toronto, ON: University of Toronto Press.
– 1998b. "Race, Space, and Prostitution: The Making of the Bourgeois Subject." *Canadian Journal of Women and the Law* 10, no. 2: 338–76.
Richards, S. 2001. "Islam Is Against This Kind of Act." *The Gazette*, 13 September: B4.
Roy, A. 2003. *War Talk.* Cambridge, MA: South End Press.
Said, E. 1978. *Orientalism.* New York: Random House.
– 1981. *Covering Islam.* New York: Pantheon Books.
Schneider, W. 1977. "Race and Empire: The Rise of Popular Ethnography in the Late Nineteenth Century." *Journal of Popular Culture* 11, no. 1: 98–109.
Schnurmacher, T. 2001. "Images of Celebration Tell the Story." *The Gazette*, 14 September: A19.
Sevunts, L. 2001. "Refugees Fear Mood Change." *The Gazette*, 14 September: A19.
Shaheen, J.G. 1984. *The TV Arab.* Bowling Green, OH: Bowling Green State University Popular Press.
Shohat, E., and Stam, R. 1994. *Unthinking Eurocentrism, Multiculturalism and the Media.* London and New York: Routledge.
Smith, M., and Philps, A. 2001. "Delta Force to Ride Planes: U.S. Anti-terrorism Squad in New Role." *The Gazette*, 14 September: A4.
Spector, N. 2001. "Deja vu for Israelis: Scenes of destruction and pain are familiar to people who are used to being attacked for who they are." *The Gazette*, 12 September: B3.

Stam, R., and Spence, L. 1985. "Colonialism, Racism and Representation: An Introduction." In *Movies and Methods, Vol. 2*, ed. B. Nichols, 632–49. Berkeley: University of California Press.

Statistics Canada. 2001. *Quebec: Largest Proportion of Roman Catholics.* Government of Canada, Ottawa, ON, Canada. http://www12.statcan.ca/english/census01/Products/Analytic/companion/rel/qc.cfm.

Stott, R. 1989. "The Dark Continent: Africa as Female Body in Haggard's Adventure Fiction." *Feminist Review* 32, Summer: 68–89.

Thobani, S. 2003. "War and the Politics of Truth-Making in Canada." *Qualitative Studies in Education* 16, no. 3: 399–414.

Todd, S. 1998. "Veiling the 'Other,' Unveiling our 'Selves': Reading Media Images of the Hijab Psychoanalytically to Move Beyond Tolerance." *Canadian Journal of Education* 23, no. 4: 438–51.

United Colours of Benetton. 2003. http://www.benetton.com/press.

van Dijk, T., ed. 1985. *Discourse and Communication*. New York: de Gruyter.

– 1991. *Racism and the Press*. London: Routledge.

– 1993. *Elite Discourse and Racism*. Thousand Oaks, CA: Sage.

Wallace, B. 2001. "West Anxiously Courting a Willing Iran: With its leader's 'remarkable' conversation, Islamic state opens door to a new relationship." *The Gazette*, 22 September: A13.

Watanabe, T. 2001. "Extremists Distort Holy Tenets to Justify War." *The Gazette*, 27 Sesptember: B1.

Waters, P. 2001. "Twisting the Faith: Islam is a serene religion, but can be warped into a form of totalitarianism." *The Gazette*, 15 September: B1.

Wyn Davies, M., Nandy, A., and Sardar, Z. 1993. *Barbaric Others: A Manifesto on Western Racism*. London: Pluto Press.

Yegenoglu, M. 1998. *Colonial Fantasies: Towards a Feminist Reading of Orientalism*. Cambridge and Melbourne: Cambridge University Press.

Contributors

JEANNETTE ARMSTRONG is director of the En'owkin International School of Writing in Penticton, Canada. A dedicated advocate of indigenous rights, she was recently appointed a traditional member of the Indian Penticton Band and to the Council of Listeners in the International Testimonials and Violations to Indigenous Sovereignty. She is an award-winning artist and writer whose publications include *Looking at the Words of Our People: First Nation Analysis of Literature* (1993), *Breath Tracks* (1991), video scripts, poetry and music collaborative recordings, and the critically acclaimed novel *Slash* (1990). She has also collaborated with Native architect Douglas Cardinal on *The Native Creative Process: A Collaborative Discourse between Douglas Cardinal and Jeannette Armstrong*.

FRANCES HENRY, FRSC, now professor emerita at York University, is one of Canada's leading experts in the study of racism and antiracism. Her most recent books include co-authoring a third edition of *The Colour of Democracy: Racism in Canadian Society* (in press) with Carol Tator, widely used in universities as a text. She has also co-authored *Challenging Racism in the Arts*, (1998). Her most recent work on racist discourse in the media is *Discourses of Domination: Racism in Canada's English Language Press*. She has a new book on racial profiling in progress.

YASMIN JIWANI is assistant professor in the Department of Communication Studies at Concordia University. Her research interests focus on race and gender intersections in media representations, social policy analysis, especially anti-violence policies, and identity formation. Her present work deals with the gendered narratives of war and representations of the Orientalized body in the news media post-9/11.

She has written several articles on intersectionality and media including "The Eurasian Female Hero(ine): Sydney Fox as the Relic Hunter, forthcoming in the *Journal of Popular Film and Television*, and a forthcoming book on race, gender, and violence.

JO-ANNE LEE is assistant professor of Women's Studies at the University of Victoria. She has published in the areas of adult education, multiculturalism, immigrant women, and racialized girls and young women.

JOHN LUTZ is associate professor of History at the University of Victoria. His research interests are in BC colonial history and First Nations history. He has published several articles on First Nations in BC and the Pacific Northwest and his book *Makúk: Aboriginal Work & Welfare* will be published in 2005.

MINELLE MAHTANI is an assistant professor in the Department of Geography and Program in Journalism at the University of Toronto. She works in the areas of "mixed race" identity, media and minority representation, critical journalism, and women of colour in geography. Her work has been published in several important collections including J. Ifekwunigwe (ed.) *Critical Mixed Race Reader*; P. Hubbard, R. Kitchin and G. Valentine (eds.), *Key Thinkers on Space and Place*, and the journal, *Ethnicities*. She is the former Associate Strategic Counsel for IMPACS: Institute for Media, Policy and Civil Society.

PAUL MAYLAM is chair of the Department of History at Rhodes University, South Africa, and has been a professor in that department since 1991. His publications include *A History of the African People of South Africa* (1986), an edited collection with I. Edwards entitled *The People's City: African Life in Twentieth-Century Durban* (1996), *South Africa's Racial Past: The History & Historiography of Racism, Segregation and Apartheid* (2001) and articles in the *Journal of Southern African Studies* and *African Affairs*.

ROY MIKI is a professor of contemporary literature in the English Department at Simon Fraser University. He is well known as a writer, poet, editor, and cultural activist. His most recent work is *Redress: Inside the Japanese Canadian Call for Justice* (2004). Among his other publications are an award-winning edited collection of poetry, *Pacific Windows: Collected Poems of Roy K. Kiyooka* (1997); a collection of essays, *Broken Entries: Race, Subjectivity, Writing* (1998); and *Surrender* (2002), which received the Governor-General's Award for Poetry. He has also written and edited books on William Carlos Williams, George Bowering, and bpNichol.

ROXANA NG is a professor in the Department of Adult Education and Counseling Psychology, Ontario Institute of Studies in Education, the University of Toronto. Her work is grounded in her involvement in the feminist movement and her experience as an immigrant woman and woman of colour. She has edited several collections, most recently *Anti-Racism, Feminism and Critical Approaches to Education* (1995) with Pat Staton and Joyce Scane, and *Community Organization and the Canadian State* (1990) with Gillian Walker and Jacob Muller. She is also the author of *The Politics of Community Services: Immigrant Women, Class and State* (1988).

ALI RATTANSI is visiting professor of sociology at City University London. His publications include the edited collections *Racism, Modernity and Identity* (1994) with S. Westwood; *"Race," Culture, and Difference* (1992) with James Donald; and *Ideology, Method and Marx: Essays from Economy and Society* (1989). He is also the author of *Marx and the Division of Labour* (1982) and articles in *Economy and Society, Sociology*, and *Labour History Review*.

ANN LAURA STOLER is Willy Brandt distinguished professor and chair of the Department of Anthropology at the New School University in New York. She has been active in ethnographic and archival research on questions related to social inequality in Indonesia, colonial Vietnam, the Netherlands, and France for the past twenty-five years. The most recent of her many books and journal publications are *Carnal Knowledge and Imperial Power; Race and the Intimate in Colonial Rule* (2003); *Race and the Education of Desire: Foucault's History of Sexuality and the Colonial Order of Things* (1995); and an edited collection with Frederick Cooper, *Tensions of Empire: Colonial Cultures in a Bourgeois World* (1997).

CAROL TATOR is course coordinator in the Department of Anthropology, York University. She has worked on the frontlines of the anti-racism and equity movement for over twenty-five years. She has published widely on the subject of racism including three books co-authored with Frances Henry, *The Colour of Democracy: Racism in Canadian Society, Challenging Racism in the Arts: Case Studies of Controversy and Conflict,* and *Discourses of Domination: Racial Bias in the Canadian English Language Press*. She and Frances Henry have just completed a major study on racial profiling and a book based on this research is forthcoming.

Index

Abella, Rosalie, 163
Aboriginal peoples, 13, 35–7, 39, 41–2, 163, 166–7
Aboriginal perspectives, 22
activists, 3, 4, 7, 10, 12, 22, 24, 26, 43–4, 98, 126, 128, 196; militant women, 187
Adachi, Ken, 97, 104
Afghanistan, 183, 187, 193, 196
African American culture, and young British blacks, 58
African Canadian, 35, 161
African Caribbean identity, 54, 61–2, 84
Africanization, 51
Afrikaner nationalism, 140–7
Ahmed, Sara, 100
Aix-en-Provence. *See* Provence
Alexander, C., 55–6, 59, 69
alien-Asian, 100
alliances, and multiethnic women, 88
ambassador. *See* metaphor
ambivalence, 180. *See also* framing
anti-colonial critique, 99
anti-equity, 161
anti-globalization movement, 38

anti-immigrant: discourse, 194; sentiment, 179, 194–5
anti-racism: critical literacies of, 4, 26; versus non-racism, 38–9
anti-racist organizations, 122
apartheid: discourse of, 155; impact of, 138; policies, 143; roots, 153
Arab women, 186
Asian British. *See* British Asian
Asian Canadian, 36–9, 100, 161
Asian gangs, 69
Asian vote, 64
Asians: Uganda, 51; East African, 51
assumptions, 161, 165, 168, 170–1, 174–5
authenticity, 22

Back, L., 59–60
backlash, 183, 195, 197; discourse of, 179; stories 191–4
Barthes, R., 182
B.C. Security Commission, 102
Bell, David, 87
Bernal, Martin, 5–6, 8
betrayal, theme of, 55, 189

bias, 6, 9, 161, 163, 165, 168, 170–2, 174–6, 182, 185, 191
Bill to Repeal Job Quotas, 164
binaries, in news reporting, 194–5
bin Laden, Osama, 190
biodiversity, 23, 41
biological essentialism, 156
biracial. *See* mixed race
black masculinity, 58, 70
body: abject, 100; black, 51; and *Enowkin*, 31; gendered, 178; guards, 129; limbless, 96; of literature, 138; orientalized, 178–97; politic, 108; in the present, 101; shape, 58; as spectacle, 96; of writing, 144
Bonnett, Alistair, 7, 18
boundaries: black British, 54; crossing, 89; Japanese Canadian, 95; policing, 132; racialized, 86, 99
Briskin, Linda, 38–9
British Asian, 48, 59–62, 66–70
British National Party (BNP), 67–8, 71
Britishness: brown, black, and Asian, 48, 51, 55;

Muslim, 66; test, 67. *See also* British Asian
buppie, 56
burqa, 182, 184, 187, 190
Butler, Judith, 105

Canadian Human Rights Commission: Annual Report 1996, 164
Canadianization, strategy of, 104
capitalism, 37, 148; and economic globalization, 38; and racial discrimination, 149. *See also* industrial capitalism
censorship, cultural, 119
Charter of Rights and Freedoms, 106
cheap labour thesis, 149
childhood, racialized, 96
Chinese, 22, 36, 40, 70, 87; and African Asians, 52; Canadian, 35, 46; and ethnic stereotypes, 87; immigrants, 39
Chirac, Jacques, 115, 124
class: and alienation, 55; analysis, 150; domination, 149; and racialization, 80; and sexuality, 50; working, 64–5, 150
cognitive decolonization, 4
colonial representations, 179
colonialism, Dutch and French, 115
colonization, 33; of aboriginal peoples, 37, of Africa, 142
colonizing codes, 99
coming out, 87
Commission for Racial Equality, 68
common sense, 4, 5, 39, 40, 43, 172, 178; and the Front National, 122, 134; and media reports, 23; and popular culture, 179; racist and materialist, 22; and repository of images, 181; and representation of an Other, 178; and science, 155
Commonwealth Immigrants Bill, 1968, 51
communication: and crossing boundaries, 89
computer technology, 189
conflict: and racial division, 145
conservatism, 8
covertness, 84–5
Cresswell, Tim, 78–9
critical discourse analysis (CDA), 161
critical literacies of anti-racism. *See* anti-racism
cult of the man, 126
cultural: ambiguities, 133; hegemony, 4–5; nationalism, 108; pluralism, 65; racism, 15–16, 114; violence, 61. *See also* diversity, hybridity
culture: of *bhangra* music, 61; of failure, 70; of fear, 129–30; of hegemonic whiteness, 17; of limb amputators, women oppressors, and terrorists, 66; poster, 126; racist, of police, 63; of resentment, 65; of self-sufficiency, 30

de-industrialization, 67, 71
democratic liberal values and principles, 162
demographics of blame, 128
demonstration, Front National, 118
dependency: as gendered term, 187
destabilization, 17, 65; of racialized spaces, 86; in sports and athletics, 57
difference, 22; and cooperation, 30–1; cultural, 60–1; as a microcosm, 32; racial, 36
disabilities, people with, 17, 163, 166, 175
discourse: analysis, 155, 182; of apartheid, 155; creative, 109; discrepant, 117; dominant, 175; of employment equity, 167–74; gendered, of racism, 17, 180, 197; of identity-making, resistance, and opposition, 106; of imperialism, 181; of liberalism, 164, 175; of orientalism, 179; public, 132; of racialization, 104, 176. *See also* backlash, critical discourse analysis
discrimination, 42–3, 52–3, 69, 139, 146–7, 149–51, 154–5, 163–4, 167, 173, 193; reverse, 164; systemic, 164, 175
discursive formation, 162
disguise, 17, 165, 173, 184
dispersal, 103–4, 108
dispossession: of Japanese Canadians, 98, 107, 109; and uprooting, 101
diversity, 22–5, 41, 60–1, 189; cultural, 17, 19
double-negative, 171
Dyer, Richard, 18

economic exploitation, 148
editorials: categorized, 162. *See also Globe and Mail*
education, 105, 132; and Afghani women, 185–6; and politics, 122; in schools, 114, 119, 121–2, 133
elite, 5, 20–1, 23, 131, 162, 173–5, 188, 190
embodiment: American military, 189; racial, 58
Employment Equity Act, 163–4
employment equity, and *Globe and Mail* editorials, 161–76
employment inequity, 169
enemy alien, 17, 98, 101–2, 106, 108
Enowkin, 22, 23, 26, 31–2, 41

equality, 17, 20, 106, 142, 163, 175, 185, 196; of opportunity, of outcomes, 166–7. *See also* inequality
Equal Opportunity Plan, 164
equity, 20, 139, 161–76; anti, 161; and inequity, 169–71
essentialism, 46; and anti-essentialism, 13–14; as mobilizing strategy, 13; and otherness, 181; rejection of, 156
ethical self-consciousness, 12
ethnic, 17, 48, 51–4, 61–2, 67, 69, 80, 140, 144, 148; community, 78; consciousness, 151; division, 146, 154; identity, 13, 78, 81; multi, 12, 85; superiority, 16; voices, 96–7
ethnicity, 9, 12, 13, 15, 17, 18, 36, 53, 65, 85–7, 97; accrued cultural value of, 97; Afrikaner, 149; mixed, 81; versus race, 79; racialized, 81; white, 46
ethnography, 59, 117
eugenicists, 154
exaggeration, 52, 170, 175
exclusion, 7, 9, 14, 16, 42–3, 87, 100, 116, 118, 120–1, 123, 134; and inclusion, 5, 25, 109; political, 142; social, 64–5
exploitation, 9, 17, 19, 24, 38; and cheap black labour, 139, 145, 149–50

factory work. *See* garment workers
Fairclough, N., 162
family values, 70, 132
fanaticism, 185, 188–9
Fanon, Franz, 7, 42, 58
far right groups, 3, 67, 115
father, 31, 86, 89; African Caribbean, 84; Bangladeshi, 85; of German ancestry, 82

fatherhood, failure of, 70
fatherland, 123, 132
female voters, 132
femininity, 82; ideals of, 84
feminist scholarship, 6; and anti-racism, 7; and activism, 34
feminized, nations, 187. *See also* inferiorizing, bin Laden, Orient, representation
film, 59, 70, 161, 190; and animal trickster, 82–3
First Nation, 22, 30, 80, 161; language, 33
foreignicity, 100
Foucault, Michel, 5, 43, 50, 123, 129, 181
fourth estate, 191
framing, 9, 11, 12, 53, 168, 183, 186, 190, 193; ambivalent, 187. *See also* postmodern
Frankenburg, Ruth, 18
Free Trade Agreement (FTA), 108
French nationalism, 128
French radical right, 114–34; and cultural priorities, 114. *See also* Front National
frontage, strategy of, 169
Front National, 16, 115–34; and anti-French racism, 121; poster art, 123–4, 126, 128

garment industry, 37
garment workers, 11, 23, 37–8. *See also* women
gender: politics, 130–3; and French scholarship, 132; and orientalism, 178–98; and terror, 193; and trickster studies, 82
gendered discourse. *See* discourse
Gilroy, Paul, 13, 139
global capitalism, 23–4, 38
globalization, 14, 32–3, 37–8, 65; and competition, 40–1; discourses of,

108; and intellectual left, 120; and work restructuring, 37
Globe and Mail, 20; editorials, 161–76
Goldberg, David T., 5
Gramsci, Antonio, 5, 43

Hall, Stuart, 5, 12, 43, 53; and fourth estate, 191; and new ethnicities, 15; and representation of black women, 180; and role of mixed people, 88–9; and young black British people, 55, 58
head covering. *See* Muslim women, veil
hedging: strategy of, 169
hegemonic, 5, 14–20, 26, 43, 178, 191, 195; discourse, 89; structures, 105
hegemony, 4–5, 22, 43, 144, 147. *See also* culture
hierarchy, 16, 18, 35–6, 87; cultural, 97; racial, 77–8, 83, 190
hijab. *See* veil
Historical Materialism. *See* modernism
historical wrongs: and identity, 25. *See also* Japanese Canadian
historiography, 10, 11, 24; of racism in South Africa, 138–56
history, 10, 14, 19, 24, 32, 47, 94, 97, 99–100, 108–9, 116, 126, 128–9, 134, 169, 173, 187, 189; disarticulated, 104; of racial oppression in South Africa, 138–56; reclaimed, 106
Hollywood: and orientalized body, 180
Holocaust studies, 128
Homma, Tomey, 108
Howe, Darcus, 51–2
human rights, 9, 17, 51, 72, 106, 121, 164–5, 168

hybrid identity, 14, 15, 48, 78
hybridity, 13–14, 61; cultural, 78, 117
hyperbole, 168, 170, 174–5
hyphenated, 12, 14, 18; identities, 25, 46–7, 66, 71; Japanese Canadian identity, 98; youth, 15
identity: of young black women, 58; Canadian, 81; crisis of, 96; decentred, 54; English national, 65; ethnic, 53; fixed, 104; Japanese Canadian and transnational process, 95; moving through categories of, 90; switching, 64; symbolic, 101; unified, 60. *See also* historical wrongs, hyphenated, mixed race, multiple
identity politics, 46, 97, 99, 166
ideology, 9, 11, 17, 24, 43, 153–5, 162, 175, 193; racial, and exploitation of labour, 150, 152; and text and talk, 162; white supremacist, 140
Ifekwunigwe, Jayne, 84, 90
imagined community, 161, 178
immigrant communities, 181–2
immigrants, 11, 17, 34–9, 47–9, 51, 67–8, 71, 179, 194; and Front National, 116, 118, 121, 127, 130–2; and European Union, 66
immigrant women, 11, 34–5, 37
immigration: to mother country, 47–8; and national identity, 120; and new assimilationism, 68; and public discussion, 121
immigration acts, 49–50, 98

incompleteness, strategy of, 173
individualism, 108; ideals of, 175; liberal, 8–9
individual political action, 11
industrial capitalism, 148, 151
inequality, 5, 7, 9, 26, 52
inferiorizing, 43; of Muslim men, 189–90
institutional: racism, 26, 48, 70, 81, 151; white, spaces and power, 175
institutions, 11, 24, 31, 34, 39, 52, 54, 68, 126, 129, 153, 155, 180–1, 195, 197; as collective memory, 164
intermarriage, 152
intermediate analysis, 153–4
internment: Japanese Canadian, 36, 39, 98
interpreter. *See* metaphor
Islam, 24, 178, 184–97
Islamic clerics, 185
Islamic/Muslim identity, 62–3, 69
Islamophobia, 62, 68
Israeli women, 186
issei, 99

Japanese-Canadian, 25, 36, 39, 94–109; official history, 97
Japanese Canadian Centennial, 97, 99
Japanese Canadian Redress Committee, 99
Jewish women, 186
juvenile delinquency, 119–20

keywords: women, veil, burqa, 182–3
King, Mackenzie, 102–3
Kitagawa, Muriel, 98, 101
Kogawa, Joy, 98

labour: and racial division, 149
lange, 182

language: anti-immigrant, 132; appropriation of, 120; assumptions about, 130; and displacement, 96; forms, 55; as knowledge and power, 155; of multiculturalism, 97; of racialization, 101; of redress, 106; trap, 103. *See also* linguistic, rhetorical strategies
Lawrence, Stephen, 52, 63–4, 70
Le Chevallier, Cendrine, 127, 131
legislation, 9, 20, 51, 100–1, 162–74
Le Pen, Jean-Marie, 116–34
lesbian, 70, 175; identity, 87
liberalism, 8–10, 20, 104–5, 130, 164, 166, 175, 197
liberal pluralist. *See* pluralist
liberal values, 162, 167–8, 174–6
linguistic, 182, 197; analysis, employment equity, 167–74; structures, 162; technique, 169–70. *See also* assumptions, bias, disguise, double-negative, exaggeration, frontage, hedging, hyperbole, incompleteness, metaphor, minimalization, mitigation, negative imagery, numbers game, oversimplification, parallelism, pejorative words, personalization, ridicule, sarcasm, sentiment, substitution, topoi, trivialization
linguistic crossover, 58–9
literacy: critical, 4, 24; of listening, 4; new, 22–3, 26

Making History, Constructing Race, 21–2

Index

Mandela, Nelson, 138
marginality: as positive, 89–90
Marquard, Leo, 9, 10, 144–5
Marxism, 8, 9
Marxist: narratives, 49–51; theory, 148, 150–1, 154, 156
mass uprooting, 98, 101, 104, 108
materialist analysis, 9–12, 22, 149–56
media, 20; British, 23, 58, 66–7, 70; and the Front National, 115–34; North American, 23; and political discourse, 107; and racism, 139. *See also* employment equity, *Globe and Mail*, Montreal *Gazette*
Megret, Bruno, 117, 127, 131–3
Megretistes, 133
meritocratic viewpoint, 175
merit principle, 165
metaphor, 14, 31, 71, 77–90, 97; ambassador and interpreter, 77, 81, 88–9; fly on the wall, 89; of excess, 123; spy, 77, 85, 86–8; technique of, 155, 172; translator, 88; trickster, 77, 81, 82–5
metis and *metis(se)*, 84
metissage, 14
Miki, Art, 107
Miles, Robert, 6, 42–3, 69, 79
minimalization, strategy of, 170–1
mining, in South Africa, 148–50
minorities, 19, 39, 68, 98–9, 104, 107, 161, 182, 191, 194; ethnic, 49, 51–3, 61, 67; racial, 13, 175; sexual, 17; women, 38, 163. *See also* visible
miscegenation, 4, 50, 152
misogyny, and religion, 178

mitigation, 175, 197
mixed race, identity, 12, 14, 18, 58, 77–90
modernism, 13; and materialism, 9, 10, 11; and modernist thinking, 8; rise of, 5. *See also* postmodern
Montreal, 181–2
Montreal *Gazette*, 178–98
multiculturalism, 12–17, 24, 46–7, 62, 65, 68, 71–2, 97–8, 105, 115–17, 121; discourses of, 105; and the Left, 17; as social policy, 14, 81; state legislated, 81
multiple identities, 11
multiracial. *See* mixed race
multiracialism: tradition of, 152
Muslim: demonized, 64; discrimination, 69; gendered, 178–98; identity in Britain, 62–71; looking, 21; men, 188–91; racialization, 21, 43; women, head coverings, 21, 184–6, 192. *See also* backlash
myth, 20, 47, 49, 77, 103, 161; and central narrative, 174–5; socially constructed, 88

naming, 6, 14, 18, 197; implications of, 101; process of, 90; social versus personal, 105. *See also* self-naming
narrative, 47–50, 69, 70, 82–90, 121; central, 174–5; dominant, 97–8, 105; family, 104; meta, 197
national agenda, 100
National Association of Japanese Canadians, 97, 106–7
National Front. *See* Front National
National Party, 143, 147
nation as plural, 107

nation state, 12, 15, 42, 44, 62, 95–100, 105–6, 108, 161
Nazi, 143
negative imagery, 161, 173
neo-liberal: state, 24; values, 108
new ethnicities, 12
New World Order, 120
nisei, 98, 101, 102
Nisei Mass Evacuation Group, 102
non-racialism, 138–9
non-racialized, 57
non-racism, 38–9
non-racist, 59–60; future, 23; veneer, 25
North American Free Trade Agreement (NAFTA), 108
numbers game, as strategy, 168, 170–2, 174

Okanagan First Nation, 22, 30–1
Omi, Michael, and Winant, Howard, 14
Ontario Human Rights Code, 164
Orient, 6; as feminized terrain, 180
orientalism, 6, 19, 99, 181; and gender, 178–98; meta-narrative of, 197
orientalist tropes, 185
Other, 6, 9, 15–18, 42, 61, 83, 88, 145–6, 180–1; of European background, 96; and exoticization, 196; and Front National, 122; and media portrayal, 161–2; men as, 178; and Muslims, 21; and other others, 97; sexualized, 7, 57
Ouimet, Émilie, 193
oversimplification, strategy of, 175

Pakistan, 52, 60–4, 69, 183–5, 187–8, 191, 195
parallelism, technique of, 172

parenting, 17, 116, 119, 120, 122, 133
parole, 182
pejorative words, 174
personalization, 171
phenotype, 6, 18, 35, 42, 79, 81, 86
pluralist analysis, 140–54; liberal, 153; primordialist, 140–1, 153
political agenda, 140, 144, 146–7, 153–4; and employment equity, 168
political right wing, and employment equity, 162
politics: of appropriation, 121; of belonging, 65; of comparison, 114; contemporary racial, 114; global, 108; of recognition, 96. *See also* gender
post-9/11. *See* September 11, 2001
post-apartheid era, 138–9
post-colonial, 12, 16, 42, 51, 60; representations, 179–80
poster art, 123–26, 128
postmodern, 12–14, 25, 54, 61; approach to racial order, 155–6; frame, 13, 48, 53; frameworks, 11; historical beginnings, 10–12; social theory, 5
postmodernism, 10, 11, 25; vulgar, 54
post-national citizenship, 71–2
post-racist world, 4
post-war: identity, 108; immigration, of black and Asian colonial and postcolonial subjects, 47, 49; Labour government, 71; labour shortages, Britain, 48, 50; migration, 51; reaction against Nazism, 143; years, 10
power, 4–5, 11–13, 17, 19–21, 23, 32–3, 37–8, 43, 78, 84, 87, 90, 101, 106, 109, 120, 126, 132, 134, 140, 152–3, 161–2, 174–5, 188–90, 197; and colonialism, 180; defined, 130; and knowledge, 155
pre-industrial South Africa: and racial order, 151–2, and roots of apartheid, 153
press. *See* media
primitivism, 187–9
primordialist. *See* pluralist
prisoners of war, 102
Provence: sites of Front National victory in, 118; racial politics of, 115
Provincial Elections Act of B.C., 100
public debate, immigration and multiculturalism, 15, 115, 121

quotas: Bill to Repeal Job, 162, 164; employment, 165–6, 173; immigration, 121; racial, 139

race: and class, 152; relations in South Africa, 146; as social fabrication, 35–6; versus ethnicity, 79
race riots, 67
racial: categories, 115, 138, 144; differences, divinely ordained, 141; hierarchies, 83; oppression in South Africa, 138–56; politics, 115; profiling, 186; regimes, 123; state, 14
racialization, 6; and acts of resistance, 83; assumptions, 139; defined, 42; and internment, 109; positive aspects of, 88; process of, 79, 105–6. *See also* childhood, class
racialized: discourses, 117; identities, 12–14, 18, 80, 84, 88–9; regimes, 115; subjectivities, 12–14. *See also* women

racism: defined, 42; distorted, 120; experience of, 55; and First Nations, 30–2; and history of France, 115; history of, in South Africa, 138–56; immorality of, 121; and the modern state, 129; and the Nazi state, 128; rise of, 5; scientific, 154–5; sexualized, 57; across time and space, 36. *See also* anti-racism
racist: ideologies, 4; practices, 3; visions, 114
Rankean tradition, 143
Rattansi, Ali, 11–15, 18, 23–6, 46–72
redress, 25; brief, 106; movement, 98–109; and racial categories, 138–9; settlement, 108
reductionist, 8; conclusions, 151; rejection of, 156
refugee, 17, 66, 68, 71, 188–9; system, in Canada, 194–5
religion, 15, 17, 20–1, 43, 60, 69, 104, 145, 178, 184, 187, 190
religious: cleavage, 145; fundamentalism, 7, 21, 70
repatriation, 103–4, 127
representation, 4, 7, 10–12, 20–3, 42, 69, 84, 95, 107, 109, 147; and employment equity, 163–5, 174; feminized, of subject nations, 179; historical, 178–9; media, 161, 180–97; white, 7
reverse discrimination. *See* discrimination
revisionist analysis: South Africa, 148–53
Revolutionary Association of Women in Afghanistan (RAWA), 196
rhetoric, 21, 104, 121, 126, 187; and slippage, 120

Index

rhetorical: arguments, 164; strategies, 161, 172, 175
ridicule, 169–71, 175
Roberts, Barbara, 35
Roediger, David, 19
Root, Maria, 77
Rothenberg, Paula, 18, 19

Said, Edward, 5, 8; and orientalism, 6, 179–82
sansei, 98, 105
sarcasm, technique of, 171–2
schools. *See* education
security, 101–2, 129, 193; airport, 186; home, 123, 128; job, 37; national, 21, 124, 142, 195; as trope, 130; urban, 116, 119
segregation, 139, 142–3, 146–9, 152–4
self-naming, 13
sentiment, 70, 89; anti-immigrant, 179, 194; hostile, 41; playing to, 172
September 11, 2001: 6, 21, 24, 43, 66, 109, 178–98
Sewell, Tony, 70
sexuality, 7, 21, 48, 50, 51, 58, 180–1
sexualized Other. *See* Other
sexualized racism, 49, 50, 57
shin-issei, 98
soccer. *See* World Cup
Social Exclusion Unit, 64
social justice, 17, 106–7, 174
South Africa, 138–56
space: discursive, 24, 81, 121; and out of place paradigm, 90; public, 21, 56, 118; racist, 83–8, 118; social and cultural, 96; third, 14; transformed, 97
spy. *See* metaphor
state: apparatus, 49, 51; British, 48; as disciplinary, punitive, exclusionary, 120; housing, 130;

intervention, 71; media partnership, 21; modern, 129; nation, 12, 14, 42, 44, 95–7, 99–100, 105, 108, 161; policies, 54; power, racialized, 20; racial, 12, 14, 20; sanctified racism, 21, 129; welfare, 66, 68, 129
Stoler, Laura Ann, 3, 16, 24–5, 85, 114–34
strategies: anti-racism, 13; of Canadianization, 104; of containment, 193; covert, 84–6; discursive, 14, 182; of emasculation, 190; of extremist racist parties, 24; of female trickery, 84; of the mining industry, 150; of multiple identity, 85; recruitment, 127; hidden, of resistance, 12, 87; survival, 85. *See also* linguistic techniques, rhetorical strategies
subject positioning, 11, 94, 107, 194
substitution, technique of, 174
suicide bombers, 186–7, 197
Sunahara, Ann, 98, 102
surveillance, 11, 116, 130, 186
syncretism, 55, 60–1

Taguieff, Pierre-André, 8, 120, 122
Taliban, 184–5, 188, 193–4, 196
teleological question, 153
terminology, 4, 181. *See also* metaphor
threshold, 89, 133
topoi, 172–3
translator. *See* metaphor
transnational corporations, 44, 108
trickster. *See* metaphor
trivialization, 56, 169–70, 173, 175, 180

tropes, 61, 83, 130, 185, 189, 197. *See also* orientalist, security
Truth and Reconciliation Commission (TRC), 138
turf, 22

United Nations, and indigenous nations, 34
Untold, 56–8

Valentine, Gill, 87
Van den Berghe, Pierre, 144–5
Van Dijkian critical linguistic analysis, 162
Vaz, Keith, 63
veil, 182, 184, 187, 191, 193, 197
vigilantism, 118
visible minorities, 4, 48, 81, 106, 163, 166
vision: different, 25; of the future, 65; of a global village, 17; of multiculturalism, 72; of a post-racist world, 4; racist, 114–34; utopian and nostalgic, 134
Vitrolles, 116–30
voice: accessed, 182, 191, 195–6; barker's, 95–6; collective, 99; community, 32; of disenchanted Others, 96; ethnic, 96–7; influential, 68; isolated, 24; of Japanese Canadians, 107; lost, 168; privileged, 20; public, 97

Ware, Vron, 18, 19
war: in Afghanistan, 66; Cold, 108–9; efforts, 102; First and Second World Wars, 10; Front National, civil, 117; Gulf, 62; in Iraq, 69; Japan, 103–4; movies, 105; occupation, 128; orientalizing, 178–97; Taliban, 188; against terror, 43, 66; Third World War, 189; and

trade, 43; between tribes, 145; World War II, 36, 39. *See also* post-war, prisoners of war
warfare, 39
War Measures Act, 101
war-time trauma, 106
weapons of mass destruction, human, 188
Weekes, D., 58
welfare, 41, 133; for immigrants, 118; payment, withholding, 119–20; state, 66, 68, 129
Western historiography. *See* historiography
Western racism, 188
white, 7; able-bodies males, 162, 165–6, 174; binaries, 12, 14–15; ethnicity, 46; frontier expansion, 146; island race, 47; labels, 4; men 52; passing as, 86; racial purity, 152; racism, 145; women, 50–52

white flight, 68
white representations. *See* representation
white supremacist, 7; groups, 123; ideology, 140
whiteness, 12, 15, 18–19, 21, 47, 83, 150, 174; and Christianity, 142; and cultural whites, 18; hegemonic, 17–18; masquerade, 83
Winant, Howard, 14
Windrush, S S Empire, 47, 49, 51, 71
women: bodies of, 180; Caribbean, 52; of colour, 4, 152, 186, 190; elderly, 130; garment workers, racialized, 11, 21, 23; gay, 87; as keyword, 182–3; minority, 38; mixed race, 13, 18, 78–82, 89; oppressors of, 64, 66; as signifiers of culture, 180. See also Muslim women, white women, immigrant women
working together across differences, 22
World Cup: French victory, 115–17; and multiculturalism, 116

xenophobia, 68, 114–5, 121, 128

Yegenoglu, M., 179
youth: Asian, 61, 67; Bangladeshi and Pakistani, 69; black British, 54–5, 69; ethnic minority, 19, 61; family control of, 119–20, 124; hyphenated, 15; identity, 60; race riots, 66; urban, 19; white, 20, 56, 61; workers, 55